The People's Pictures

The People's Pictures: National Lottery Funding and British Cinema

By

James Caterer

CAMBRIDGE
SCHOLARS
PUBLISHING

The People's Pictures: National Lottery Funding and British Cinema,
by James Caterer

This book first published 2011

Cambridge Scholars Publishing

12 Back Chapman Street, Newcastle upon Tyne, NE6 2XX, UK

British Library Cataloguing in Publication Data
A catalogue record for this book is available from the British Library

ISBN (10): 1-4438-3307-X, ISBN (13): 978-1-4438-3307-3

For Annie, who first took me to the pictures.

TABLE OF CONTENTS

LIST OF ILLUSTRATIONS

List of Tables

ACKNOWLEDGEMENTS

The seeds of this project were sown whilst I was employed at the Arts Council of England between 1998 and 2002. For their guidance and knowledge during this period, I am grateful to Moss Cooper, Sarah Macnee, Neil Sweet and Rebecca Holdcroft. Much later, my research into this organisation and its equivalents across the UK was kindly assisted by Isabelle Andrews, Scott Royal, Michael Clarke, Linzi Nelson, Lorraine McDowell and Anneli Jones. The staff at the BFI National Library were always very helpful, as was John Flahive, who provided access to the production files for *Stella Does Tricks*. Luc Roeg at Artists Independent supplied a fascinating script draft of the unproduced *Jack Sheppard and Jonathan Wild*. Special credit is due to my interviewees for their invaluable information and opinions: Deborah Allison, Adam Barker, Andrea Calderwood, David Curtis, Mark Dunford, Ben Gibson, John Preston, Benjamin Ross, Frances-Ann Solomon, Richard Taylor and Samantha Taylor. My regards are also extended to the academic staff and postgraduate community formerly of the University of East Anglia, particularly Andrew Higson for his tireless support, but also Charles Barr, Peter Krämer, Lawrence Napper, Nathalie Morris, Jon Stubbs, Harri Kilpi, Hannah Hamad and Pietari Kääpä. Thanks to my fantastic colleagues at Oxford Brookes University: Daniela Treveri-Gennari, Lindsay Steenberg, Warren Buckland, Paolo Russo, Alberto Mira and Paul Whitty. Hayley Brierley-Roberts provided expert copy editing. Finally, and most of all, thanks to Stuart.

This project was financed by a doctoral award from the Arts and Humanities Research Council.

INTRODUCTION

This book is a detailed study of the British film industry in its political context. It provides a snapshot of a relatively brief but typically tumultuous period, from 1995 to 2000, and focuses upon the introduction and early years of a new cultural policy mechanism: National Lottery funding for film. When I began to research this project in 2003, those five years felt dangerously close and present, to the extent that it was difficult to close them off as a moment in history. But as I put the finishing touches to this book in the summer of 2011, this is clearly no longer the case. In the intervening years, an entire political dynasty has run its course. Under New Labour, public expenditure on education, the health service and the arts significantly increased, and the impact of National Lottery funding became tangible in new public buildings up and down the country, from the Tate Modern in London to the Baltic in Gateshead. The UK Film Council, which took over the distribution of Lottery money to filmmakers from the Arts Councils in 2000, provided a decade of relative stability in film policy terms, and was then unceremoniously dumped by the incoming coalition government in 2010. One of the final projects to have received financial support from the Film Council, *The King's Speech* (2010), swept the boards during awards season early in 2011, and has also been an enormous popular hit, generating over £45 million at the UK box office.[1] Therefore, given all this water under the bridge, what particular value does the late 1990s continue to hold for British film historians of the twenty-first century?

The years between 1995 and 2000 were a period of innovation and experimentation which irrevocably altered the relationship between British cinema and the state. Over this period, the four Arts Councils of England, Wales, Scotland and Northern Ireland ploughed £135 million of Lottery funding into filmmaking, assisting over 400 film and video projects.[2] This

[1] Adam Dawtry, "Shuttered Film Council reaps rewards for BFI," *Variety*, March 14, 2011, 4.

[2] This figure is calculated from data provided for the purposes of this project by the four Arts Councils of the UK, and contained in my awards database. This data is available online at James Caterer, "The People's Pictures Appendices," *Google Sites*, https://sites.google.com/a/brookes.ac.uk/jamescaterer/.

significant financial boost was accompanied by an ambitious plan which aimed to reform the structure of the film industry. Under this plan, three private consortia of companies, known as "franchises" were granted privileged access to Lottery funding, which could be spent on script development, production or distribution. By the year 2000, new industry "super-body" the Film Council was ready to take over the bulk of film funding from the Arts Council of England, and also to absorb other key elements of the public funding support for the UK film industry. In terms of its dramatic financial and institutional changes, this was a period comparable only to the years immediately following World War II, which saw the introduction of the National Film Finance Corporation, the Eady Levy, and the Group Production Plan. The lively debates which took place around these transformations in the public sphere are also vital for this project, as they illuminate the contested status of cinema in our national life.

The source of the film industry's newfound *largesse*, the National Lottery itself, was introduced by John Major's Conservative Government in 1994 to generate revenue for designated "good causes"; initially sport, heritage, charities, the Millennium celebrations, and the arts. This raised the question of whether the production of more home-grown feature films was really as worthy a "cause" as the maintenance of the nation's concert halls, its historic buildings, or its parks and leisure facilities. In addition, the system of distributing Lottery money to the arts through the four Arts Councils of the home nations meant that filmmaking was placed on an equal funding basis with opera, ballet or the visual arts. The coronation of cinema as a state-sanctioned art form, deeming it worthy of public protection and preservation, is problematic both for arts traditionalists and for *laissez-faire* economists, all of whom argue that industrial leisure commodities, such as films, should be provided by market forces alone. However, such market forces, acting with impunity since the film industry's deregulation in the early 1980s, had produced a malnourished production sector largely reliant on television for its funding and talent, whilst Hollywood consolidated its hold over the UK's distribution and exhibition networks. If this is what had become of the UK's national cinema, was this situation acceptable? If not, what could be done to improve the fortunes of the UK film industry?

Whilst researching this book, my primary aim has been to document and contextualise these debates in order to forge a greater understanding of this period, as well as its importance for the larger history of national cinema in the UK. Therefore, in the first three chapters to follow I investigate the history of film policy within the UK, and consider the extent to which historical precedents informed the design of the Lottery mechanism. I then explore the reasons for the system's development and how it worked in practice, where the money was spent, and what kinds of films and filmmakers benefited. These questions are posed in order to reveal the underlying processes at work. However, whilst these socioeconomic processes and their histories are significant within themselves, they become most fascinating when considered in conjunction with their end products—the corpus of Lottery-funded films. For this reason, unusually for a work concerned with film policy, the second half of this book is textually focused. A wide range of Lottery-funded feature films, shorts and artists' film and video projects are discussed, compared and analysed. Here, my working hypothesis is that these texts provide invaluable lenses through which the UK's complex and shifting film production ecology might be brought into focus.

Around one in every five UK feature films produced in the late 1990s benefited from National Lottery funding;[3] it is therefore important to note that the category of Lottery-funded feature films, although sizeable, remains a minority of the total output of the film industry during this period. Many of the most profitable and influential films released between 1995 and 2000 had no involvement with the scheme. As such, the reasons for separating out the Lottery-funded films from the rest of the pack need to be considered carefully. Does this method produce a representative sample of the industry as a whole, or are certain types of films more likely to fall within the Lottery remit, producing a more internally consistent grouping? Or do the differences lie not within the films themselves, but in the ways in which they are consumed by critics and audiences? With regard to these questions, a productive initial example is provided by Andrew Kötting's Lottery-funded feature film *Gallivant* (1997). This project grew out of Kötting's long-running relationship with the Arts Council, and was also supported by Channel Four and the British Film Institute (BFI). In September 1995, it became one of the first film projects to receive a National Lottery award through the Arts Council of England.[4] More recently, it has benefited from a beautifully packaged DVD released by BFI publishing. This is therefore a film which has received high levels of support from public institutions during its production and its subsequent consumption.

[3] As detailed in Chapter Three, 120 of the 608 features which went into production during this period had support from National Lottery funding.
[4] For more details on *Gallivant*'s production history, see Chapter Five.

In this light, Margaret Dickinson's remark that *Gallivant* "reaches the public carrying a cultural burden" opens up a series of issues surrounding the nature of public patronage and its effects, both upon the cultural artefacts which it helps to create and the ways in which they are interpreted.[5] Dickinson's comment should be considered in the context of her work as a historian both of British film policy and of the independent filmmaking sector.[6] It is taken from her review of *Gallivant* in the avant-garde and art cinema journal *Vertigo*, wherein she describes the film's "cultural burden" as a complication for her own reviewing process. For Dickinson, this "burden" is one which not only weighs the film down—suggesting that it may creak or even collapse under the weight of institutional expectation—but also somehow insulates it against criticism. In a sense, by expressing her own reservations about a film which had been so whole-heartedly embraced by the public sector, Dickinson presumably feels that she is betraying her strong support for the concept of public funding for artists' film. Other critics came to the film with entirely different axes to grind. Alexander Walker of London's *Evening Standard*, for example, was a vocal critic of National Lottery funding for filmmaking, and frequently used his film reviews to tot-up the amounts of public money that had been wasted. His discussion of *Gallivant* brusquely concludes that "the budget was £334,306, including £150,465 Lottery funding. Unlikely that the punters or the picture makers will see a penny of it back."[7] Walker had a preference for art cinema which meant that, for once, he could bear this loss; overall, however, his argument was clear: the "burden" associated with Lottery-funded cinema was financial rather than cultural, and was borne by the British public.

For Dickinson, this "burden" is a specifically cultural one, as *Gallivant* was funded for reasons other than the commercial. However, the history of film policy in the UK demonstrates that *economic* goals have most often been the first concern of the state when it has opted to intervene in national cinema. In the 1920s, the film industry became the focus of wider debates concerned with protecting British economic interests against mounting international competition—both at home and in the Empire.[8] Following the first Cinematograph Films Act in 1927, the Board of Trade held

---

[5] Margaret Dickinson, "Gallivant," *Vertigo*, 1:7 (Autumn 1997): 28.
[6] e.g. Margaret Dickinson, ed., *Rogue Reels: Oppositional Film in Britain, 1945–1990* (London: BFI, 1999).
[7] Alexander Walker, "Around the coast in weird ways," *Evening Standard*, September 18, 1997, 27.
[8] Margaret Dickinson and Sarah Street, *Cinema and State: The Film Industry and the British Government 1927–1984* (London: BFI, 1985), 5-7.

responsibility for the film industry until the early 1990s. With film firmly categorised as an industrial activity, successive governments implemented primarily economic film policies: the quota system, the "Eady Levy", tax incentives, and public funding bodies, such as the National Film Finance Corporation, later known as British Screen, were all designed to bolster the production of British feature films aimed at a wide audience. But running alongside these policies have been other schemes driven by different sets of motives. John Grierson's documentary film units, the BFI and the Arts Council have all channelled small amounts of public money into non-mainstream film culture, as more recently have European initiatives and broadcasters, particularly Channel Four. The cultural aims of such initiatives work on a variety of scales, ranging from notions of projecting the national interest, to providing a space for collective debate on issues of national importance, to giving voice to the culturally disadvantaged, or even to romantic ideals of personal expression. One of the most important ambitions of the Arts Councils in the early years of National Lottery funding for film production was to bring together these economic and cultural drives to produce a wide range of films, encompassing expensive period dramas, medium-budget comedies, and more economical short films and artists' film and video works. Films funded through a combination of these objectives are therefore given a particular "mandate" to operate in the public interest.[9]

Populism and Film Funding

The title of this book takes its cue from John Major's description of the new charitable gambling mechanism at its launch in 1994. By christening the scheme "the people's lottery", Major was not only responding to early criticisms of the scheme—particularly the decision to hand the operating licence to a private consortium with shareholders—but was also invoking a complex and potent descriptive label.[10] Ascribing the ownership of a policy to the people is a rhetorical strategy associated with "populism", a political doctrine with great emotive power but little in the way of fixed content. As Paul Taggart has noted, populism is essentially an empty

[9] I am borrowing the concept of the "mandate" given to filmmakers from Simon Blanchard and Sylvia Harvey's discussion of independent cinema. Blanchard and Harvey, "The Post-war Independent Cinema—Structure and Organisation," in *British Cinema History*, ed. James Curran and Vincent Porter (London: Weidenfeld and Nicholson, 1983), 226–227.

[10] John Major cited in Anon., "Don't tax the poor to amuse the rich," *Daily Mail*, November 15, 1994, 10.

vessel, making it an invaluable tool for politicians of every ideological persuasion.[11] It was crucial to the beginnings of democracy in the United States, but has also been strongly associated with Marxist socialism. Within recent British politics, populism has been appropriated in a wide variety of ways, from the semi-humorous nickname of the left-leaning Sheffield City Council during the 1970s and 1980s, "the people's republic of South Yorkshire",[12] through to Margaret Thatcher's vision of a home and share owning democracy, and to Tony Blair's eulogy for Diana, Princess of Wales, "the people's princess." Major's invocation of populism in relation to the National Lottery was founded upon Conservative neo-liberal economic principles, which state that the freedom of the market is more democratic than state intervention, and yet the mechanism was designed with philanthropic intent. This created a further implication for the best use of the proceeds: the money raised should be spent on what the ordinary people of the country want, not on some fossilised, elitist ideal of national culture. In this manner, the National Lottery was handed to the mythical stewardship of the Everyman.

The status of populism is especially contested within the area of cultural activity. The notion of "cultural populism" has an added set of connotations associated with the breakdown of barriers between high and low culture, or what Richard Hoggart refers to as "the tyranny of relativism."[13] Cultural populism is one of the key principles enabling film and media studies to be considered as serious disciplines within academia, although it is by no means an unchallenged truism.[14] More broadly, in the public sphere, cultural populism validates activities which have, at various points, been excluded from the rarefied domain of state-sponsored culture; here, the trajectory of the Arts Council itself is indicative. As established by the economist and Bloomsbury intellectual John Maynard Keynes in 1946, its remit was initially restricted to opera, ballet and classical theatre, but over time many more art forms have joined this list, including film, video and television, all of which were granted their own separate

---

[11] Paul Taggart, *Populism* (Buckingham: Open University Press, 2000).

[12] "The people's republic of South Yorkshire" was reportedly coined by Conservative MP Irvine Patnick during the period of David Blunkett's leadership of the council, 1980-1987. See Rachel Sylvester, "The blind boy who never stopped fighting," *Daily Telegraph*, December 16, 2004, 6.

[13] Richard Hoggart, *The Tyranny of Relativism: Culture and Politics in Contemporary English Society* (New Brunswick: Transaction, 1998).

[14] See Jim McGuigan, *Cultural Populism* (London: Routledge, 1992).

department in 1986.[15] The types of films sponsored by this new department were restricted by both finance and cultural sensibility to low-budget, often avant-garde works. The arrival of the National Lottery in 1995 promised previously unimaginable amounts of public funding to filmmakers, upon the understanding that British popular cinema would be a major recipient. As noted in Chapter One, however, the distribution of National Lottery funds to filmmakers was certainly not the first attempt to supporting popular cinema in the UK through public intervention. Thus, the quota legislation introduced in 1927 in effect provided exhibition space, which was filled by populist fare, whilst the Eady Levy was designed to reward box-office success in the hope of stimulating further hits. The Lottery scheme generated its own versions of long-running debates, which are worth rehearsing here before the films are considered in detail.

In the case of Lottery funding for film, the competing interests of commerce and culture were heightened by the scheme's resources, which were ample enough to make a real impact on production levels. Nonetheless, such resources were subject to the peculiarities of a selective award mechanism administered by institutions with largely cultural remits. Assessment criteria were designed to implement these remits, and these criteria could, in themselves, become the focus of debate.[16] Overall, the National Lottery's principal constraining factor was one of "additionality", a concept which attempted to ensure that previously existing funding, both private and public, was not simply replaced by the Lottery's proceeds. The logical corollary of this idea is that Lottery funding for film production should not simply aim to produce the same types of films already being made by the industry, but, by definition, these are the most popular types of films. Further aggravating the issue of risk and return was the fact that Lottery awards to filmmakers were considered as investments rather than straight-forward grants, and therefore some measure of return or "recoupment" was to be expected. Each of these tensions proved particularly problematic within the realm of Lottery funding for popular cinema. For instance, some producers argued that easily available finance would distort the market, and vociferously objected to the idea of filmmaking "by

---

[15] The Arts Council of Great Britain had been making film documentaries about artists since the early 1950s, but such activity was overseen by the Visual Arts Department.

[16] See the account of the debate over the concept of "public benefit" in Chapter Two.

committee".[17] Demonstrating that a film project would be of benefit to the public and would provide additionality (or added value) for the film industry was often easier for those filmmakers with an art cinema sensibility and access to the long-running arguments in favour of supporting this type of activity. Higher expectations of profitability also meant that the failure to recoup Lottery money invested in ostensibly "commercial" cinema would later become damaging for the scheme.

In several senses, the stakes were high for Lottery-funded popular cinema, but the potential rewards for the film industry were also considerable. It was hoped that providing a reliable flow of good quality British films could begin to change audience tastes and build demand for home-grown popular cinema alongside Hollywood imports. With cinema attendances rising year on year throughout the 1990s, and further exploitation windows opening thanks to continuing technological advances, the dream of a film industry supported largely by domestic audiences was becoming a possibility for the first time since the period following World War II.[18] This is not to underestimate the importance of the international market where, in theory at least, Lottery-funded hits could generate large amounts of income, off-setting inevitable disappointments, but a sustainable national film industry was considered the best breeding ground for these same breakthrough successes. Optimistic objectives such as these are driven by one crucial assumption: that UK films produced in the popular cinema mode would, in fact, prove to be genuinely popular with domestic audiences. Of course, this is not always the case, largely because of the fact that Hollywood films are the most widely consumed product within British film culture. A strictly populist viewpoint might therefore question the value of supporting home-grown popular cinema at all and, to some extent, this thinking can be observed behind the decisions to award Lottery funding to bigger-budget international co-productions. However, the wholesale support of Hollywood production by British public funds would have been both deeply unpopular and entirely unnecessary, which illustrates that, within the arena of public funding, the populist drive is inevitably tempered by competing factors.

---

[17] See the comments made by Simon Perry and Duncan Kenworthy in Adam Dawtry, "Whole Lotto Shakin' in Brit Film Funding," *Variety*, May 6, 1996, 23, 26, 214.

[18] Gerald Kaufman's 1995 Select Committee report on the UK film industry concludes that "The growing audience is the key to a flourishing industry." Department of National Heritage (DNH), *The British Film Industry*, Cmnd. 2884 (London: HMSO, 1995), 39.

Viewpoint and Methodology

The Arts Councils' five-year involvement with the UK film industry was a period of experimentation which now forms an invaluable case study of cultural policy in practice; however, I have opted to concentrate particularly upon the Arts Councils for another reason. This focus allows me to make use of my own personal history as an employee of the Arts Council of England's Lottery Unit between 1998 and 2002. Whilst this book is certainly not a first-person account—as the majority of the information found herein is in the public domain—it would be disingenuous to ignore the implications of my closeness to this research topic. In practical terms, this closeness facilitated certain methodologies, particularly the building of my awards database made up of data obtained directly from the four Arts Councils. This database provides many of the statistics found throughout this book, and forms the basis of the extensive and original statistical analysis found in Chapter Three. My own experience within this system also encouraged me to speak directly to several of the key policy-makers and practitioners involved in this period, and the resulting interviews were crucial in terms of challenging and developing my arguments. Here I share Maggie Magor and Phillip Schlesinger's position that the "actors pursuing competing interests in the policy process" deserve far more scholarly attention than they have previously received.[19] More broadly, I have been careful to signal those moments in this project when my viewpoint specifically impacts upon the threads of my argument. In this way, I hope this book represents a productive balance between objective evidence and subjective experience.

Given my personal involvement in many of the issues and debates discussed in this book, it is vital to be transparent about my opinions and objectives. The initial impetus for this project was a desire to shed light upon a set of institutional circumstances which were badly misunderstood and misrepresented within the public arena. The dominant assumption about this period was—and, to some extent, still is—that it was a terrible misjudgement to allow antiquated cultural institutions like the Arts Councils to have any responsibility over a large-scale economic activity, such as filmmaking. Whilst it is certainly true that the problems of the UK film industry were not miraculously solved by five years of Lottery investment, I would suggest that the Arts Councils were not solely to blame for this outcome. In addition, there were certain positive results of

[19] Maggie Magor and Philip Schlesinger, "'For this relief much thanks.' Taxation, film policy and the UK government," *Screen* 50:3 (2009): 299.

the scheme which would not have occurred without the Arts Councils' involvement, such as the unusually "joined up" spectrum of artists' film and video, short films and feature length art cinema, which took place at the Arts Council of England. Other areas were more problematic, particularly the failure to achieve a consistent level of box-office success for larger budget feature film projects, although I maintain that it is just as important to evaluate failure and consider the lessons it may offer as it is to celebrate success. If my own detachment from this topic has grown during the course of this project, my belief that cinema is just as deserving a recipient of National Lottery funds as arts centres, swimming pools or heritage landmarks remains undiminished.

In Chapter One of this book, I consider the UK's previous economic and cultural film policies in relation to the recent development of National Lottery funding. In particular, the occasionally fractious relationship between the Arts Council of Great Britain and the British Film Institute provides an instructive backdrop to the situation of the 1990s. Chapter Two forms a narrative history of the development of National Lottery funding for film as an instance of cultural policy in practice. Here I examine key concepts, such as the principle of "additionality", and explore vital debates, such as that which surrounds the notion of the scheme's "public benefit". The two key policy changes which affected the latter stages of this period are also discussed in detail, namely the Lottery Franchise scheme and the establishment of the Film Council, which ended the Arts Council of England's involvement with the film industry in April 2000. In Chapter Three, I interrogate these developments through the use of statistical analysis, which provides some predictable and some surprising results. For example, it is usually assumed that a major failure of the Lottery film production scheme was that it did not take sufficient account of distribution, but my analysis suggests that this is an unfair assessment. Chapter Three also contains extensive evaluation of the scheme's other difficulties, such as the failure of some Lottery-funded film projects to reach production. The truncated production history of one of these projects, *Jack Sheppard and Jonathan Wild*, is examined, along with an example of an expensive Lottery-funded "flop", *Amy Foster* (1998).

The final two chapters of this book are driven by the most challenging and rewarding objects of film policy analysis: the films themselves. Chapter Four considers how the populist rhetoric of the Lottery affected the film production scheme; in particular, I examine a range of Lottery-funded comedies in light of the economic and cultural objectives they were expected to fulfil. The chapter concludes with a case study of the one major Lottery-funded hit of the period, *Billy Elliot* (2000). In Chapter

Five, I focus upon the "art" of the Arts Councils, providing a survey of the art cinema made with the involvement of National Lottery funding. Here I argue that, perhaps contrary to expectations, the populist intervention of the Lottery produced a distinctive legacy of art cinema projects made up of artists' film and video work, short films, and feature-length art cinema. I also provide a case study of a Lottery-funded art-house film, which is centrally concerned with the artistic process and its relationship to the public sphere: the Francis Bacon biopic *Love is the Devil* (1998). This film was initially developed by the Production Board at the British Film Institute, which was a small-scale but nevertheless vital lifeline for British art cinema in the 1970s and 1980s. As this book goes to press in 2011, the BFI are taking on the responsibility of large-scale commercial film funding for the first time, which makes the many mistakes and selected small victories of the Arts Council's five-year encounter with the British film industry all the more topical, important and relevant.

CHAPTER ONE

FILM POLICY, INDUSTRY AND CULTURE

> Exhibitors *know* that the fostering and strengthening of British production can be a fortifying bulwark against the monopolising aggression of our American cousins.[1]
>
> *Kinematograph Weekly*, 6 August 1925

> A radical shift of policy was sanctioned: it became the avowed intention to intervene in the cultural drift of things in order to establish a British Art Cinema......[2]
>
> Peter Sainsbury on BFI Production in the 1970s

> The Arts Council will announce on Thursday that it is financing five or six films, from Hollywood-style blockbusters to art-house 15-minute shorts...[3]
>
> *The Independent*, 18 September 1995

These three statements are selected from the multitude of voices that have contested film policy in the UK for more than three-quarters of a century. Each describes a moment of change for the industry: the beginnings of economic protectionism in the late 1920s; the stirrings of an explicitly "cultural" approach to the development of national cinema at the British Film Institute (BFI) in the 1970s; and the arrival of National Lottery funding for film production in 1995, which set out to combine the economic and the cultural strategies. The "monopolising aggression" of Hollywood is a central theme across this history, but this issue was particularly fraught during the 1920s, as American movies consolidated their stranglehold on the international market. As Margaret Dickinson and Sarah Street point out, during this period, the film industry became the focus of a wider political debate concerning the protection of British

---

[1] Charles Lapworth, "Production—and the exhibitor," *Kinematograph Weekly*, 102:955, August 6, 1925, 26.

[2] Peter Sainsbury, "Independent British Filmmaking and the Production Board," in *Catalogue*: *British Film Institute Productions 1951-1976* (London: BFI, 1977), 11.

[3] Marianne Macdonald, "Lottery goes into the blockbuster business," *The Independent*, September 18, 1995, 1.

economic interests at home and abroad—a question thorny enough to lead to the Conservatives' General Election defeat in 1923.[4] As a result, quota legislation was introduced to protect the interests of the British film in 1927, and the industry was placed under the auspices of the Board of Trade. Thus categorised as an industrial activity, successive governments implemented primarily economic film policies: the quota system formally sanctioned a guaranteed proportion of cinema screen time for British films; the "Eady Levy" redirected revenue from the profitable exhibition sector back to the cash-starved producers; and public funding bodies, such as the National Film Finance Corporation, later known as British Screen, provided direct financial help to encourage production.

Running alongside these broadly fiscal policies have been other schemes driven by different sets of motives. The "radical shift in policy" at the BFI during the 1970s is one example of such attempts, which can be grouped together loosely under the heading of "cultural" initiatives. The early years of state-sponsored filmmaking in the UK were led by John Grierson and the documentary film units at a time when the BFI's aims were modest and educational. Following World War II, a new model of direct intervention in cultural activity was provided by the setting up of the Arts Council of Great Britain, which began to channel small amounts of public money into film activity outside of the mainstream, as did the BFI. In later decades, television broadcasters—in particular Channel Four—would also engage with "the cultural drift of things". Subsequently, in 1995, these two divergent motives came together in the shape of National Lottery funding for film production administered by the Arts Councils, which was a mechanism constitutionally charged both with supporting the previously unsupported *and* with making money. From "Hollywood-style blockbusters" to "art-house shorts", the Lottery promised to heal the commerce/culture rift and thus deliver a new unified policy for cinema in the UK. This convergence of previously discrete interests provides a tempting narrative arc through which to explain the subsequent successes and failures of the new system. In reality, of course, the situation was more complex than this narrative allows.

An important problem with this narrative concerns the contested definition of the term "cultural", as it has been utilised in film policy. This, in turn, reflects the complex set of meanings which have built up around the word "culture" itself.[5] In its more general sense, "culture" refers to the

---

[4] Margaret Dickinson and Sarah Street, *Cinema and State: The Film Industry and the British Government 1927–1984* (London: BFI, 1985), 5-7.
[5] See Raymond Williams, *Culture* (London: Fontana, 1981), 10-14.

"way of life" of a particular social grouping, most often nations or states. Thus, "British culture" is the shared social construction which contains notions of national identity, from high ideals, such as parliamentary democracy, to banal (yet richly symbolic) traditions, such as the cup of tea. However, "British culture" also refers more specifically to the intellectual and artistic activity originating in this country, which then may go on to circulate internationally. An even more narrow definition differentiates between high and low (or popular) culture, a delineation which has particular importance in the debates around cinema. Therefore, "cultural" issues within film policy have drawn on any or all of these definitions: censorship is an attempt to maintain a set of shared (or imposed) ethical values; the fear of "Americanisation" resulting from too many Hollywood movies implicitly suggests that British culture is superior to that of "our American cousins"; and notions of "propaganda" make the link between representation and national identity explicit. However, in recent years, the cultural question of film policy has tended to concentrate upon the support of (high culture) art cinema to compensate for the failure of the market to provide such activity. In this sense, it tends to be perceived in opposition to the economic drive to create a sustainable national film industry.

The fact that most cinema is produced via an industrial rather than an artisanal process means that questions of culture and economics cannot be separated easily. For example, in the 1920s and 1930s, at the same time as the growth of interest in film as an art form exemplified by the establishment of the London Film Society and the publication of the journal *Close Up*, there was also keen public debate surrounding the cultural effects of mainstream cinema. An oft-repeated slogan of the time, "trade follows the film", contains an understanding of film's potential to influence audiences in their consumer choices.[6] The mechanisms chosen to deal with this problem may have been largely economic, but the motivations and purposes of each were at least as much cultural as they were financial. Similarly, it is difficult to completely exclude questions of an industrial nature even from the most stridently "cultural" policy decisions. For example, Peter Sainsbury's achievements as Head of Production at the BFI in the 1980s were built around a closer allegiance of

[6] Paul Swann attributes the origin of this slogan to a speech made by the Prince of Wales in 1923. Swann, *The British Documentary Film Movement, 1926–1946* (Cambridge: Cambridge University Press, 1989), 10.

the organisation's production, distribution and exhibition activities.[7] These complexities are vital and provide much of the richness of debate that surrounds film policy. Nevertheless, historically, there has been a clear separation between those who wished to place the mainstream industry on a stronger footing and those who believed in helping filmmakers on the margins—not least in terms of the scale of the resources available to each. The Lottery certainly changed this equation, for the first time bringing many millions of pounds of public money within the reach of all filmmakers, whether driven by art, profit, or a combination of the two.

At this point, it is important to remember that the focus of this book is on institutions which have broadly cultural rather than industrial remits. In particular, the Arts Councils carry the responsibility for the nation's artistic heritage, and have tended, through the influence of their founder, John Maynard Keynes, to privilege high culture ideals. If only for this reason it is worth attempting to maintain a separation between issues of economics and culture within the following contextual history, although the connections and interplay between the two will not go unnoticed. The first section of this chapter considers each of the major initiatives taken by the British government to support film as an industry prior to the influx of National Lottery money in 1995. Quota protectionism, the Eady Levy, the National Film Finance Corporation (later British Screen) and its off-shoot the "Group Production Plan", European co-productions and tax incentives are each examined in terms of their objectives, successes and failures, and the corresponding debates provoked by each. Without being too prescriptive, the purpose is to illustrate the developments and continuities in these debates across the decades, particularly insofar as they provide useful precedents for the Lottery-funded era. The second section concentrates on the historical initiatives which have aimed to support non-mainstream film activity within the UK, again tracing a path which eventually leads to the late 1990s. The early history of state-supported filmmaking is focused upon the documentary film movement, driven by John Grierson's charisma and artistic ambition. In the post-war period, the emergent Arts Council was also involved in documentary film production, and later provided consistent support for avant-garde "artists' film". The BFI's own investment in "experimental" filmmaking created an artificial rift between the two organisations, which sheds light upon later tensions. Finally, Channel Four's commitment to innovation brought a new audience to the avant-garde, as well as providing vital support for

---

[7] For an illustration of his financial acumen, see Peter Sainsbury, "The Financial Base of Independent Film Production in the UK," *Screen*, 22:1 (1981): 41–53.

independent feature films. The chapter concludes with a brief overview or "map" of the film policy environment as it existed prior to the influx of National Lottery money in 1995.

Industrial Initiatives

In 1925, as politicians debated the protection of British interests against foreign competition and the idea that "trade follows the film" took hold, the Federation of British Industries (FBI) presented a memorandum to the Board of Trade, which was important enough to warrant publication in full by the trade paper *Kinematograph Weekly*.[8] It contained one suggestion that proved particularly influential:

> The proposal favoured by the Federation and their associated bodies, which may better be called the "Quota" system, is that the exhibitor shall, by legislation, be required to show a reasonable percentage of British films in his program.[9]

In Germany, "renters" (distributors) were obliged to handle one local film for every imported one of equal length; this was a high quota level, but one which applied at the point of distribution rather than exhibition.[10] In Britain, a lower *exhibitors'* quota of 12%—eventually rising to 37%—was considered "reasonable". By providing a guaranteed share of the domestic market for British pictures, it was hoped that the confidence of investors would increase, thereby stimulating production. In the following issue, *Kinematograph Weekly* published a selection of "trade views" on the memorandum, which seemed broadly in favour of adopting the quota system.[11] As the measure progressed through Parliament, it faced some opposition from the exhibition sector, but the cinema managers were placated by a reduction in their initial quota level to just 5%. At the same time, 7.5% of films handled by renters would have to be British, thereby allowing exhibitors a vital element of choice.

Although both measures were designed to boost the production of British films, the protection of the domestic market is a very different strategy to the large-scale direct investment represented by Lottery funding.

---

[8] Federation of British Industries, "To Revive Production: FBI's Summary of the Rival Plans," *Kinematograph Weekly*, 102:955, August 6, 1925, 30–1.
[9] FBI, "To revive production," 30.
[10] Dickinson and Street, *Cinema and State*, 18.
[11] Anon., "F.B.I.'s "plans" under the microscope: Trade views and counter-suggestions," *Kinematograph Weekly*, 102:956, August 13, 1925, 49–52.

The quota system created an (arguably) artificial demand for British product rather than simply increasing the supply and hoping for success. However, the results of the two measures, at least in terms of the number of films being made, were roughly comparable. As Figure 1-1 demonstrates, both interventions caused an immediate leap in the number of UK films being made, with an increase of 66% in 1928 and 64% in 1996. Each "boom" also triggered concerns over sustainability; between 1925 and 1936, 640 new production companies were registered in the UK, but by 1937, only 20 were still operating.[12]

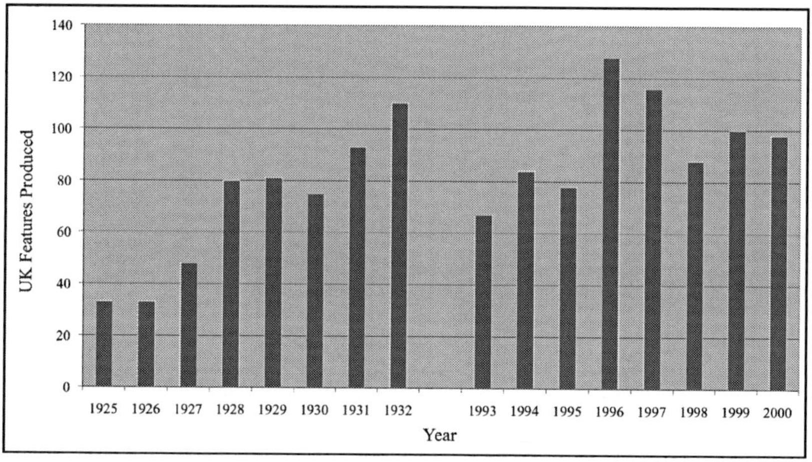

Fig. 1-1: Number of UK feature films produced 1925–1932 & 1993–2000[13]

However, the most important difference between the two systems is the effect upon budgets or the amount invested per film. Because the 1927 Cinematograph Films Act failed to include a minimum cost criteria, it transpired that some renters (many of which were American subsidiaries) chose to fill their quota by making or acquiring cheap British films without the production values of their Hollywood equivalents—the so-called "quota quickie" effect.[14] As a result, fairly or otherwise, the quota became

[12] Dickinson and Street, *Cinema and State*, 76.

[13] Eddie Dyja (ed.), *BFI Film and Television Handbook 2002* (London: BFI, 2001), 30.

[14] As Lawrence Napper has demonstrated, not all of these "quickies" were despised by audiences. Napper, "A despicable tradition? Quota-quickies in the 1930s," *The British Cinema Book,* 2nd ed., ed. Robert Murphy (London: BFI, 2001), 45–59.

associated with a decline in the "quality" of British films, which in these terms is nearly always synonymous with "cheapness" rather than any subjective measurement of worth. Although Lottery funding tended to have an opposite, inflationary effect on budgets, the films produced under this system would also face criticism over their quality and, perhaps ironically, their extravagance.

The quota was an indirect method of controlling exhibition in order to increase British production, and a logical extension to this idea was a physical redirection of the money taken at the box office back to producers. The Eady Levy was introduced in 1950 for this purpose.[15] Named after Sir Wilfred Eady, a treasury official central to film policy under the then President of the Board of Trade Harold Wilson, the Levy and the new National Film Finance Corporation formed Wilson's notable legacy for the film industry. As with the quota, the idea was taken in modified form from Europe; France and Italy had introduced similar systems in 1948 and 1949, respectively. In 1950, Eady outlined the British equivalent which would see a reduction in Entertainment Duty in return for higher cinema seat prices, with a proportion of this increased revenue being payable into a production fund. An important difference between the British scheme and its European precedents was that the fund was not specifically targeted to encourage certain types of production, but rather allocated according to box-office earnings of films. To all intents and purposes, this was an automatic subsidy for the industry at a time when to name it as such would have had severe political implications. Memories of the disastrous experiment with import restrictions, the Dalton Duty, which three years earlier had caused a near catastrophic complete boycott of the UK industry by Hollywood, were still fresh and painful. By comparison, the Levy was a modest imposition on cinemagoers, and its structure rewarded success rather than encouraging risky ventures. It was intended to be temporary, but was extended and became statutory in 1957, only being removed in 1985.

The effects of the Levy are less easy to quantify than those of the quota. The mechanism once more served to highlight the crucial importance of definitions; the precise criteria for qualification as a "British" film under successive Films Acts would have wide-ranging implications. Under the 1948 legislation, a production company was required to be registered as British in order to qualify for payments from the fund, but there were no restrictions placed upon the nationalities of stockholders or the source of the production money invested. This contributed towards a

---

[15] Dickinson and Street, *Cinema and State*, 224–226.

dramatically increased involvement in "British" production by American capital during the 1950s and 1960s, which was also driven by the break-up of the studio system, favourable sterling exchange rates, and the need to release millions of US dollars "frozen" by the British government in the aftermath of the war.[16] Bigger budget international films, such as *Tom Jones* (1963) and *Goldfinger* (1964), were allowed to benefit substantially from the Eady Levy fund, leading to the criticism that it was helping those who least needed to be helped. Very similar attacks would later be made on the Lottery film production fund. Although *The Independent*'s prediction of Lottery-funded "Hollywood-style blockbusters" was not entirely accurate, several major international production companies were involved in making films which received Lottery money, amongst them, Miramax (*Mansfield Park* (1999) and *Love's Labour's Lost* (1999)) and Columbia TriStar (*Amy Foster* (1998) and *Still Crazy* (1998)). Lottery awards were connected to box-office success in a different way: the expectation was that they would be repaid to the Arts Council should the productions show a profit, a process known as "recoupment"; this proved to be equally problematic given the relatively poor performance of the majority of the films.

Whilst the primary function of the Eady Levy was to act as a hidden subsidy for the commercial film industry, it was also channelled into smaller-scale "cultural" initiatives, such as the Children's Film Foundation and the BFI Production Board. However the most significant single recipient of the fund was the National Film Finance Corporation (NFFC). The idea for a state films bank which would make loans to support production had been around for a long time; it was one of the unsuccessful recommendations put forward by the FBI's memo published in *Kine Weekly* in 1925. It wasn't until 1948 that the Board of Trade began to give the notion proper consideration, which was largely owing to the perilous financial situation of British Lion, the independent production company born out of the quota period, which had recently been acquired by Alexander Korda.[17] Some fifteen years earlier, Korda had scored a sizeable commercial hit in the US with *The Private Life of Henry VIII* (1933), but had since struggled to repeat this success. Harold Wilson was advised that British Lion's collapse would effectively remove all competition from the major combines, Rank and ABPC, but found it impossible to sanction such preferential assistance to a single company. The result was the National Film Finance Corporation, which had an initial

[16] See Jon Stubbs, "The Eady Levy: A Runaway Bribe? Hollywood Production and British Subsidy in the Early 1960s," *Journal of British Cinema and Television* 6:1 (2009): 1–20.

[17] Dickinson and Street, *Cinema and State*, 211–219.

annual budget of £5 million, £3 million of which immediately formed a loan to British Lion. The NFFC's official brief was to supplement (rather than compete with) private finance through the provision of small amounts of "end money" to a large number of projects.[18]

One interesting off-shoot of the NFFC was an ambitious experiment in utilising public funds to encourage a restructuring of the film industry.[19] The motivation for the "Group" production plan was explained by Lord Reith, then NFFC chairman, in the following terms:

> Few independent producing companies are organised to carry out a programme of production with the economies and other advantages of continuity. The Corporation intends to examine the possibility of financing groups of independent producers, working together to achieve these benefits but without sacrificing individuality.[20]

Three subsidised groups were set up, the first two in co-operation with each of the major combines, Rank and ABPC, and the third, known as "Group 3" and led by John Grierson, would remain at arm's length from the film business and support new talent. On the one hand, then this was a bold attempt to reconfigure the industry and provide the advantages of "continuity": spreading risk across a slate of projects; holding rights to films in order to create a back catalogue; and forging stable creative teams. However, the scheme also hoped to provide opportunities for innovation, experiment and "individuality", and as such, its aims were split between the industrial and the cultural realms.[21] Industrially, the experiment was not a great success; the two commercially driven groups produced just 19 films between them. Both collapsed after a few years in operation, largely owing to the two powerful combines quickly losing interest.[22] Grierson's

---

[18] "End money" was defined as the part of a film's budget (usually 30%) not covered by the loan raised on the distributor's guarantee. See Julian Petley, "Cinema and State," in *All Our Yesterdays: 90 Years of British Cinema*, ed. Charles Barr (London: BFI, 1986), 37.

[19] Richard Dyer MacCann, "Subsidy for the Screen: Grierson and Group 3, 1951-55," *Sight and Sound*, 46:3, March 1977, 168–173.

[20] Lord Reith, *1st Annual Report of the National Film Finance Corporation* (5 April 1950) cited in Dyer MacCann, "Subsidy for the Screen," 169.

[21] Although Grierson's Group 3 did provide opportunities for unproven directors Lewis Gilbert and Phillip Leacock, and the scheme even uncovered a new British star, Joan Collins.

[22] Sue Harper and Vincent Porter, *British Cinema of the 1950s: The Decline of Deference* (Oxford: Oxford University Press, 2003), 21–27.

Group 3 survived a little longer, producing 22 subsidised features with an average budget of £50,000 before it was wound-up in 1955.

For Richard Dyer MacCann, the Group 3 features are characterised by a split between two impulses: the 1930s documentary tradition and the more contemporary Ealing comedy mode.[23] In this sense, they echoed the practical tensions between the high-minded idealist Grierson and the industry-savvy Michael Balcon, who, as well as being head of production at Ealing and therefore associated with Rank, was also an advisor to the NFFC and chairman of Group 3. Balcon's view here, as with his involvement with production at the BFI, was that "experiment" was akin to research and development for the commercial industry, whilst Grierson clung to his belief that audiences' tastes could be educated and changed for the better. Group 3's Technicolor documentary of *The Conquest of Everest* (1953) was a commercial success, less topical, and more didactic films were abject failures.[24] One-off hits could not save the entire Group plan from rapid dissolution, which clearly left few benefits for the industry in terms of the key goal of continuity. It was this same desire for continuity that motivated a similar experiment which took place fifty years later with the assistance of Lottery money—the so-called Lottery "Franchise" scheme. Thus, in 1997, another three umbrella organisations were set up, each representing alliances with key industry players. It was hoped that the franchises would encompass development, production and distribution activities to make and release a varied slate of Lottery-funded films. As with the Group plan, two of the franchises—The Film Consortium and Pathé Pictures—were fraught by internal power struggles and personality changes, whilst the third, DNA Films, proved very slow to show results.[25]

Taken together, the NFFC, the Eady Levy and the quota were the three major planks of economic film policy for the following three decades. The rapid decline in cinema audiences during the 1960s and 1970s meant that the quota and the Levy became increasingly ineffective, and both measures were abolished during Margaret Thatcher's first term in office.[26]

---

[23] Dyer MacCann, "Subsidy for the Screen," 170.

[24] e.g. Cyril Frankel's *Man of Africa* (1953), which Balcon considered "terrible", resulting in its recutting and the removal of Grierson's favourite "lyrical" passages. Dyer MacCann, "Subsidy for the Screen," 172.

[25] For a more detailed comparison between the two schemes, see James Caterer, "Reinventing the British Film Industry: the Group Production Plan and the National Lottery Franchise Scheme," *International Journal of Cultural Policy* 17:1 (2011): 94-105.

[26] John Hill, "British Film Policy" in *Film Policy: International, National and Regional Perspectives*, ed. Albert Moran (London: Routledge, 1996), 101–105.

A few years later, the NFFC was replaced by the public/private partnership organisation British Screen, with new shareholders Channel Four, Cannon, Rank and Granada adding investment to the government allocation, which, by now, had shrunk to just £1.5 million per year. Despite meagre resources, British Screen's achievements throughout the late 1980s and 1990s are not inconsiderable; from 1986 to 1989, it had a stake in 45 films and saw some commercial success (e.g. *Scandal* (1989)). John Hill notes that the organisation "managed to defy the gloomy forecasts of its early critics"[27], whilst David Hancock of trade journal *Screen Digest* goes even further, stating:

> British Screen was probably the most successful public funder of films in the world in terms of the amounts repaid by producers after a film's release, averaging above 50 per cent of the amount granted.[28]

Against this background of modest success, in 1994 the Arts Council sought British Screen's involvement in an experimental Lottery scheme known as The Greenlight Fund. The idea behind this fund was to attract directors "of international repute" into the industry through larger awards made to films with budgets between £3 million and £10 million.[29] *Wilde* (1997), *The Land Girls* (1998), and *Topsy Turvy* (1999) all benefited from this money, which was administered via British Screen.[30] However, the Greenlight Fund was difficult to reconcile with British Screen's policy of "additionality": the idea that "Money can only be granted if the film otherwise would not be made."[31] Films at this higher budgetary level are very likely to have large international companies involved, and so it becomes increasingly difficult to argue that they could not have been financed entirely by the market. The principle of additionality was also central to National Lottery funding as a whole, and was particularly problematic within the context of the entrepreneurial film industry. Many argue that, in order to create a stronger film industry in the UK, it is important to fund films with strong commercial potential, whilst others

---

[27] Hill, "British Film Policy," 104.

[28] David Hancock, "Profile of the Film Industry," in *The UK Cultural Sector: Profile and Policy Issues*, ed. Sara Selwood (London: PSI, 2001), 302.

[29] ACE, "National Lottery: The Greenlight Fund," *National Lottery Pack for Film Production Applicants* (London: ACE, 1997), separate note.

[30] The legacy of this scheme could be felt in the Film Council's "Premiere Fund" which had an early success with Robert Altman's *Gosford Park* in 2001.

[31] Martin Dale, *The Movie Game: The Film Industry in Britain, Europe and America* (London: Cassell, 1997), 194.

point out that such projects should be able to find financing without the involvement of public money.

The influence of European film policy upon Britain's initiatives—particularly the quota and the Eady Levy—has already been noted briefly. As Anne Jäckel describes, the national film industries of Europe have a long history of co-operation and co-production driven largely by a shared resistance to Hollywood domination.[32] From the late 1980s onwards, the increasing political integration of the European Economic Community meant that Pan-European cultural policies began to emerge. The first of these to affect the film and television industries, the MEDIA programme, was piloted in 1987 and then launched in 1990 with a budget worth around €180 million for the first five years.[33] The programme focused upon three areas neglected by production funding: training, development and distribution; the most important of these was distribution, which received around 50% of the annual budget during the scheme's first phase. This was initially run along selective lines, giving preference to low-budget projects which might otherwise struggle to achieve a theatrical release, but following a series of controversial decisions, an automatic system took over which became available to all European films.[34] Development activities accounted for around 30% of the MEDIA budget and included the European Script Fund, through which individual scriptwriters could apply for support whilst the script was delivered. Training funds went towards research and broadening the skills base of young independent producers, and claimed 20% of the overall budget. The MEDIA schemes were renewed in 1995 and again in 2001, and were later joined by Eurimages, a direct subsidy fund paid by subscription of each of the member states, which would provide up to 20% of a co-produced film's budget.[35]

Martin Dale argues that, whilst the European initiatives were originally designed to provide "seed money" with the aim of stimulating a flourishing commercial industry, in time, they tended to become an unwieldy conglomeration of the cultural control mechanisms of each of

---

[32] Anne Jäckel, "European Co-Production Strategies" in *Film Policy: International, National and Regional Perspectives*, ed. Albert Moran (London: Routledge, 1996), 85–97.

[33] European Parliament, "Factsheet 4.18.0—Media and Sport Policy," *European Parliament*, September 30, 2004, accessed February 2006, http://www.europarl.eu.int/facts/4_18_0_en.htm.

[34] Dale, *The Movie Game*, 208.

[35] Britain was only briefly a member of this scheme, joining in 1992 and then withdrawing by 1995.

the member states.[36] This criticism needs to be considered in the light of Dale's antipathy towards the "subsidy trap" and the European "cultural ghetto", but the idea that bureaucracy and creativity are inherently incompatible is certainly not limited to supporters of Hollywood's "democratic" approach. According to this argument, bureaucracy is, at best, inefficient and, at worst, corrupt, with the filmmaker frustrated at every turn by form-filling and committees. Terry Illot, whose research on the economics of European cinema was supported by the MEDIA programme, has since suggested that the scheme's first incarnation "did little more than facilitate hundreds of meetings in expensive hotels all over Europe".[37] In the BFI's 1996 *Handbook*, Illot speaks out against a "production-at-all-costs" philosophy which "is killing European cinema", therefore viewing the arrival of National Lottery money with some concern.[38] In this sense, European subsidy can be seen as a direct forebear of the Lottery system, with the new mechanism expected to inherit the problems of the old. Whilst this may be a fair comparison for the subscription fund Eurimages, it is difficult to compare the Lottery to the larger MEDIA framework, which has actually spent very little on production. Nonetheless, the idea that the Lottery was rashly throwing money into filmmaking without considering audiences became widespread, and was influential in shaping the later development of the fund, such as the decision to allow the three franchise companies to spend Lottery money on development.

Tax incentives are the most complex and opaque of the measures taken by the Government to encourage UK film production. Their detailed workings are all but impenetrable for those without an extensive knowledge of accounting procedures and, as such, are often absent from less specialised accounts of film policy. Notably, the amounts of public money channelled into the industry via this route are immense: by the time of its review in 2004, Section 48 of the 1997 Finance Act had already benefited the industry to the tune of £6 billion.[39] This clearly dwarfs the £135 million of National Lottery money spent on film production between 1995

---

[36] Dale, *The Movie Game*, 210.

[37] Terry Illot, "UK Film, Television and Video: Overview," in *BFI Film and Television Handbook 1996*, ed. Eddie Dyja (London: BFI, 1995), 21.

[38] Illot, *BFI Film and Television Handbook 1996,* 31.

[39] This estimate was cited by the Paymaster General, Dawn Primarolo, at the House of Commons Standing Committee on the Finance Bill on May 24, 2004. See HMSO, "House of Commons Standing Committee A (pt 5)," Column 367, *UK Parliament*, accessed April 2006, http://www.publications.parliament.uk/pa/cm200304/cmstand/a/st040525/am/40525s05.htm.

and 2000; however, despite this tax breaks have rarely been as contentious a matter for public debate. John Hill dates their arrival in the UK to 1979 when the Inland Revenue changed the law on "capital allowances" to make film production much more attractive to City investors. This measure helped contribute to a short-lived wave of success enjoyed by the UK industry exemplified by *Chariots of Fire* (1981) and its production company Goldcrest.[40] This financial incentive was withdrawn in 1986 and was later reinstated under the 1992 Finance Act as Section 42, which was joined five years later by Section 48. Fundamentally, the mechanism works by allowing a certain amount of film production costs to be offset against the tax payable by a registered individual or company. For Section 48, which was aimed at "low budget" films costing less than £15 million, this meant production companies could receive up to 15% of the budget upfront.[41]

The key difference between the tax incentives and National Lottery funding for film production is that both Section 42 and Section 48 are non-selective tools:

> As long as the eligibility criteria are met, any film can qualify for tax incentives without interference from Government in its cultural merit or how it is produced.[42]

This lack of "interference" is considered preferable by opponents of the selective grant-giving system, such as Martin Dale. In theory, tax relief should result in bigger-budget commercial films which are more able to compete with Hollywood product—both at home and internationally. In practice, however, similar schemes in place around the world have had mixed results; a good example here is the box-office failure and critical contempt faced by films produced during the Canadian tax shelter boom of the late 1970s.[43] Much like quota protectionism, tax incentives have been criticised for producing films, regardless of their quality. Indeed, some commentators allege that, under certain circumstances, it is preferable for

---

[40] See Jake Eberts and Terry Illot, *My Indecision is Final: The Rise and Fall of Goldcrest Films* (London: Faber and Faber, 1990).

[41] See UK Film Council, "Tax Relief for the production of low budget British films," *UK Film Council*, accessed September 2005, http://www.ukfilmcouncil.org.uk/usr/downloads/BFC_UKFCI/finance/ Tax_Relief_Sale_Leaseback.pdf.

[42] HM Treasury, *Reform of Film Tax Incentives: Promoting the Sustainable Production of Culturally British Films* (London: HMSO, 2005), 7.

[43] Peter Urquhart, "You should know something—*anything*—about this movie. You paid for it," *Canadian Journal of Film Studies*, 12:2 (Fall 2003): 64–80.

investors to back poor films as they are less likely to be distributed and therefore incur further costs. The National Lottery contains checks in the system designed to avoid absurdities such as this; the Arts Councils were required to ensure that all funded projects reached the widest possible audiences. For film production, this meant an engagement with the complexities of distribution where, as Chapter Three demonstrates, the system did make some progress.

Broadly speaking, the principal objective of all economic film policy is to produce a successful and sustainable industry capable of competing for both domestic and international audiences. There have been a range of different methodologies applied within different historical contexts in an attempt to try and reach this goal, with each method potentially considered as a precedent for aspects of the National Lottery-funded period of the 1990s. The quota solution chose to create demand for British product in order to stimulate supply, whereas the Lottery invests directly in producing a greater number of films in the hope that some will succeed. However, both interventions tend to implicitly devalue the films produced by raising uncomfortable issues concerning the nature of the "demand" for British films: do British audiences really want to see more locally produced films in cinemas? The Eady Levy tried to reconnect the exhibition and production sectors within a fragmented industry, but through a mechanism which rewarded success, and which therefore increased the power of larger concerns, exacerbating rather than combating international conglomeration. In theory, at least, the Lottery system subscribes to a rhetoric of "additionality", which should support local innovation over international co-operation, but this logic was extremely difficult to apply to the film industry at the turn of the millennium. Similarly, the NFFC and British Screen wrestled with issues of the public/private split in film finances, whilst tax incentives appear to remove the public decision-making process from the system entirely.[44] However, by devising the National Lottery as a selective rather than an automatic mechanism, and then choosing the Arts Councils as gatekeepers—not only for the traditional arts world but also for the film industry—the government ensured that economic objectives would at least be complicated by, if not entirely balanced with, cultural concerns.

---

[44] On the development of tax incentives since 2000, see Maggie Magor and Philip Schlesinger, "'For this relief much thanks.' Taxation, film policy and the UK government," *Screen* 50:3 (2009): 299–317.

Cultural Concerns

If the BFI Production Board's 1970s policy shift towards British art cinema was truly as "radical" as Peter Sainsbury claims, it would then be possible to infer that this moment was the first time that the state had chosen to intervene in the cinematic "cultural drift of things." However, this would be to overlook the various initiatives which were in existence long before the 1970s, and which worked to provide help, however limited, for filmmakers outside of the mainstream film industry. Sainsbury was part of a generation of politicised film policy-makers, whose manifesto of "independent cinema" was influenced by the radical cultural theory of academic discourse and the artistic avant-garde.[45] This generation sought to define itself against not only the narrow economic motivation of the majority of film policy interventions, but also the "paternalistic" character of their predecessors in the cultural domain.[46] John Grierson, father of the documentary film movement and head of its state-funded nucleus, was the prime representative of this paternalism, who spoke with the Victorian language of social uplift and moral improvement. However, amongst his contemporaries, Grierson and his team of filmmakers were, themselves, considered radical aesthetes, largely owing to the openly acknowledged influence of Soviet cinema on their work. Grierson's aesthetic legacy in terms of the British social realist tradition has been discussed elsewhere,[47] but what is more important within the context of this chapter is the space which he determinedly carved out for a new mode of film production, which relied on an unusual combination of state patronage and industrial sponsorship.

The first institutional home for Grierson's project was provided by the Empire Marketing Board (EMB). This body was set up by the Conservative government in 1926 with the aim of taking full economic advantage of the Dominions without having to resort to unpopular tariffs and restrictions.[48] An important area of the Board's work was in publicity,

---

[45] Here "independence" refers not just to financial autonomy but also to freedom from the formal and ideological constraints of mainstream cinema. The Independent Film-Makers Association, formed in 1974, was a key organisation in this regard.

[46] See Sylvia Harvey's discussion of Grierson in "The 'Other Cinema' in Britain," in *All Our Yesterdays*, ed. Charles Barr (London: BFI, 1986), 225–251.

[47] e.g. Andrew Higson, *Waving the Flag: Constructing a National Cinema in Britain* (Clarendon: Oxford, 1995).

[48] Paul Swann, *The British Documentary Film Movement, 1926-1946* (Cambridge: Cambridge University Press, 1989), 21–22.

both in terms of improving the Empire's image at home and abroad and in promoting particular industries or products. Grierson impressed the Board with his passionate belief in the cinema as a propaganda tool, and following the relative success of his actuality film on the herring industry, *Drifters* (1929), which was booked in many commercial picture houses, he was given rein to establish Britain's first state-sponsored film unit in 1930. As Paul Swann describes, Grierson and his civil servant accomplice Stephen Tallents were not above using ungentlemanly tactics to defend their own interests in constant battles with the Treasury, who considered them wasteful, and the film trade, who saw them as unfair competition. Creative accounting procedures were sometimes employed: for example, Grierson received £7,500 for a film about the Port of London authority which he never intended to make; instead, the money was spent on other projects closer to his heart.[49] His ability to work the civil service system to his advantage and a natural flair for publicity meant that Grierson's film unit outlived the EMB itself, moving to the General Post Office (GPO) under advantageous terms in 1933. It survived here after Grierson's resignation in 1937 and the outbreak of war in 1939, which provided the basis for the government's propaganda efforts, the Ministry of Information's Crown Film Unit.

Grierson's diverse team of filmmakers worked to produce a range of products within their public service remit. There were simple instructional films on topics as banal as how to tie a parcel; bigger-budget projects intended for cinema release, such as Basil Wright's *Song of Ceylon* (1934) and low-budget advertisements which were treated as creative experiments by expatriate animators like Len Lye and Norman McClaren. Despite their corporate heritage, these wildly colourful promotional films are now considered forerunners of a modernist avant-garde movement in Britain.[50] This paradox of artistic freedom flourishing under the constraints of an organisation which combined commercial and public service interests is one which, for some, makes Grierson's entire project problematic. In retrospect, the films produced by his unit can feel compromised by the effects of patronage. For example, Stuart Hood criticises *Song of Ceylon*—which was originally commissioned as publicity for the Ceylon Tea Company—for avoiding the difficult political questions of colonial labour

[49] Swann, *The British Documentary Film Movement*, 45.
[50] See Sarah Street, *British National Cinema* (London: Routledge, 1997), 157–158.

and economic exploitation.[51] However, this charge of white-washing was not one which would have made much sense to Grierson's critics of the time, who generally considered his team as a repository of left-wing politics. A far more common contemporary attack on the work of the unit was that it had failed to find an audience with the general public. Even the bigger-budget productions were rarely seen in cinemas, instead being pressed into service amongst the growing non-theatrical release circuits. Sixty years later, and with the intervening shift of the public service drive towards the far more significant non-theatrical exhibition mechanism of television, it is perhaps not surprising that the Lottery-funded feature documentaries found similar difficulty in securing cinema releases.[52]

A key reason for the failure of Grierson's documentary movement to reach a broad swathe of the cinema-going public was that the film trade had made sure that documentaries would not qualify as quota under the initial legislation, and the films were therefore instantly unattractive to exhibitors.[53] This conflict provides an early example of tension between those representing the economic interests of the film industry and the champions of cultural film policy. According to Dickinson and Street, film trade organisations were also instrumental in the effective neutering of the emergent British Film Institute.[54] The idea for the body had come from a report published in 1932 by the Adult Education Institute, "The Film in National Life".[55] This argued for a wide-reaching organisation with functions including training, advising education authorities, and improving public taste, with possible interests in film distribution and development. It would be funded by a percentage of the proceeds from the Sunday opening of cinemas and by subscription membership. The film trade began to lobby the government amidst fears that the new body would exercise unfair control over exhibition—or worse, move into production. As a result, the

---

[51] Stuart Hood, "John Grierson and the Documentary Film Movement" in *British Cinema History*, eds. James Curran and Vincent Porter (London: Weidenfeld and Nicholson, 1983), 102.

[52] e.g. Isaac Julien's *Franz Fanon: Black Skin, White Mask* (1996) and Kevin McDonald's *Donald Cammell: The Ultimate Performance* (1998). Both were joint-funded with the BBC and well-received at international festivals but failed to find theatrical distribution.

[53] The only way that documentaries could qualify was if they were of "special entertainment value", which was very difficult to prove. Dickinson and Street, *Cinema and State*, 35.

[54] Dickinson and Street, *Cinema and State*, 47–52.

[55] Commission on Educational and Cultural Films, Chair. Sir Benjamin Gott, *The Film in National Life* (London: Allen and Unwin, 1932).

fledgling Institute concurred that it would "have to be in a position of undisputable commercial disinterestedness."[56] Born in 1933, the BFI's remit was restricted to educational and archival purposes by its constitution and its lack of resources, and it would be some years before it was in a position to exert direct influence over "the cultural drift of things."

Both the problems faced by Grierson's documentary movement and the beginnings of the BFI demonstrate that the British film industry as a whole has tended to resist moves towards the cultural provision of filmmaking.[57] In contrast, the inception of the Arts Council of Great Britain (ACGB) in 1945 gave the film trade little cause for concern. The Arts Council's direct precursor, the Committee for the Encouragement of Music and the Arts (CEMA), was a product of the wartime government's increased willingness to intervene in matters of culture, driven by the need to keep up civilian morale. A small team of the great and the good of the British arts decided upon the allocation of limited grants to support both professional and amateur music-making, and found particular success with classical concerts performed in munitions factories.[58] Following the war, CEMA's example led to the new body which would claim stewardship over the arts in peacetime. The Arts Council's first Royal Charter, published in 1946, contains an ornate statement of intent which had been drafted by John Maynard Keynes. The Charter proposes that the Arts Council be set up:

> for the purpose of developing a greater knowledge, understanding and practice of the fine arts exclusively, and in particular to increase the accessibility of the fine arts to the public throughout Our Realm, to improve the standard of execution of the fine arts and to advise and co-operate with Our Government Departments, local authorities, and other bodies on any matters concerned directly or indirectly with those objects.[59]

This touchstone for early Arts Council policy was changed little in the subsequent Charter of 1967, which set up the semi-autonomous Scottish

---

[56] John W. Brown and Alan Cameron, *The Times* (August 9, 1932), cited in Dickinson and Street, *Cinema and State*, 51.

[57] A notable exception in this regard is the oft-stated desire to produce British films for British audiences, although this "cultural" motive is clearly also in the economic interest of producers.

[58] Andrew Sinclair, *Arts and Cultures: The History of the 50 Years of the Arts Council of Great Britain* (London: Sinclair-Stevenson, 1995), 33.

[59] Arts Council of Great Britain (ACGB), *Draft Charter of Incorporation of the Arts Council of Great Britain* (London: ACGB, 1946).

and Welsh Committees, and it survived the organisation's break up into the three Arts Councils of England, Scotland, and Wales in 1994.

The Charter works because it manages—though perhaps with some strain—to yolk together several competing agendas. The dominant voice here is that of Keynes himself, former advisor to the Treasury, sometime associate of the Bloomsbury group, and unapologetic elitist.[60] It was Keynes who inserted the crucial modifier "fine" before the more inclusive "arts", thus banishing folk, community or popular arts, including cinema, from the Council's remit. There is clearly a tension between the lofty ambitions of the first aim—"greater knowledge, understanding and practice"—and the populism of the second clause's insistence on "accessibility". According to Richard Witts, this ambivalence mirrored disagreements between Keynes and other former members of the Council, such as the composer Ralph Vaughan Williams, an advocate for amateur involvement in the arts.[61] Another suggestion, to add a commitment to assist the livelihoods of struggling artists, was simply ignored in favour of improving standards of execution. The final section, which promises to advise and co-operate with other branches of Government, is crucial because it indicates the level of autonomy granted to the body. This institutional independence from Parliament was the organisation's defence against the criticism that it would reduce the nation's art to the status of political propaganda.[62] The "arm's-length principle" was not only supposed to safeguard the integrity of creative expression, but also to ward off possible comparisons between democratic British cultural policy and those vigorous interventions instigated under the totalitarian regimes of communism and fascism.[63] Whether or not this independence was illusory depended on the differing styles of successive governments. In the 1990s,

---

[60] Andrew Sinclair's official history of the organisation casts Keynes as a tireless worker and passionate advocate for the fine arts, whereas Richard Witts' less reverent account emphasises his vested interests and colourful private life. Sinclair, *Arts and Cultures: The History of the 50 Years of the Arts Council of Great Britain* (London: Sinclair-Stevenson, 1995), 25–76. Richard Witts, *Artist Unknown: An Alternative History of the Arts Council* (London: Little, Brown and Co., 1998), 10–153.

[61] Witts, *Artist Unknown*, 150–151.

[62] Anna Upchurch notes that Keynes was strongly opposed to bureaucracy and government interference. See Upchurch, "John Maynard Keynes, The Bloomsbury Group and the Origins of the Arts Council Movement," *International Journal of Cultural Policy*, 10:2 (2004): 203–217.

[63] John Pick, *The Arts in a State: A Study of Government Arts Policies from Ancient Greece to the Present* (Bristol: Bristol Classical Press, 1988), 87–95.

the "arm's-length" principle became a useful corroborative of the hands-off rhetoric associated with "the people's Lottery".

Whilst the text of the Arts Council's Charter remained essentially static from this point onwards, an important change was signalled in 1967 by the removal of the contentious word "fine". This reflected a gradual move across the organisation towards those activities previously considered insignificant by Keynes—one of which was filmmaking. There had been those who had wanted film to be on the list of subsidised art forms right from the moment of CEMA's transformation: as its parting shot, CEMA had commissioned reports from across the arts world concerning the best way of continuing its work in peacetime, with one of these pleas for support deriving from the documentary film movement, led by Paul Rotha, Harry Watt and Basil Wright.[64] But, the highbrow Keynes was uninterested in the cinema, which, due to its dominance as the mass cultural medium of the 1930s and 1940s, was overwhelmingly associated with the working and lower-middle classes—or "the mob", as Keynes' associate John Christie would often phrase it.[65] Keynes believed that the activities within which he was involved—namely the performing arts of opera, theatre, ballet and classical music—were the most suitable beneficiaries of public funding. As time progressed, further panels and art form departments were added to the structure of the Arts Council, but its core activities and the recipients of the majority of its funds remained allied with Keynes' tastes.[66] Nonetheless, despite the documentarians' ignominious rejection, within a decade, the Arts Council had started to fund the making of films, including *The Stained Glass at Fairford* (1956), which was directed by Basil Wright.[67] This and other films recording the nation's art treasures began a relationship between the Visual Arts Department and cultural filmmaking, which eventually led to Lottery funding for "Artists" Film and Video".

The Arts Council's Visual Arts Department works differently to those representing the performing arts. One principle reason for this is that it owns and manages a major national asset: the "Arts Council Collection" of artworks. The collection began under CEMA in 1942, and now comprises

[64] Sinclair, *Arts and Cultures*, 42.

[65] Witts, *Artist Unknown*, 46.

[66] This was also true for the Lottery awards: in 1995/6 dance, drama and opera accounted for 62% of the total spend, whilst film production received just 0.9%. ACE, *2nd Annual Report and Accounts 1995/6* (London: ACE, 1996), 99.

[67] The film was shot in colour and had a commentary written by John Betjemen. See BFI, *Catalogue: British Film Institute Productions 1951–1976* (London: BFI, 1977), 25.

over 6,800 works from at least 1,700 different painters, sculptors, photographers and filmmakers, valued for insurance purposes at £25–£30 million.[68] Its emphasis on the acquisition of contemporary British art means that the department has had to engage more thoroughly with the present climate rather than simply preserving an artistic heritage, and it also has a strong tradition of promoting accessibility to the general public. During the war, one of its original purposes had been to tour exhibitions around the country, bringing art to towns without galleries; this function developed into "a comprehensive and economic machinery of art-circulation throughout the country."[69] The decision to make cheap documentary records of significant exhibitions on film was a natural extension of this "machinery", which began to occur from around 1950 onwards.[70] A diverse range of subjects included Botticelli, Magritte, Giacometti, Stanley Spencer, Henry Moore and Francis Bacon.[71] The films were funded by the Arts Council but were produced by the BFI, who, which would then also distribute them to the eager aspirational audiences of the regional film societies. There is even record of one film, *The Pre-Raphaelite Revolt,* showing at the Curzon Soho in London alongside Luis Buñuel's *Belle de Jour* (1967).[72] The success of this experiment with broadening public access to art through film would later change the Arts Council's relationship with the BFI from co-operation to direct competition.

After its humble beginnings in the early 1930s, the BFI grew steadily in membership and influence despite continually meagre resources.[73] The Festival of Britain in 1951 brought an opportunity for the organisation to begin to make its mark on exhibition thanks to the construction of the Telekinema—later the National Film Theatre (NFT)—as part of London's revamped South Bank. Producing programming for the Telekinema led to the idea of a small rolling fund to assist new directors in the creation of short films which could act as their route into the commercial industry.

---

[68] Witts, *Artist Unknown*, 373–375.

[69] Early Visual Arts officer Bill Williams cited in Witts, *Artists Unknown*, 377.

[70] The Victoria and Albert Museum's archive of art and design contains papers relating to this activity which date back to 1950. See Victoria and Albert Museum, "ACGB: Film, Video and Broadcasting Department," *V&A*, accessed October 2005, http://www.vam.ac.uk/vastatic/wid/ead/acgb/acgb-56.html.

[71] List from Sinclair, *Arts and Cultures*, 115; Butler, *The Art of the Film*, 155. For more details on the Francis Bacon film see Chapter 5.

[72] Sinclair, *Arts and Cultures*, 167.

[73] The BFI's annual grant from the Cinematograph Fund was just £9,000 until 1944 when it jumped to £14,000, rising again to £31,500 in 1948. Butler, *The Art of The Film*, 27.

Michael Balcon of Ealing Studios became Chair of the so-called "Experimental Film Fund" in 1952, and managed to obtain a grant of £12,500 from the proceeds of the new Eady Levy.[74] For some, this "Experimental" tag was misleading. As Christophe Dupin describes, the new committee was careful to separate itself from more radical strands of filmmaking:

> it did not see experimentation as a practice *against* the industry, but clearly *on its behalf* and *to its benefit.* The sort of experimentation that the Committee certainly did not have in mind was, for example, avant-garde cinema.[75]

The fund's remit, to support new talent with limited funding, production facilities and a first screening at the NFT, saw some success thanks to the self-identified "Free Cinema" group, which included Karel Reisz, Tony Richardson and Michael Grigsby. Each made short films with assistance from the fund before going on to direct within the commercial film industry. However, these ambitious and articulate young directors were also active within the BFI's film culture with their contributions to its publication *Sight and Sound*, and curation of special programmes of films for exhibition. Between 1956 and 1959, the Experimental fund therefore enabled lively debate and a sense of renewal within British cinema.

During the 1950s and 1960s, both the BFI and the Arts Council had become involved in cultural filmmaking, albeit with different objectives. By the late 1960s, however, the Experimental Film Fund had run out of money, and the Arts Council needed a change of direction. During this period, fringe arts organisations were developing as alternatives to the Arts Council, which had already gained a reputation of being essentially conservative and "out of touch" with the radical avant-garde.[76] A turning point was reached in 1968 when the sculptor (and later video artist) David Hall received Arts Council support to make *Vertical*, an early structuralist piece, intended not just as a record of Hall's sculpture but as an artwork in its own right. Visual Arts officer Rodney Wilson recognised the potential

---

[74] Butler, ...*The Art of The Film*, 149.

[75] Christope Dupin, "Early Days of Short Film Production at the British Film Institute: Origins and Evolution of the BFI Experimental Film Fund (1952–66)," *Journal of Media Practice,* 4:2 (2003): 84.

[76] Visual Arts officer David Curtis, interview with the author, October 22, 2004. The following account of the ACGB-BFI "spat" is based on Curtis' recollections. All subsequent further quotations from Curtis are from this interview unless attributed otherwise.

in this cross-over area, and accordingly began to encourage artists to make similar films.[77] Wilson then hired David Curtis, who had previously worked with artist Malcolm Le Grice at the London Arts Lab, in the hope that Curtis' expertise and contacts would help revitalise Arts Council provision for what was now referred to as "artists' film" rather than "films about artists". The new team decided to end the previous co-production arrangement with the BFI by directly commissioning these works from the artists themselves, thus creating a new distribution mechanism known as the Arts Council's film tour. This consisted of three vans equipped with projectors which toured the country, showing the annual collection of documentaries in art galleries, schools and universities.[78]

The Arts Council's growing interest in and control over cultural filmmaking provision sparked complaints from the BFI, which felt that the larger organisation was directly encroaching upon what should be their natural territory. This resulted in an enquiry headed by Richard Attenborough, who, at the time, was a member of both the BFI and the Arts Council boards. Curtis recalls that the enquiry had been expected to rule in favour of the BFI, but the report published in 1973 surprised onlookers with its recommendation that "the Arts Council should embrace and encourage film-making as a fine art activity."[79] The committee thereby set up an arbitrary and almost meaningless distinction between film as a "fine art form", which was the province of the Arts Council, and "experimental" activity, which was to continue to be supported by the BFI. This could only serve to exacerbate the rift between the two organisations as they continued to compete for extremely limited public resources to support very similar types of activity. The ruling resulted in the first official acknowledgment of filmmaking within the Arts Council's structure: the "Artists' Films Subcommittee" was set up in 1973, although it was still under the Visual Arts umbrella rather than recognised in its own right. Importantly, this provided a consistent level of support for avant-garde filmmaking throughout the 1970s, until the time that Rodney Wilson finally set up a dedicated Film, Video and Broadcasting department

[77] Eric White notes that ACGB produced 39 films between 1966 and 1973: 26 documentaries, and 13 "specially made by artists exploring the visual and conceptual aspects of the medium." White, *The Arts Council of Great Britain* (London: Denis Poynter, 1975), 191.
[78] In 1969–70, 2 projector units toured for 43 weeks at a cost of £5,500. ACGB, *Twenty-fifth Annual Report and Accounts, year ending March 1970* (London: ACGB, 1970), 22.
[79] Arts Council of Great Britain, *Report of the Arts Council Film Committee of Enquiry* (London: ACGB, 1973), 6.

in 1986.[80] The mixed media title of the new department reflected the increasing use of video as a more accessible technology than celluloid, as well as growing acceptance of the potential of television as a distribution mechanism suitable for a varied mixture of output.

It was around this point that the BFI's "radical" policy shift, as identified by Peter Sainsbury began to take shape. Fundamentally, this was a move into the production of low-budget features which aimed to be formally experimental and ideologically challenging, often showing a strong influence from European art cinema. The *locus classicus* of these productions was *Radio On* (1979), written and directed by film critic Christopher Petit, and indebted to the "New German Cinema", especially Wim Wenders.[81] The Experimental Film Fund had become the Production Board in 1965, and began to receive its income directly from the BFI rather than independently.[82] The first production officer was the Australian Bruce Beresford, who oversaw Don Levy's *Herostratus* (1967), an esoteric and abrasive call to arms for the new British art cinema. This policy continued to gain momentum under Mamoun Hassan, who would later take charge of the final days of the NFFC, and under Sainsbury himself from 1975 onwards. Sainsbury's natural sympathies were with "independent cinema", but he was also keen to establish viable delivery mechanisms: in 1970 he had helped to establish one of London's key art-house venues, The Other Cinema.[83] This experience of the exhibition sector led to a new interest in sales and promotion within the Board's policy:

> the production, distribution and exhibition of films are aspects of a single creative activity: an indivisible process of creative work and communication.[84]

---

[80] Arts Council of Great Britain, *42nd Annual Report and Accounts, 1986/7* (London: ACGB, 1987), 18.

[81] Geoffrey Nowell-Smith's comment, that *Radio On* was "a film without a cinema" obliquely emphasised the importance of the BFI's production policy. See "Radio On," *Screen*, 20:3/4 (Winter 1979/80): 29–40.

[82] Butler, *The Art of the Film*, 150–156.

[83] Despite a high-profile campaign to save the venue, the Other Cinema closed its doors in November 2004 due to increases in Soho rental costs. See Paul Ardendt, "Last Reel for Soho Cinema?" *Guardian Unlimited*, October 21, 2004, accessed April 2005, http:// www.guardian.co.uk /arts/news/story/0,,1331943,00.html.

[84] Peter Sainsbury, "Production Policy," *The New Social Function of Cinema—Catalogue: British Film Institute Productions, 79/80* (London: BFI, 1981), 9.

This "indivisible process" meant building relationships with filmmakers such as Peter Greenaway and Derek Jarman, whose early work was in the realm of avant-garde experimentation. Sainsbury convinced both to move into full-length narrative feature films with production values high enough not to deter the less radical section of the art-house audience. Films such as *The Draughtsman's Contract* (1982) and *Caravaggio* (1986) therefore achieved a level of visibility within British film culture, which would have been unthinkable for *Radio On*, and were also successful internationally, particularly in Europe.[85] Sainsbury's successors Colin MacCabe and Ben Gibson were able to build upon this foundation throughout the 1980s and 1990s.

A key strength of the BFI during the 1980s came from its subvention deal struck with the new force in broadcasting, Channel Four. This arrangement, forged between the Chief Executive of Channel Four, Jeremy Isaacs, and Sainsbury, then Head of the BFI's Production Board, meant that the broadcaster would automatically match the Institute's investment in any projects of their choosing in return for a seat on the Board and the rights to broadcast the resulting films. One emblematic production resulting from this arrangement was Isaac Julien's *Young Soul Rebels* (1991), an attempt to produce a "cross-over" film which aimed for success outside of the country's art-house venues.[86] Channel Four had already produced several modest hits under its own Film on Four banner (e.g. *My Beautiful Laundrette* (1985)), and was becoming a vital life-line for the commercial film industry, which had lost public support under Margaret Thatcher's deregulation. However, the broadcaster's remit, "to encourage innovation and experiment",[87] also reinvigorated the artists' film and video sector. The channel invested directly in community access video workshops, including David Hall's London Video Arts, although initial results were hampered by a lack of consistent scheduling.[88] The Arts Council's new Film, Video and Broadcasting Department went into partnership with Channel Four to produce programming strands, such as *The 11th Hour* (1988–1994), which represented an "exponential rise in the

---

[85] See Amy Lawrence, *The Films of Peter Greenaway* (Cambridge: Cambridge Uni. Press, 1997); Michael O'Pray, *Derek Jarman: Dreams of England* (London: BFI, 1996).

[86] See Isaac Julien and Colin MacCabe, *Diary of a Young Soul Rebel* (London: BFI, 1990).

[87] Great Britain, *Broadcasting Act 1980* (London: HMSO, 1980).

[88] Rod Stoneman, "Sins of Commissioning," *Screen*, 33:2 (Summer 1992): 127–144.

production of experimental work for television".[89] These late-night broadcasts raised audiences for such previously marginal activity to unprecedented highs: in 1992, it is estimated that around 6 million people saw them;[90] therefore, it can be seen that the collaboration between the Arts Council and Channel Four served to satisfy the same urge towards "accessibility" that Keynes had only reluctantly allowed into his charter, and which had driven the Council's first encounters with the moving image over forty years before.

Conclusion

In 1995, National Lottery funding for film production became the latest in a long line of state interventions in the UK's film industry. Viewed from the perspective of these historical initiatives, the new mechanism can be seen to share certain objectives, advantages and problems with its predecessors. Similar to the quota system, Lottery funding for film aimed to increase the number of feature films produced by the industry, but it did so with direct subsidy rather than by altering market conditions through legislation. Whilst the quota drove down the amounts of money invested in each film, creating the so-called "quickies", Lottery funding tended to inflate budgets, although they remained considerably lower than the amounts invested in comparable Hollywood films. The Eady Levy was designed to reward box-office success, and hence faced criticism for supporting those film companies least requiring state assistance, and in a similar fashion, the Arts Councils' support of popular cinema was partially driven by the logic of recoupment. Probably the most suggestive point of comparison is provided by the National Film Finance Corporation's "Group Production Plan" of the early 1950s, which bears a striking resemblance to the National Lottery franchise scheme, both in terms of its design and its effects. Given this similarity, it is important to consider the extent to which the implementation of Lottery funding for filmmaking was genuinely shaped and influenced by such precedents. Were mistakes corrected and lessons learned, or do the

[89] Rod Stoneman, "Incursions and inclusions: the avant-garde on Channel Four 1983–93," in *The British Avant-Garde Film, 1926–1995: an Anthology of Writings*, ed. Michael O'Pray (Luton: University of Luton Press, 1996), 285–296.
[90] Michael Mazière, "Institutional Support for Artists' Film and Video in England 1966–2003," *British Artists Film and Video Study Collection*, accessed April 2004.http://www.research .linst.ac.uk/ filmcentre//maziere/paper.html.

persistent underlying problems of the UK film industry tend to lead towards similar, yet entirely unconnected, solutions?

Such questions inform my own detailed account of the development of National Lottery funding for film production, which is found in the following two chapters. However, at this point, it is worth pausing to summarise the key components of the film-funding environment into which the Arts Councils entered as distributors of Lottery revenue. The abolition of the Eady Levy and the quota in the early 1980s had left the film industry almost entirely deregulated, although the semi-privatised British Screen continued to provide assistance. Television had become a vital source of funding for low- to medium-budget features, with Channel Four assisting in the production of several films which enjoyed international success, including *The Crying Game* (1992), and *Four Weddings and a Funeral* (1994). As a result, the broadcaster's film operations were expanding, and the international ambitions of PolyGram Filmed Entertainment and the growth of Working Title provided further cause for cautious optimism. Public funding for international co-productions was available through the new European MEDIA initiatives, and tax incentives provided large-scale financial assistance, although the availability of these two sources varied from year to year. Low-budget art cinema continued to find a home at BFI Production, and producers outside of London could access small amounts of regional and national funding through various organisations, such as the Scottish Film Production Fund. Before it was devolved into its constituent home nations, The Arts Council of Great Britain also provided limited grants for artists' film and video projects. The new source of revenue provided by the National Lottery would have a significant impact upon each of these pre-existing resources and institutions, not least upon the Arts Councils themselves.

CHAPTER TWO

ARTS FUNDING MEETS FILM FINANCE

The Arts Councils' brief encounter with the UK film industry presents an opportunity to examine the workings of film policy in practice, as competing agendas from the public and private spheres actively negotiate with one another. This scenario also represents a collision between what Jim McGuigan has termed cultural policy "proper", referring to the long-established structures and institutions which have shaped the relationship between British culture and the state—such as the Arts Council—and cultural policy "as display"; the National Lottery acting in the interests of "national aggrandisement".[1] The most prominent and infamous example of this "aggrandisement" was the Millennium Dome project, but it is also possible to view the support of the film industry in this light, especially within the changing political climate caused by New Labour's image-conscious style of government, and the coinciding media discourse of "Cool Britannia".[2] This media-fuelled resurgence of national pride was predominantly triggered by the music and fashion industries, but it also provided a context within which several of the debates that have traditionally surrounded national cinema could productively be renewed. For example, film's ability to articulate modern or nostalgic notions of British (or English, Scottish, Welsh and Irish) national identities—both at home and across the international arena—was just one of the qualities making it suitable as a recipient of National Lottery funding. Nonetheless, it is important not to forget that this type of policy "on display" could only be achieved with a considerable amount of work going on behind the scenes.

The aim of this chapter is to bring to light the often overlooked or misunderstood effort involved in the realm of policy "proper" through a detailed examination of the early years of National Lottery support for the

---

[1] Jim McGuigan, *Rethinking Cultural Policy* (Maidenhead: Open University Press, 2004), 63–64.

[2] See Peter Oborne, *Alistair Campbell: New Labour and the Rise of the Media Class* (London: Aurum, 1999); John Harris, *The Last Party: Britpop, Blair and the Demise of English Rock* (London: Fourth Estate, 2003).

film industry. Building upon the historical overview provided by Chapter One, I will consider the continuities and departures represented by this new funding mechanism in order to understand how it came into being and how it worked. Before this history can be constructed, there is an additional context to consider: that of the National Lottery itself. This distinctive form of "charitable gambling" has its own set of predecessors, both in the United Kingdom and internationally. Its launch in November 1994 was a moment that provoked intense media scrutiny and set the terms for many of the debates to follow. Such debates have fed into the issues already associated with arts funding in general, and with the support of cinema in particular, and influenced the decision-making of the key personalities and institutions involved. It is well worth considering the procedural details of the resulting system as they articulate the purposes and the problems of this policy. The initial "pilot year" of National Lottery funding for film production in 1995–1996 was followed by a more complex range of measures, including the Lottery Franchise scheme and the policy review, which led to the creation of the Film Council in 2000 and which subsequently removed the Arts Council of England from its gatekeeper role. These developments will be considered here as part of a narrative relating the fortunes of UK film policy in the 1990s, before the evaluative questions raised by this narrative are dealt with at length in Chapter Three.

Lottery Precursors

The introduction of the UK National Lottery in 1994 was a significant development for state-supported culture, but the system was not without its historical and international precedents. Different versions of this "charitable gambling" mechanism have existed in England since the Elizabethan period, and have more recently spread in popularity across the world. Historian C. L'Estrange Ewen has detailed the many and varied benefits to English civilisation, which were made possible by the previous State Lotteries. This list includes the building of Westminster Bridge, the founding of the British Museum, and the colonisation of the State of Virginia, as well as "the encouragement of the Fine Arts".[3] Despite such worthy results, the English State Lottery was abandoned by George IV amidst much pomp and ceremony. In October 1826, Londoners witnessed

[3] C. L'Estrange Ewen, *Lotteries and Sweepstakes: an Historical, Legal and Ethical Survey of their Introduction, Suppression and Re-establishment in the British Isles* (London: Heath Cranton, 1932), 240–242.

processions headed by purple silk banners proclaiming, "All Lotteries end for ever on Tuesday next",[4] and *The Times* confirmed that the Lottery had indeed "breathed its last".[5]

Fig. 2-1: "All Lotteries End For Ever" in 1826

This unpopular decision was prompted by ethical concerns: the lotteries had become synonymous with profiteering, scandal and moral degradation. Diarist William Hone's 'Epitaph' for the State Lotteries contends that they were outlawed for encouraging "a spirit of Speculation and Gambling among the lower classes of the people, thousands of whom fell victim to their insinuating and tempting allurements."[6] The idea that the 'Lottery

[4] L'Estrange Ewen, *Lotteries and Sweepstakes*, 241.
[5] William Hone, *The Every Day Book, Or, A Guide to the Year, Vol. II* (London: William Tegg, 1868), 750. First published weekly, January 1825–December 1826; Anon., 'State Lottery', *The Times* (October 19, 1826), 3.
[6] Hone, *The Every Day Book*, Vol. ii, 763.

myth' effectively exploits the most financially vulnerable in society is one which was reprised upon the system's revival 168 years later.

The prohibition of the State Lotteries in England left a gap between public expenditure and private philanthropy for several generations. During this period, Royal patronage of the fine arts continued and was augmented by investment from the wealth of the mercantile classes. London's first public art gallery at Dulwich College contained the private collection of Sir William Bourgeois, willed for posterity upon his death in 1811.[7] The founding of the first National Gallery in 1824, paid for with a grant from Parliament, signalled that the state was taking increased responsibility for the nation's artistic treasures, a trend which continued with the establishment of the Victoria and Albert Museum and the Royal College of Art, both of which were built on land purchased by the Government.[8] In 1852, Queen Victoria inaugurated a parliamentary Department of Science and Art, proclaiming that "The advancement of the Fine Arts and of Practical Science will be readily recognized by you as worthy of the Attention of a great and enlightened Nation."[9] This department developed into the Board of Education with responsibility for funding museums, galleries and libraries as well as schools, therefore combining several senses of the complex noun "culture": knowledge and learning, artistic endeavour, and national aggrandisement. Robert Hewison has described the modern trajectory of cultural funding in developed countries as the patronage of the government gradually replacing that of the Church, the Crown, the aristocracy, and the bourgeoisie.[10] However, unlike previous forms of patronage, the state pays for culture using public money—either in the form of taxation or, as in the UK since 1994, with the proceeds of the National Lottery. This use of public finance has important implications for the types of culture which are validated or ignored.

Internationally, state lotteries increased both in numbers and in scale throughout the twentieth century. In 1930, for example, the Irish Free State exploited its independence from British control by establishing the Hospital Sweepstakes to finance an improved health infrastructure. Because

---

[7] Dulwich Picture Gallery, "Gallery History," *DPG*, accessed February 2006, http://www.dulwichpicture gallery.org.uk /history/default.aspx.

[8] John Pick, *The Arts in a State: A Study of Government Arts Policies from Ancient Greece to the Present* (Bristol: Bristol Classical Press, 1988).

[9] Queen Victoria cited in Andrew Sinclair, *Arts and Cultures* (London: Sinclair-Stevenson, 1995), 17.

[10] Robert Hewison, *Culture and Consensus: England, Art and Politics since 1940* (London: Methuen, 1995), 301.

large-scale lotteries were still outlawed at this point across the rest of the British Isles, the Sweepstakes were enormously popular and tickets were sold worldwide, albeit illegally.[11] France reintroduced a nationwide lottery in 1936, and in 1964 the United States saw its first state lottery system in New Hampshire. From the 1980s onwards, as economic historian Andrew Douglas demonstrated, European lotteries grew exponentially. This boom, combined with the reduction in trade barriers within the European Union after 1992, meant that losing large amounts of potential revenue overseas became a real possibility.[12] Douglas also notes that the importance of moral objections to so-called "soft" forms of gambling had significantly diminished since World War II. An important ethical barrier against the principle was removed in 1956 when Premium Bonds were introduced within the UK. This system of state investment has interest paid as random prizes, and therefore reinstated a form of gambling onto the government's balance sheet. In 1978, the Royal Commission on Gambling chaired by Lord Rothschild recommended the reinstatement of nationwide charitable gambling in the UK with the proceeds to be spent on the arts, sport and other good causes.[13] Mrs Thatcher's Methodist affiliation effectively ruled out this possibility, despite the fact that her government's cuts in public spending were having detrimental effects in precisely the areas which a Lottery might benefit. Indeed, the Arts Council suffered funding freezes during the 1980s which meant that, adjusted for inflation, its income had fallen in real terms by 19%.[14]

During his tenure as Chancellor of the Exchequer, John Major oversaw several above-inflation increases in arts spending, and when he succeeded Margaret Thatcher as Prime Minister in 1990, he planned to reorganise provision for the arts, sport and heritage within a new department of state.[15] Major argued that the new Department of National Heritage needed an additional source of finance if it was to have any significant impact, and the idea of a National Lottery was floated once again. The chairman of the Home Affairs Select Committee, Sir Ivan Lawrence,

---

[11] Andrew Douglas notes that between 1930 and 1986 the 201 Irish Sweepstakes paid out Ir £275m in prizes and raised Ir £133m for the countries hospitals. Douglas, *British Charitable Gambling 1956–1994: Towards a National Lottery* (London: Athalone, 1995), 411.

[12] Douglas, *British Charitable Gambling*, 403–409.

[13] The Royal Commission on Gambling, chair Lord Rothschild, *Final Report*, Cmnd. 7200 (London: HMSO, 1978).

[14] Hewison, *Culture and Consensus*, 247.

[15] John Major, *John Major: The Autobiography* (London: Harper Collins, 1999), 405.

produced a Private Member's Bill on the policy in 1991, with a White Paper and full Bill following in March and December 1992, respectively.[16] Issues discussed herein included a notable reduction in moral objections to gambling, and the potential competition for charitable revenue from Europe. In 1993, the introduction of a National Lottery became an official pledge in the Conservative Party's manifesto for the General Election.[17] Major's political opponents may have considered the policy as a desperate act of populism from a failing Tory dynasty, but following his party's surprise re-election, the Lottery quickly gained Royal assent.

The Department of National Heritage (DNH) identified five "good causes" to be the beneficiaries of Lottery proceeds: the arts, sport, charities, heritage and the upcoming Millennium celebrations. The government put the system out for private tender, and there was significant press interest in which applicants would be granted the operating licence, particularly when the celebrity entrepreneur Richard Branson declared his intention to run the system on a not-for-profit basis.[18] This was not the case for several of his competitors, including the eventual winners Camelot, a consortium of business interests which included Cadbury/Schweppes and computer manufacturer ICL. Under the terms of the licence agreement with Camelot, for every pound spent on a Lottery ticket, 28p would go to good causes, 50p would top-up the prize fund, 10p would cover running costs (including Camelot's profits) and, equally controversially, 12p would go back to the Exchequer as taxation.[19]

In line with the so-called "arm's-length" principle, each of the organisations selected to distribute Lottery funds would be independent from direct government control. Accordingly, the DNH was required to set up two new organisations to handle charity awards and the Millennium projects against a very tight timetable, as the launch of the system was scheduled for just over a year after the 1993 General Election. It can therefore be suggested that the decision to allocate the responsibility for arts, sports and heritage Lottery funding to previously existing bodies was,

---

[16] Great Britain Home Office, *A National Lottery Raising Money for Good Causes*, Cmnd. 1861, (London: HMSO, 1992); Great Britain House of Commons, *National Lottery etc. Bill* (London: HMSO, 1992).

[17] Conservative Party, *The Best Future for Britain: The Conservative Manifesto 1992* (London: Conservative Central Office, 1992), 44–46.

[18] Raymond Snoddy and John Ashworth, *It Could Be You: The Untold Story of the National Lottery* (London: Faber and Faber, 2000), 86–104.

[19] Director General of the National Lottery, *Annual Report 1994/95* (London: HMSO, 1995), 10.

above all, a matter of political expediency.[20] The recently devolved Arts Councils of England, Scotland and Wales, and the independent Arts Council of Northern Ireland, were given the task of distributing Lottery money into the arts sector. All of the Lottery distributing bodies were required to concentrate on funding capital infrastructure, primarily buildings and equipment, rather than revenue expenditure, such as wages and running costs. They were asked to prioritise projects which could demonstrate a significant element of "partnership funding" already committed from other sources. Applications from all organisations, large and small, must be considered, with no possibility—initially, at least—of soliciting the projects which best fitted into their long-term strategies.[21] Each of the requirements set down in the Lottery legislation would have direct effects upon the systems put in place to deliver the funding, and consequently also impact upon the sectors which received the money.

The controls placed upon the use of National Lottery funds represented attempts to manage political tensions within the system as a whole. For example, the "partnership funding" requirement was used to argue that the extra money was being used as "seed capital" to attract further private investment, rather than simply replacing it. Other pieces of the system proved more difficult to defend from its critics, the numbers of which included the Australian composer and philanthropist Denis Vaughan. Vaughan had previously been an influential voice arguing in favour of the introduction of a lottery system; he had put the idea to Margaret Thatcher as early as 1987.[22] However, Vaughan's utopian dream of a "Lottery Foundation independent of government and the Arts Councils" was frustrated, and when Camelot was awarded the licence to operate the Lottery as a commercial concern, he was furious to learn that £85m a year would be lost to company profits.[23] Such charges of profiteering and sleaze are perhaps not so far removed from the debates that led to the State

---

[20] Sports funding went to the four Sports Councils of the UK, whilst heritage funding was allocated to the trustees of the National Heritage Memorial Fund, a body created in 1980.

[21] Arts Council of England (ACE), "Statement of Compliance with Policy and Financial Regulations," *2nd Annual Report and Accounts 1995–6* (London: ACE, 1996), 99–102. Also see Anthony Everitt, "Catch-22 of the Lottery," *The Guardian*, May 30, 1994, Section 2, 11.

[22] Michael Binyon, "Denis the Menace and the Great Lotto Rip-Off," *Times Online*, December 29, 2003, accessed January 2004, http://www.timesonline.co.uk/article/0,,585-942548,00.html.

[23] Peter Lennon, "The Composer, the Lottery and the Fat Cats who will Hit the Jackpot," *The Guardian*, September 24, 1994, 27.

Lottery's downfall in 1826; however, Vaughan continued to argue for a fairer, non-profit-making Lottery system which would use the arts and sport to tackle widespread and destructive "spiritual poverty".[24] This may sound like an antiquated, even puritanical notion of the function of artistic activity within society, but Vaughan's views would find echoes in the incoming Labour government's ideology.[25] They also find expression within the narrative of the hit Lottery-funded film of 2000, *Billy Elliot,* whose eponymous young hero ballet dances his way out of hardship to success on the London stage.

Here it is important to make a distinction between Vaughan's noble objections and the views of the right-wing press on the moral responsibilities of the National Lottery. This stance is exemplified by the *Daily Mail*'s editorials during the launch week in November 1994. One prototypical column attacked the "self-important quangos" who, it suggested, would hijack the Lottery's proceeds for the purposes of the "cultural elite". Like Vaughan, the *Mail* believed in the Lottery's potential to improve social conditions, but it took a more literal view of the best way to achieve such desired improvements:

> Lottery tickets should buy green spaces for those trapped in the dereliction of the inner cities. Not white elephants for the year 2000. Lottery tickets should pay for beds for the elderly. Not seats at the opera for businessmen on expense accounts.[26]

This type of emotive populism creates rousing leader inches, but it betrays a stubborn misunderstanding of both the mechanism and the purpose of the National Lottery. At the time of its launch, the money raised for the five good causes was split evenly between the five separate distributors. Therefore, the notorious award made by the Arts Council for the renovation of the Royal Opera House in Covent Garden had no direct effect on the amount of money available to charitable causes.[27] More importantly, however, the *Mail*'s argument disregards a founding principle of the Lottery system: that of "additionality".

---

[24] Binyon, "Denis the Menace".
[25] See Chris Smith, *Creative Britain.* London: Faber and Faber, 1998.
[26] Anon., "Don't Tax the Poor to Amuse the Rich," *Daily Mail*, November 15, 1994, 8.
[27] For an eloquent, if partisan, explanation of this logic from the then Chairman of the Arts Council, see Grey Gowrie, "Let the Bids Roll In," *The Guardian*, August 6, 1996, 13.

The provision of additionality in the National Lottery legislation was designed to alleviate one fear expressed by many commentators before its launch, namely: "Will lottery money become a substitute for government expenditure?"[28] As early as 1968, the then Chancellor, Roy Jenkins, had proposed a lottery system to support sectors of society where additional expenditure could be described as "desirable but not essential".[29] "Essential" services would continue to be funded through general taxation, whereas those "desirable" extras would benefit from the new, "additional" source of income; Jenkins' definition therefore relies on a distinction between society's "wants" and its "needs". The obvious problem with this idea lies in the qualitative judgement, which must be made as to any given sector's importance relative to all others. For example, Denis Vaughan regards the arts as absolutely essential for British society, but for the *Mail,* seats at the opera are mere extravagances. Nonetheless, Jenkins' separation of the essential from the desirable was passed down through the political generations to become a clear influence upon the Lottery White Paper of 1992. Here, the government states that the money raised for the good causes must fund projects additional to those which would otherwise be paid for by taxation.[30]

The question of additionality is heightened in the case of the Lottery when compared with general taxation, partly because of the element of choice implicit in the decision to buy a lottery ticket. The public feel that Lottery money belongs to them in a way, which is different to general taxation. This psychological ownership was encouraged by political rhetoric of the time, particularly John Major's, who stated that, "This is in every sense a people's lottery."[31] The tactic of labelling the Lottery as belonging to "the people" creates problems for those with the responsibility of distributing the proceeds; if this money represents an emotional investment as well as a fiscal one, it should not be surprising that the public have strong reactions to the more contentious decisions. This was especially the case during the early stages of the Lottery's reintroduction, when the system was a national obsession, exceeding all estimates of its

---

[28] Michael Church, "The Arm's Length Way to Wave Goodbye," *The Observer*, January 17, 1993, 45.

[29] Roy Jenkins cited in Snoddy, *It Could Be You*, 29.

[30] Great British Home Office, *A National Lottery Raising Money for Good Causes*, Cmnd. 1861 (March 1992), paragraph 41.

[31] John Major cited in Anon., "Don't Tax the Poor to Amuse the Rich," *Daily Mail*, November 15, 1994, 8.

potential popularity.[32] Sales of tickets in the first 20 weeks were worth £1.2 billion, around £300 million more than had been forecast.[33] As a consequence of its success, the Lottery seemed to offer a solution for even the most intractable of arts funding deficiencies. For the first time, large-scale public investment in the UK film industry became a real possibility. However, funding the film sector, where private enterprise intersects with public cultural concerns, stretches the logic of additionality to its limits. The public's emotional investment in such an industry was sure to provoke as much as placate.

Towards Lottery Funding for Film

> Even today, you cannot make a living as a feature-film producer in England. You really can't. Even I couldn't, and I was doing well. What it must have been like for other people I shudder to think.[34]
>
> David Puttnam on the 1980s.

> If you are a [British] producer, your opportunities in terms of the overall growth of the market have never been so good.[35]
>
> Former PolyGram CEO Stuart Till in 1998.

The above two statements on the changing fortunes of British film producers are separated by a period of almost ten years. The most obvious question they raise is: what happened in the intervening period to create such an apparent turnaround? Part of the answer to that question is the arrival of National Lottery funding for film production. Puttnam's perspective comes from a period when state support for British cinema had reached its nadir; he had nonetheless found success as an independent producer, as well as developing a close association with Goldcrest, the company responsible for the notion that "the British were coming".[36] He moved further and further away from the domestic industry, eventually all the way to Hollywood, having a brief period of tenure as head of

---

[32] Christopher Leake, "Britain's Luckiest Numbers," *Mail on Sunday*, November 20, November, 1994, 1.

[33] Andrew Culf, "Pay and profits justified by success, says Camelot," *The Guardian*, June 7, 1995, 3.

[34] Jake Eberts and Terry Illot, *My Indecision is Final: The Rise and Fall of Goldcrest Films* (London: Faber and Faber, 1990), 103.

[35] Louise Tutt, "Greater Expectations," *Screen International,* 1142, January 23, 1998), 24.

[36] This famous phrase was uttered by screenwriter Colin Welland as he won an Oscar for *Chariots of Fire* in 1982.

Columbia Pictures in 1986. Stuart Till's career developed less erratically; with a background in advertising, he became Chief Executive of PolyGram Filmed Entertainment (PFE) in 1992. PFE was an ambitious off-shoot of the Dutch music company PolyGram, and therefore typical of the international entertainment industry's trend towards multi-media conglomeration during this period.[37] Through its subsidiary Working Title, PFE was involved in the production or distribution of the majority of successful British films throughout the 1990s, from *Four Weddings and a Funeral* to *Bean*.

Neither Puttnam nor Till would seem to have been in the position of needing support from public funding mechanisms. Nonetheless, their careers converged in the middle of the 1990s through shared ambitions in the political arena. Puttnam became an influential member of the panel which advised the Arts Councils on their investments in film production, and Till led the Labour government's Film Policy Review Group which eventually resulted in the setting up of the Film Council in 2000. The process of reconciliation between the state and the film industry is often considered to date from a seminar held by Margaret Thatcher at Downing Street in June 1990.[38] Thatcher invited the industry's great and good, including Puttnam and his Goldcrest associate Richard Attenborough, to discuss ways in which the government might be able to offer them a financial lifeline. As with the beginnings of the National Lottery itself, and indeed much of the British political agenda in the early 1990s, competition with Europe seemed a vital motivating factor. The Prime Minister conceded that in order to create a level playing field for British filmmakers in Europe she would have to overcome her aversion to state subsidy and provide some direct economic support. This policy review resulted in a little extra money for European co-productions via British Screen, and the creation of a British Film Commission to attract lucrative overseas productions into the UK. However, building links with Europe or sustaining an infrastructure to service Hollywood blockbusters were only partial solutions to the industry's difficulties, with the big question remaining: what measures could be taken to stimulate home-grown film production?

---

[37] See Stephen Prince, *A New Pot of Gold: Hollywood Under the Electronic Rainbow, 1980–1989* (Berkeley, University of California Press: 2000).

[38] An entertaining account of the strange events that day is provided by the artist and filmmaker Isaac Julien. See Isaac Julien and Colin MacCabe, *Diary of a Young Soul Rebel* (London: BFI, 1990), 14–21.

It is worth pausing for a moment to consider this assumption in more detail. For some economists and commentators, there is no actual requirement for the British film industry to produce its own films. Michael Walsh summarises these arguments in his work on the relationship between the American and British film industries following the First World War.[39] The central idea is one of "comparative advantage". This theory states that the most sensible use of international economic resources is for each state to concentrate on the production of commodities in which it enjoys a natural advantage. This allows for efficient, specialised producers which can yield additional economies of scale, producing a trade surplus which can be used to purchase other types of goods. In this sense, only a handful of nations have the comparative advantage of an efficient, specialised movie industry combined with a large enough domestic market to amortise the high initial costs of production—most obviously the United States and India. Britain was capable of sustaining a film industry on the basis of its strong domestic market during the peak of cinema's popularity in the 1930s and 1940s, but declining audiences since the introduction of television means that this has not been the case for several decades. However, this country does have a legacy of highly skilled technicians and facilities, as well as a renowned tradition of training for stage actors and directors, and a more recent comparative advantage in high-tech post-production technology. These factors have led some commentators to conclude that the film industry in the UK should renounce attempts to compete with the world's more efficient nations and become "Hollywood East". Some go even further and argue that the very idea of competition between nation states is now irrelevant in the face of global entertainment industries.[40]

The main problem with the logic of comparative advantage is that it assumes homogeneity of product, with consumers who only care about price and supply. Whilst this may be the case for industrial commodities, such as coal or textiles, it is nevertheless known to be more difficult to apply to the products of the entertainment industries, such as music or films. Walsh explains:

> If we make the strong claim that films are cultural expressions of (among other things) national identity, or even the weaker claim that films contain references to profilmic elements which may not be comprehensible to

[39] Michael Walsh, "Fighting the American Invasion with Cricket, Roses and Marmalade for Breakfast," *The Velvet Light Trap*, 40 (Fall 1997): 3–17.
[40] See Toby Miller et al. on the new international division of cultural labour in *Global Hollywood* (London: BFI, 2003).

> audiences in another part of the world, then consumer indifference is lost and comparative advantage called into question.[41]

Different versions of both these "strong" and "weak" claims have formed the backbone of the debate over state support for the British film industry throughout the twentieth century. As discussed in Chapter One, the quota system introduced in the 1920s was based on the assumption that British audiences naturally wanted to watch British films but were not being given the opportunity to do so by the exhibition sector. By the mid-1990s, similar claims were being reformulated in policy documents, such as that produced by MP Gerald Kaufman's select committee in 1995. This report describes the film industry as "a national asset in which all may take genuine pride." It makes "an important contribution to the creative and imaginative life of the nation," and "contributes to the country's international reputation".[42] A committee invoking the language of national aggrandisement through culture is unlikely to be convinced by the argument that the UK's inherent comparative disadvantage in this sector makes any state intervention meaningless.

Despite its optimistic tone and carefully polished presentation, the 1995 report fails in its attempts to gloss over what was, by this stage, becoming an increasingly thorny issue: what to do with the impending influx of National Lottery money. The section on the role of the Lottery is introduced with this sentence:

> While neither the Government nor the industry favours large-scale direct subsidy, the Government recognises that the risks involved in making even a modest feature film are high, and that prospective financial backers are often reluctant to add to that risk by investing in films involving inexperienced or unknown film makers as producers or directors.[43]

This lengthy construction places its most controversial statement in a modest subsidiary clause at the beginning. Thus, the big problem—that neither the government nor the industry actually favours subsidy—loses its force behind the subsequent chain of common sense economics. Following this linguistic sleight of hand, the report offers British Screen as the model upon which the Arts Council of England (ACE), not the government, has decided to construct its programme of funding. It is also noted that the

[41] Walsh, "Fighting the American Invasion," 5–6.

[42] Department of National Heritage, *The British Film Industry,* Cmnd. 2884 (London: HMSO, 1995), 4.

[43] DNH, *The British Film Industry*, 18.

other Arts Councils of the home nations are to decide how the money should be used within their own territories; this is the "arm's-length" principle working in the government's favour: the Department of National Heritage (DNH) takes the credit for a scheme which it cannot logically "favour", whilst subtly shifting responsibility for the decisions away to a safe distance.

A few months before the publication of the select committee's report, ACE had officially announced that a portion of its funds raised by the National Lottery were to be made available to the British film industry. This decision had been reached as a result of persistent lobbying from industry bodies, particularly the Producers Alliance for Cinema and Television (PACT).[44] Certain issues remained contested, such as the legal definition of film production as the creation of a capital asset, rather than as revenue expenditure. The restriction of Lottery funding to capital projects had been included in the legislation as a further guarantee of additionality: the Arts Council were already providing revenue funding for large arts organisations through taxation, with the fear that this would be cut and replaced with the new funding stream. However, the film industry differed from institutions, such as the Royal Opera House, in the crucial respect that it had not received significant protection from market forces for a generation, and that there was therefore very little public investment to "replace". Another important difference between funding films and other arts projects was that the Lottery money was to be an equity investment rather than a straight-forward grant; recoupment was expected. In public, the chairman of the newly established Lottery Panel, Peter Gummer, spoke of his confidence that Lottery funding for film production would "lever in additional money, attract new investors and encourage investment in high-quality projects previously considered too risky."[45] Around £10 million was pledged for a pilot scheme to last for one year, during which time the Panel would assess the suitability of the mechanism it had chosen to deliver Lottery funding into the film industry.

Initially, this mechanism was almost identical to that which applied to all other "art forms" chasing their share of the money. Production companies were invited to put in applications on a single project basis, and were required to demonstrate that their organisation was financially viable, and also that funding from other sources was already in place. Applicants were also required to address the more abstract question of the "public benefit"

---

[44] DNH, *Second Report from the National Heritage Committee: The British Film Industry, Vol. 1* (London: HMSO, 1995).

[45] Peter Gummer cited in Adam Dawtry, "Brit Pix Win Lottery Subsidy Money," *Variety*, April 10, 1995, 21.

which would result from their completed film. The assessment process sometimes included a period of consultation with other bodies: for example, in England, British Screen's script reading expertise would be used to assess the project's potential quality. Amongst the smaller home nations, the work of assessment was outsourced to make efficient use of limited finances, although the ultimate responsibility remained with the respective Arts Council. In Northern Ireland, this work was carried out by the Northern Ireland Film Council, —a small integrated agency combining funding from regional and national sources to support local production.[46] This agency received the applications and their supporting material from ACNI, sent out scripts to a range of freelance readers, and corresponded with the applicants if further information was required, before compiling their summary report.[47] Such reports contained comments from the readers on the script, an evaluation of the key creative personalities involved and the viability of the budget, and finally, a recommendation either to fund or to reject the project. Similar arrangements were also set up in Wales (with Sgrin) and Scotland (with the Scottish Film Production Fund). The first Lottery awards for film production were announced by the Scottish Arts Council in August 1995.[48]

The arrival of Lottery funding represented a major structural upheaval for the Arts Councils, which was especially evident in England where the bulk of the money was allocated. The resulting process has been described by Richard Witts as "bolting on a unit sometimes twice as rich as its presumed boss".[49] During the late 1990s, the "old" Arts Council of England received around £190 million a year from taxation to spend on the annual work of its client list. The new Lottery unit, established under director Jeremy Newton in 1995–1996, committed £340 million in its first year of operation.[50] The Lottery unit was physically separated from ACE's prestigious premises at Great Peter Street, London, with its views of

---

[46] The Northern Ireland Film Council became the Northern Ireland Film Commission in 1997. In 2002 it was renamed as the Northern Ireland Film and Television Commission, and in 2007 it became simply Northern Ireland Screen.

[47] According to then Chief Executive Richard Taylor, the Northern Ireland Film Council's income rose from £400k per annum in 1994 to over £2m in 2002 as a result of processing the Lottery applications on behalf of ACNI. Interview with the author, February 2006.

[48] Rhys Williams, "Lottery Handout for Film Projects," *The Independent*, August 26, 1995, 6.

[49] Richard Witts, *Artist Unknown: An Alternative History of the Arts Council* (London: Little, Brown and Company, 1998), 510.

[50] ACE, 2rd *Annual Reports and Accounts 1995–6* (London: ACE, 1996), 10.

Westminster. Instead, it was situated in Portland House, a functional 1960s office tower block located near Victoria Station. Speaking from my own experience as an employee of the Lottery unit, the cultures of the two "wings" were extremely different. Placed on a steep learning curve, the new unit was characterised by frenetic activity and a flexible approach to procedure; thus, in the early days, the activity of film production was treated no differently than the provision of new instruments for a brass band in Huddersfield or the major building projects, such as the Royal Opera House's renovation. Two Lottery officers were hired as film specialists, and alongside their colleagues from different disciplines they fielded applications, consulted external assessors, including British Screen and the BFI, and made recommendations to the Lottery Advisory Panel, who made the final decisions.[51]

It soon became obvious that there were fundamental differences between the tasks of funding film production and the other activities supported by the Lottery unit. Film Officer Mark Dunford likened the situation to "trying to bang square pegs into round holes."[52] For example, the DNH policy directions on the use of National Lottery money contained a requirement of "the widening of public access" to whatever activity was being supported.[53] For a new arts centre, this requirement is relatively easy to quantify; market research tools exist which can be used to demonstrate the extent of the potential audience for such a venue. For film projects, however, this requirement demands an engagement with the complexities of film distribution networks, which multiplies the number of organisations involved. Other difficulties were caused by the fragility of film financing deals, which, by their nature, require careful and strategic tendering. The officers were soon arguing that they needed to be able to collect different types of information and assess the applications in a different way, which subsequently led to a separate application form for film projects and revised assessment criteria, which were published in 1997. This, in turn, began a process of separation between the Lottery unit, now renamed "Capital Services", and the new Lottery Film department. Staff numbers for the new department grew; a new director, Carolyn Lambert, was hired, and the need for more space meant that they, too, were soon physically separated from the other officers on a different floor of Portland House.

---

[51] One of these Officers, Mark Dunford was hired based on his experience at the BBC, the Communications Policy Research Centre, and the BFI. Interview with the author, July 2004.

[52] Email interview with the author, July 2004.

[53] Arts Council of England (ACE), "Guidelines," *National Lottery Funding for Film: Application Pack* (London, ACE, 1997), 5.

These internal pressures, caused by difficulties in marrying the ideology of Lottery funding with the practicalities of the film industry, were also reflected in public debates during this period. A good example is the argument that surrounded the notion of "public benefit", which was to be one of the criteria against which applications would be judged suitable or unsuitable for Lottery funding. ACE's guidelines warned film producers that they would "need to demonstrate that the proposed subject will promote the public good".[54] The obvious lack of clarity of this statement was exploited by journalists, such as *The Independent*'s David Lister, who claimed this meant that only "politically correct" films would be eligible for funding. Lister cited another of the DNH's requirements; that people with disabilities be encouraged to participate in film production, as further evidence that left-wing tokenism would dominate the awards. He also speculated that this prerequisite would, by definition, rule out movies which were "likely to be commercially successful."[55] This article prompted ACE's National Lottery director Jeremy Newton to reply forcefully, claiming that there was no contradiction between "public benefit" and likely commercial success. Newton argued that "many commercial films do serve the public good by virtue of their high artistic quality or by their capacity to raise significant social issues."[56] By September 1995, as ACE announced their first crop of film awards, they had reportedly decided to take "an extremely broad view of what defines public benefit."[57]

There are interesting parallels between these arguments and those surrounding the idea of "public service" in British broadcasting. Paddy Scannell noted that this concept originated as a pragmatic response to the twin technological limitations of early broadcasting: scarcity of available wavelength and lack of a box-office mechanism.[58] This meant that a "public utility" approach was most sensible, leading to a monopolistic BBC funded by the licence fee. However, by the mid-1980s, this situation had changed dramatically. In 1986, the Peacock Committee report on the financing of the BBC redefined British broadcasting as a "market", driven

---

[54] ACE, "Guidelines," *National Lottery Funding for Film: Application Pack*, 8.

[55] David Lister, "'Correct' Films to get Lottery Cash," *The Independent*, April 6, 1995), 8.

[56] Jeremy Newton, "Films that Serve the Public Good," *The Independent*, April 7, 1995, 18.

[57] Marianne MacDonald, "Lottery goes into the Blockbuster Business," *The Independent*, September 18, 1995, 1.

[58] Paddy Scannell, "Public Service Broadcasting: The History of a Concept" in *Understanding Television*, eds. Andrew Goodwin and Paddy Scannel (London: Routledge, 1990), 11–29.

by the forces of competition, and its audience as "consumers" with the power of choice. This perspective therefore alters the idea of "public service" to "simply any major modification of purely commercial provision resulting from public policy."[59] Thus, public service broadcasting survives deregulation thanks to ideas of "market failure", or the acceptance that market forces alone cannot be relied upon to provide everything that society deems important.[60] In the context of television, this is closely tied with notions of "quality"; the BBC's classic defence of its corner is to highlight declining standards in commercial broadcasting. Within the film industry, the most obvious public service/benefit provided by interventionist policy is simply more British films being made. Strictly speaking, the resulting publicly-funded films will therefore be "uncommercial" by definition, in that the market left alone would probably not support their production.

The Independent's critique, cited above, also raises questions of elitism and accessibility. Lister uses the term "political correctness" to attack a pluralist stance, which places an emphasis on the voices of minorities over those of the majority. In response, Newton shifts "public benefit" back into the realm of "quality", and points out the democratic potential of pluralism: the raising of "issues" to be debated by society as whole. But perhaps no manner of renegotiation could appease those commentators who fundamentally disagreed with the idea that Lottery funding for film production was in the public's interest. The most notorious examples of this response were provided by Alexander Walker's regular attacks on the system from his position as film critic for the London *Evening Standard*. These tirades began in November 1995 with an article entitled "Lottery Millions Will Be Wasted on Films."[61] Here, Walker accuses the Major government of naked opportunism and getting itself off the hook with the film industry by gifting them funds from outside the Treasury. He opposes the definition of films as capital assets, necessary in order to make them eligible for Lottery funding, claiming that filmmaking is "an irrational, unsafe and often wildly wasteful gamble with only a slim chance of winning." He also argues that the film industry is in no need of further "government largesse", citing the £17 million annual grant given to the

[59] Alan Peacock (chair), *Report of the Committee on Financing the BBC,* Cmnd. 9824, (London: HMSO, July 1986), para. 580, cited in Bob Franklin, ed., *British Television Policy: A Reader* (London: Routledge, 2001), 26.

[60] I am grateful to Prof. Shaun Hargreaves Heap who argued this case at a UEA film studies research seminar on the future of the BBC in March 2004.

[61] Alexander Walker, "Lottery millions will be wasted on films," *Evening Standard*, November 24, 1995, 9.

BFI as proof of its riches, and presumably confusing the entire running costs of this public body with the small amounts it was spending on film production at that point.[62]

When Walker rhetorically questions who will benefit from the scheme, his answer is not the nation or the community, but rather the "bank accounts of privately owned production companies and the pockets of individual film people." His mistrust of filmmakers' motives is illustrated by a cartoon showing a director helping himself to large amounts of public money. This article therefore sets out the key points of Walker's critique: filmmakers neither need nor deserve public handouts, and the industry should be left alone to sort out its own problems. As the resulting films were released, he would often use his newspaper reviews to draw attention to the amounts of public money wasted on those he disliked, whilst more positive verdicts frequently omitted the film's Lottery-funded status.[63]

Walker's final book on the UK film industry, published posthumously following his death in 2003, gives detailed attention to Lottery funding for film, including his involvement in Gerald Kaufman's Select Committee readings, which led to its introduction. In a retrospective round-up of the Lottery's early "Fool's Gold" years, he comments that:

> Subsidy was essential to the British—or any—film industry, either in direct grants or tax relief, but subsidy on this scale, applied by people lacking time and judgement, and utilised by others lacking talent and commitment to anything but paying their own salaries upfront, was bound to fail.[64]

This argument is flawed by Walker's misunderstanding of the "scale" of Lottery funding compared with tax relief, which has seen far greater sums of public money pass into producers' pockets—largely without the checks of a selective grant-giving system. His assessment of the Arts Councils' commitment to filmmaking is unfair given the time and energy spent

---

[62] In 1995, BFI Production's annual allocation from the Institute's overall budget was £500,000. Then Head of Production, Ben Gibson, interview with the author, March 2004.

[63] Alexander Walker's negative reviews emphasising Lottery funding: *Beautiful People* ("From Farce to Worse," *Evening Standard*, September 16, 1999, 31); *Plunkett and Macleane* ("Highway Yobbery," *Evening Standard*, April 1, 1999, 37); and *Simon Magus* ("Devil Makes Mischief," *Evening Standard*, May 15, 2000, 30). Glowing review omitting Lottery funding: *The Tango Lesson* ("Sally puts on her dancing shoes," *Evening Standard*, November 27, 1997, 27).

[64] Alexander Walker, *Icons in the Fire: The Decline and Fall of Almost Everybody in the British Film Industry, 1984–2000* (London: Orion, 2004), 275.

setting up an entire new department, and the "judgement" of its staff members was augmented by the skills and experience of many external assessors, including the BFI and British Screen. Finally, Walker's condemnation of all subsidised British filmmakers as talentless cynics is clearly ridiculous: he is an unabashed elitist, but he forgets that the careers of his favourite art-house auteurs Peter Greenaway, Sally Potter or even Lynne Ramsey would have been unthinkable without cultural subsidies. Walker's increasingly strident attacks on the Arts Council came to be viewed by many other critics as sheer bloody-mindedness, or even sour grapes for the failure of Gerald Kaufmann's advisory committee to take his advice, that the film industry "is not a business for any public body to have dealings with."[65]

Walker was fond of repeating a memorable comment made by Simon Perry, Chief Executive of British Screen, who, when interviewed by *Variety* on Lottery funding for film production in 1996, stated:

> What they're doing is releasing pure heroin onto the street, rather than the diluted methadone that everyone's used to... So they had best be sure they get it right.[66]

As a supplier of the "diluted methadone" himself, Perry is clearly speaking partly from a position of concern over the future of his own organisation, but he is also markedly proposing that too much subsidy could be a bad thing for an industry which was managing reasonably well, against the odds. Perry's statement was much repeated partly because it is expressed using a seductive and topical metaphor, as the furore caused by *Trainspotting* (1996) had yet to die down. The successful producer of *Four Weddings and a Funeral*, Duncan Kenworthy, concurred that, despite meagre resources, "at least we haven't got that awful subsidy culture you see in other countries."[67] Kenworthy's bad object here is clear enough: European cinema, with its incurable addiction to protectionism and state handouts. Of course, it is easy to be dismissive of public subsidy when you make the kind of films that have no need for such, and Kenworthy may have lived to regret this statement as he later became joint head of the Lottery-supported franchise company, DNA. Perhaps it should not go unnoticed that these were the kind of quotations sought by a journalist working for the American trade paper, *Variety*—a publication

[65] Walker, *Icons in the Fire*, 213.

[66] Simon Perry cited in Adam Dawtry, "Whole Lotto Shakin' in Brit Film Funding," *Variety*, May 6, 1996, 26.

[67] Duncan Kenworthy cited in Dawtry, "Whole Lotto Shakin'," 26.

traditionally aligned with the free-market discourses of Hollywood and the powerful Motion Picture Association of America (MPAA).

With many commentators critical of the scheme and the government admitting that no-one involved in the review process seemed to favour "large-scale" direct subsidy, it becomes possible to lose sight of the reasons why the money was committed in the first place. As detailed in the previous chapter, many of the arguments in favour of the intervention are familiar from the history of British cinema's "protracted but tenacious struggle for survival".[68] These include the need to protect the industry against Hollywood domination, the desire to compete on an equal footing with Europe, or the various benefits offered by a vibrant domestic "cinema culture". However, the major difference in the 1990s was quite simple: this time round, the money to help was suddenly there, in unprecedented quantities. The runaway success of the National Lottery had built up a momentum of its own, appearing, at times, to drag decision-makers along in its wake. Partly for this reason, during the "pilot year" of the scheme in 1995–1996, the Arts Councils and the Department of National Heritage looked at a range of options which would refine and target the effects of this increased revenue. One of these was an ambitious plan concerned with not only delegating a significant element of the decision-making process into the industry, deflecting possible criticisms, but also attempting to tackle the film industry's deep-seated and long-running problems. This bold attempt to restructure the UK film industry was known as the Lottery "franchise" scheme.

The Franchise Scheme and Pathé Pictures

During the initial "pilot year" of National Lottery Funding for Film Production, up until March 1996, the idea which had the most significant impact upon the future of the system came not from policy-makers but from within the industry itself. The Producers Alliance for Cinema and Television (PACT) was founded in 1991 to represent the interests of independent feature film, television, animation and interactive media companies.[69] Thus it follows in a long tradition of professional bodies and lobbying organisations for the UK film industry, such as the Film Producers' Group of the Federation of British Industries (FBI), and the

---

[68] Margaret Dickinson and Sarah Street, *Cinema and State: The Film Industry and the British Government 1927–84* (London: BFI, 1985), 248.

[69] See "About PACT," *PACT*, accessed January 2006, http://www.pact.co.uk /about/

Association of Independent Producers (AIP).[70] Formed at a point when the British government was beginning to rebuild support structures for the film industry following the deregulation of the 1980s, PACT was able to contribute to the debates shaping current film policy. Its first chair, Marc Samuelson, who had previously led the AIP, spoke on behalf of producers in the Department of National Heritage review of the British film industry published in 1995. Here, he highlighted "the massive disproportion in the investment available from the UK for film production as compared to many other countries", and the inadequate budgets of most British films.[71] PACT therefore helped to convince the DNH that National Lottery money should be made available to support film production, and as it came on stream in 1995, they offered detailed guidance to help producers access this new source of investment.[72] However, PACT clearly saw itself as a lobby with the power to shape public policy rather than simply respond to it.

In early 1996, the organisation published its proposals for the use of Lottery funding for films, which would prove as influential as a similar document published by the FBI some seventy years prior.[73] The FBI had wanted a quota system to revive British production, PACT wanted Lottery "franchises". Their principal concern was that the current "ad-hoc mechanism" for handing out Lottery money on an individual, project-by-project basis would "have little impact on the structure of the film business itself."[74] Instead, they urged the DNH "to use the Lottery money to help leverage private capital investment" into the film industry by "creating British studios able to develop, produce and distribute British films". The notion of the "franchise" was related to the term's use in the competitive system of allocating regional rights for ITV broadcasters—except that the limited resource to which the successful companies would gain access was not terrestrial bandwidth but Lottery funding. The proposal stressed the importance of involving distribution networks in the scheme, and hoped that the winning bids would come from a diverse range of organisations,

---

[70] The FBI was active in the quota debate in the 1920s and the AIP began in 1976. Dickinson and Street, *Cinema and State*, 17, 243.

[71] Department of National Heritage (DNH), *Second Report from the National Heritage Committee: The British Film Industry, Vol. 1* (London: HMSO, 1995), xiv, xv.

[72] e.g. Anon, "Lottery Funding: Who Decides?" *The PACT Magazine*, 47, November 1995, 13.

[73] Federation of British Industries, "To revive production: F.B.I.'s summary of the rival plans," *Kinematograph Weekly*, 102:955, August 6, 1925, 30–1.

[74] Anon., "National Lottery Funding for British films: the PACT Proposals," *The PACT Magazine*, 50, March 96, 18.

both large and small. Finally, it was noted that the Arts Council had already responded positively to the idea and was in the process of commissioning its own feasibility study on the plan. This feasibility study was known as "The Spectrum Report", after the London-based media consultancy firm who produced it, and was published in May 1996.[75]

The Spectrum report is generally positive regarding the prospects for the UK film industry, suggesting that audiences were gradually regaining their confidence in British cinema; however, it also condemns structural inefficiencies for failing to capitalise upon this potential. It claims that only a small proportion of UK feature films ever reach profitability owing to the "cottage industry" structure of its production base.[76] UK films tended to be financed on an individual project-by-project basis, which makes it likely that much of the exploitation rights would be lost through the system of "pre-sales", where the rights to distribute a film in a given territory are sold before the film is made. By comparison, films produced by the Hollywood majors can benefit from guaranteed international distribution through their own subsidiaries, and also tend to receive far more generous print and marketing support. All of these factors combine to severely disadvantage UK-produced films—not just internationally but also in the domestic marketplace. The report argues that the key to levelling the playing field for UK films is to regain control of distribution and build larger, vertically integrated companies capable of retaining the rights to profitable projects. Around the same time, Sir Peter Middleton published the report of another DNH Advisory Committee on Film Finance, which also concluded that structural reform of the industry was essential to ensuring its survival, and recommended the reinstatement of tax relief for film production.[77]

In May of 1996, *Variety* predicted that "The British film industry is poised to embark on an extraordinary experiment... to reinvent its cottage production business."[78] By October of the same year the Arts Council had approved the initiative and called for bids to be submitted. The former head of BBC Drama and previous chairman of PACT, Charles Denton,

---

[75] Arts Council of England (ACE), "The Spectrum Report," *Lottery Film Franchising: A Feasibility Study* (London: ACE, 1996).
[76] "The Spectrum Report," 1, 38.
[77] "The Middleton Report" is often cited as the basis for the Section 48 tax relief system formally introduced by the incoming Labour government in 1997. GB Advisory Committee on Film Finance, Chair: Sir Peter Middleton, *Report to the Secretary of State for National Heritage* (London: DNH, 1996).
[78] Adam Dawtry, "Whole Lotto Shakin' in Brit Film Funding," *Variety*, May 6, 1996, 26.

was selected to oversee the new system, to field applications from interested parties, and to make final decisions of which companies would be successful. Denton's stated goals were primarily industrial rather than cultural, and he aimed to "put producers in a stronger bargaining position when they talk to the likes of Miramax and UGC."[79] Denton set up a new "advisory panel" for film at the Arts Council, putting the activity on an institutional level with dance, drama and music for the first time.[80] In February of 1997, he announced that 176 companies or consortia had registered their intention to apply for franchise status, prompting amused press reactions on the "frenetic, last-minute flurry of deals and documentation" gripping the industry.[81] Rumoured applicants included the major broadcasters, Working Title and Merchant Ivory, as well as smaller concerns, such as Ewan McGregor's Natural Nylon. In the end, only 37 full applications were considered and, just weeks after Labour's landslide election victory in May 1997, the new Culture secretary Chris Smith announced that three franchises would be granted, allocating £92 million of Lottery funds to be shared between them. After creating a competitive environment which had involved almost everybody in the UK film industry, it was expected that this decision would prove controversial, and that the winners would face intense scrutiny in the years to come.

The largest of the three franchises was Pathé Pictures, the new UK production wing of the French media giant, which received an allocation of £33 million to make a proposed slate of 35 films during the six-year lifespan of the franchise agreement. The second franchise, the Film Consortium, represented the combined interests of four independent production companies—Scala Productions, Parallax, Skreba and Greenpoint—together with the exhibitor Virgin Cinemas and agents The Sales Company. They received £30 million and planned to make 39 films. The third group, DNA Films, was the joint venture of Duncan Kenworthy and Andrew Macdonald, and promised to make 16 films with their

---

[79] At the time, UGC was one of Europe's largest exhibitors. Charles Denton cited in Andy Fry, "Interview with Charles Denton," *The PACT Magazine*, 60, February 1997, 12.

[80] Arts Council Advisory Panel on Film members: Charles Denton (chair); Mike Dibb (director); Lyn Goleby (film lawyer); Keith Griffiths (producer); Hilary King (exhibitor); Colin Leventhal (Channel Four); Claire Mulholland (ITC); Ann Pointon (TV producer); Roger Shannon (funding sector); Alex Usborne (producer); John Woodward (PACT CEO).

[81] Robin Stringer, "Now Showing: Film industry in dash for Lottery cash," *Evening Standard*, February 27, 1997, 4.

earmarked £29 million.[82] The three franchises did not simply receive cheques for their entire allocations up front, as was sometimes implied in the press surrounding the announcement. The Arts Council of England (ACE) were bound by Lottery legislation, which ruled out delegating the task of distributing the money to a third party—irrespective of how careful vetting was carried out. Strictly speaking, the franchises were only granted access to a streamlined application process, as each award still had to be signed off by ACE. However, the three companies were encouraged to use Lottery money for developing projects as well as producing them, and some projects were given money for "exploitation", to help with distribution costs. This was an important difference between the franchises and the traditional "single-project" scheme, which was to continue alongside, partly to assuage industry grumblings about "the chosen few". Another concern widely expressed at this early stage was regarding Pathé's status as a French-controlled company having access to British funding.[83]

The subsequent history of the Lottery franchises is very complex; the three consortia were buffeted by a combination of market forces and industry hostility, and each had their own strengths and problems. For the sake of clarity, the following section concentrates upon just one of the three—the biggest and most controversial of the winners, Pathé Pictures. The Pathé name is one of the most illustrious in the history of the international film business and has been associated with a variety of filmmaking activities since the founding of the original Pathé Frères in 1896. Charles Pathé's well-known *bon mots*, "I did not invent the cinema, I industrialised it", suggest the company's importance as a model of vertical integration long before the period of Hollywood dominance.[84] Those critics shocked to see a French company given access to Lottery funding should remember that Pathé has been involved in the British film industry in different capacities since 1902, including production and

---

[82] Stuart Kemp, "Many Happy Returns?" *Screen International*, 1158, May 15, 1998, 12.

[83] Alexander Walker, "You've got your £92m Lottery cash, now show us your films," *Evening Standard*, May 16, 1997, 4; Nigel Reynolds, "French Connection mars Lottery award," *Daily Telegraph*, May 16, 1997, 4.

[84] Ginette Vincendeau, "Pathé, Charles," in *Encyclopaedia of European Cinema*, ed. Ginette Vincendeau (London: BFI, 1995), 328. For more detail on Pathé's dominance of the early film industry see Richard Abel, *The Ciné Goes to Town: French Cinema 1896–1914* (Berkley: University of California Press, 1994), 19–25.

distribution activity, particularly in the newsreel market.[85] Since the 1970s, Pathé has concentrated mainly on distribution and exhibition, with the exception of a turbulent period when media magnate Giancarlo Paretti used the Pathé name as a vehicle to take control of MGM.[86] Paretti was later declared bankrupt and the company passed into the hands of French entrepreneur Jérôme Seydoux in 1990. The acquisition of Gaumont cinemas in France made Pathé the largest exhibitor in continental Europe, and the company retained its international distribution networks. Moving back into production with their new Lottery franchise wing was an opportunity for Pathé to regain a measure of the vertical integration which had originally made it a potent force in the early film industry.

The success of Pathé Pictures' application for franchise status rested upon the potential benefits of this vertical integration, which included access to its European distribution network. Neither DNA nor the Film Consortium could offer such guarantees, as their initial deals with Virgin Cinemas and PolyGram did not survive long into the period of the franchise. Pathé's application listed six of the UK's most successful producers who would be closely aligned with the new outfit: Simon Channing-Williams, Jake Eberts, Norma Hayden, Lynda Myles, Sarah Radclyffe and Barnaby Thompson.[87] Lottery funding could only be used to finance a third of each project, and so the franchises were required to demonstrate that they could attract additional sources of investment. For Pathé Pictures, this money would come from Pathé themselves, Canal+, and the banks Barclays and Coutts, as well as pre-sales in territories not already covered.[88] This means that, rather than losing Lottery money overseas, the franchise was actually bringing new investment into the British production sector. Having convinced the Arts Council's advisory panel, Pathé hired a new head of production, Andrea Calderwood. As Head of Drama for BBC Scotland, Calderwood had been involved in several high-profile successes, including *Mrs Brown*, which sparked an international bidding war eventually won by Miramax.[89] Her challenge

---

[85] Luke McKernan, "Pathé" in *The Encyclopaedia of British Film*, ed. Brian McFarlane (London: Methuen, 2003), 511–512.

[86] Stephen Prince, *A New Pot of Gold: Hollywood Under the Electronic Rainbow, 1980–1989* (Berkeley: University of California Press, 2000), 158.

[87] Between them these producers are responsible for many of the most successful British films of the previous two decades: including *Chariots of Fire* (1981); *My Beautiful Laundrette* (1985); *Dangerous Liaisons* (1988); *The Commitments* (1991); and *Secrets and Lies* (1996).

[88] Anon., "Open for business," *The PACT Magazine*, 69, Dec 1997, 10–12.

[89] Adam Minns, "Pathé lures BBC talent," *Screen International*, January 30, 1998, 5.

was to blend the rich development culture of the BBC with the commercial imperatives of European cinema distribution represented by Pathé.[90] She brought with her three projects that would become Pathé Pictures' first production slate: the Oscar Wilde adaptation *An Ideal Husband*; *Ratcatcher*, the fruits of a long relationship with director Lynne Ramsey; and *The Darkest Light*, Simon Beaufoy's first script since *The Full Monty*.

According to Calderwood, of these three films, Pathé bosses were only really enthusiastic about *The Darkest Light* owing to Beaufoy. Despite its European art cinema credentials, *Ratcatcher* "mystified" the French corporation, and *An Ideal Husband* was felt to be "too English", though its growing international cast list—which included Cate Blanchett and Julianne Moore —was a mark in its favour. Calderwood stuck to her guns on the two less popular projects, and began to find ways by which the vertically integrated structure around her could be beneficial as well as bureaucratic and unwieldy.[91] For *An Ideal Husband*, this meant involving the marketing team right from the early stages, although the issue of which star should be most prominent on the posters caused some disagreement. *Ratcatcher* was a less obvious commercial proposition, but Pathé's contacts in the French industry helped to bring it some exposure at Cannes, and the distributors organised a slow, careful release, allowing good word of mouth to spread. In 1999, *An Ideal Husband* was a genuine hit, earning back over three times its budget at the international box office, with the critical attention paid to *Ratcatcher* seemingly suggesting that Pathé had struck the correct balance between art-house and popular cinema.[92] Ironically, the project most favoured by Calderwood's bosses, *The Darkest Light*, turned out to be very difficult to sell, with its themes of racism, childhood leukaemia and the foot and mouth disease crisis. The film was barely released in Europe despite Pathé's enviable connections, illustrating that international distribution for the franchise films would have to be earned rather than granted on an automatic basis.

---

[90] Interview with the author, January 2006. All subsequent quotations are from this interview unless otherwise attributed.

[91] This "bureaucratic" charge is one which Pathé Pictures struggled to shake off, although Calderwood points out that it may contain an element of French stereotyping.

[92] *Ratcatcher* rave reviews: Andrew O'Hagan, "This is my film of the year," *Daily Telegraph*, November 12, 1999, 25; Peter Bradshaw, "Poetry from the rubbish tip," *Guardian Unlimited*, November 12, 1999, accessed June 2003, http://film.guardian.co.uk/News_Story/Critic_Review/Guardian_Film_of_the_week/0,4267,102485,00.html; Alexander Walker, "Spellbound in Glasgow's ghetto', *Evening Standard*, November 11, 1999, 30.

In May 1999, Pathé surprised the UK film industry by deciding to cut its formal links with the filmmakers named in its franchise bid.[93] The producers in question were said to have been frustrated with the company's slowness, and increasingly angry that only one of their projects had been picked up for production. Outsiders expressed "outrage" at Pathé's decision to break the terms of its original contract with the Arts Council, and concern that the Arts Council had not reacted punitively. Calderwood explains that the problem originated during the franchise bidding process, when Pathé had mistakenly given producers the impression that they would be involved in the company's decision-making processes.[94] In actual fact, this could not happen given the structure within which she was placed, as an individual making the final decisions on which projects should proceed. Calderwood still believes that this is the best management model for the film industry, with the alternative of filmmaking by committee tending to result in safe, mediocre choices. With relationships deteriorating, Pathé decided to proceed with an "open-door policy", claiming that broader access to the franchise funds was what the industry had wanted in the first place. Nonetheless, this strategy damaged the company's reputation, and the new projects coming up through the system failed to repeat the venture's early successes (Table 2-1). Kenneth Branagh's *Love's Labour's Lost* was a box-office failure, with its cast of young American stars unable to improve its chances. Michael Winterbottom's extravagant production *The Claim* had been, by Calderwood's own admission, "a very tough experience for everyone involved", and the enormous difficulties faced by Terry Gilliam's *The Man Who Killed Don Quixote*, another Pathé project at this point, are now the stuff of industry legend.

Calderwood left the organisation in June 2000 to set up her own independent production company, which had a "first-look deal" with Film Four.[95] *Screen International* reported that this would mean "more *Ratcatchers*", as well as citing an unnamed source suggesting her reputation in the industry was as somewhat of an intellectual: "Calderwood will be reading Dostoyevsky in the evenings instead of schmoozing in the bar."[96] The implication here is that Pathé was not, in the long-term, a natural home

---

[93] Anon., "Pathé Shake-up Divides Producers," *Screen Finance*, 12:9, May 13, 1999, 2–3.

[94] Calderwood, interview with the author, January 2006.

[95] In other words, Film Four would invest money in Calderwood's company in return for first refusal on any new projects.

[96] Adam Minns, "FilmFour, Calderwood first-look deal shapes up," *Screen International*, June 9, 2000, 14.

Table 2-1: Pathé Pictures features produced by Andrea Calderwood

Title (Year)	Awarded	Budget	UK Box Office
An Ideal Husband (1999)	£1,000,000	£6,350,000	£2,893,000
Ratcatcher (1999)	£615,000	£1,980,000	£432,000
The Darkest Light (1999)	£708,000	£1,946,000	£18,000
It Was An Accident (2000)	£1,507,501	£2,765,000	£31,000
Love's Labour's Lost (2000)	£1,056,909	£8,545,545	£531,000
Miss Julie (2000)	£900,000	£1,800,000	£29,000
There's Only One Jimmy Grimble (2000)	£1,695,474	£3,315,000	£355,000
The Claim (2001)	£2,000,000	£12,500,000	£245,000

for her talents. The company's strategy seemed to have drifted away from the low-budget art cinema with which Calderwood had made her name, towards either populist genre films, like football comedy *There's Only One Jimmy Grimble,* or expensive and risky ventures such as *The Claim.* Pathé's work rate was also failing to match up to the proposed 35 films over six years, and in the end they only produced 15. In response, Calderwood argues that their original target was not achievable from a standing start, and that two or three films a year is an above-average output in a UK context. It is notable that the other two franchises performed no better in this regard: The Film Consortium made 16 films rather than 30, and DNA only managed 5, missing their more modest target of 16.[97] Arguably, the fault here lies with the Arts Council's unrealistically high expectations, or their willingness to accept (and then publicise) exaggerated promises made by the would-be franchises. Calderwood also points out that Pathé's continued interest in UK production demonstrates that the franchise scheme had succeeded in "pump-priming" a company that would not otherwise have been involved in such activity.[98] The Film Consortium also still exists under the umbrella of media conglomerate Civilian Content, and DNA is now partly owned by Fox, which demonstrates that the franchises' original intentions to compete with Hollywood had undergone considerable adjustment.

---

[97] Geoffrey Macnab, "Five years of flack," *Guardian Unlimited*, October 25, 2002, accessed December 2005, http://film.guardian.co.uk/features/featurepages/0,,818782,00.html.

[98] The company recently invested in the Academy Award-winning productions *The Queen* (2006) and *Slumdog Millionaire* (2007).

Other commentators have given the franchises a more damning assessment. Robert Murphy describes The Film Consortium as "remarkably combustible", focusing on its rapid regime changes and corporate takeovers.[99] He condemns Chris Auty's strategy of converting the Consortium into a film finance company reliant on international pre-sales as "precisely the opposite of what the franchises were set up to do." His overall verdict is that "as far as changing the face of British film production, the franchise scheme has proved to be an utter failure." Murphy points out that the only period of stability in the British film industry, the 1950s, was built upon a guaranteed home market for modestly budgeted British films. However, Murphy does not make another, possibly more relevant, historical connection to that period, namely the "Group" production plan run by the NFFC between 1951 and 1955.[100] Like the franchises, the group plan was motivated by a need for "continuity" within the independent film sector, and it produced similar, ostensibly disappointing results—not least in terms of the longevity of the companies which benefited. However, the reason for the failure of the idea in the 1950s was principally the lack of interest of the two major combines, Rank and ABPC.[101] The obvious difference with the 1990s situation is that there were no major British production companies by that point—a situation which the Spectrum report, perhaps over-optimistically, hoped could be rectified by creating the Lottery consortia.

With hindsight, it seems probable that the ambitious franchise scheme would fail owing to the relatively small sums of Lottery money available. £33m investment over six years was unlikely to turn Pathé Pictures into a company with the might of the Hollywood majors; however, other side effects were more positive, such as the strengthening of the links between the UK's independent production sector and international film distribution networks. Whilst they were apparently under-productive in terms of number of films released, the franchise companies nevertheless clearly valued the support offered to their projects during the often-precarious development stage, and so it is notable that the replacement for the franchise scheme opted to specialise in this area whilst making no promises about production. Announced in 2004, the "Super Slates" had access to even smaller amounts of money but were encouraged to be

---

99 Robert Murphy, "Another false dawn? The Film Consortium and the franchise scheme," *Journal of Popular British Cinema*, 5 (2000): 31–35.

100 Richard Dyer MacCann, "Subsidy for the Screen: Grierson and Group 3, 1951–55," *Sight and Sound*, 46:3, March 1977, 168–173.

101 Sue Harper and Vincent Porter, *British Cinema of the 1950s: The Decline of Deference* (Oxford: Oxford University Press, 2003), 23–27.

strategic in their planning.[102] Again, consortia of companies were invited to apply, and seven were successful, receiving a total investment of £7.5m over three years. This time, the fact that Pathé Pictures was once again amongst the lucky few selected appears to have caused no equivalent concerns either over the company's national status or over their apparent golden touch when it came to Lottery funding applications. In any case, by 2004, the Arts Council of England had no say in any of these decisions as they had long since been replaced by a new organisation established to unify the disparate threads of public funding for film in the UK.

The Film Council

After five years of disappointing box-office results, National Lottery funding for film production finally created a runaway hit in November 2000. *Billy Elliot* had been developed at the BBC and produced by Working Title, but it also received around a third of its budget from the Arts Council of England. This crowd-pleasing tale of youthful talent overcoming economic deprivation was made for less than £3m, but went on to take over £18m in the UK and £15m at US cinemas.[103] Nonetheless, reporting on the film's recipe for success, the *Financial Times* described the Arts Council as the "tragic figure" of *Billy Elliot*'s production history, as the body had already been stripped of its powers to distribute Lottery money to the film industry.[104] Could *Billy Elliot* have saved the Arts Council this humiliation if it had arrived a few years earlier? It would certainly have boosted the organisation's confidence, as well as being a useful riposte for those who claimed that the Arts Councils' natural preference was for less commercial elitist fare. In truth, however, it would probably not have been enough to safeguard the status quo. The setting up of the film franchises had distracted civil servants and politicians from the central question of the Arts Councils' perceived incompatibility with the film sector, but as soon as Labour came into power in 1997, they set up a new Film Policy Review Group with a broadly industrial focus and an appetite for change. From this point onwards, it became increasingly likely

---

[102] Geoffrey Macnab, "Rise of the Super-Slate," *Screen International*, October 27, 2006, 20.

[103] Budget and UK box office data from Eddie Dyja (ed.), *BFI Film and Television Handbook 2002* (London: BFI, 2001), 32; US and international box office data from www.variety.com, accessed June 3, 2003.

[104] James Harding, "Film Makers Jostle to take Credit for *Billy Elliot,*" *Financial Times*, September 30, 2000, 3.

that the Arts Councils would soon be refocusing their efforts on funding the careers of real ballet dancers rather than fictional ones—irrespective of matter how plucky and popular they may prove to be.

The Film Policy Review Group was jointly chaired by the new Minister for Film, Tom Clarke, and Stewart Till, president of PolyGram Filmed Entertainment. The inclusion of a powerful industry figure right at the forefront of the review process marked a significant change in emphasis from the previous Department of National Heritage committee, which was led by the MP (and film enthusiast) Gerald Kaufman. The Review Group's members included many of the figures who had been actively involved in the Lottery franchise process, most notably Charles Denton, now representing the Arts Council of England's Lottery Film department; Chris Auty of the Film Consortium; Duncan Kenworthy of DNA Films; and Lynda Myles, who, at that point, was one of the producers formally attached to Pathé Pictures. Other key personalities included Wilf Stephenson, former head of the British Film Institute, director Ridley Scott, and representatives from distributors and cinema chains.[105] According to Clarke, the review represented "a true collaboration between industry and government, perhaps a model for other sectors of Britain's flourishing creative economy."[106] In this way, the Review Group was praised as an exemplar of New Labour's ideological project of "rebranding" British culture using the language of the media and advertising, rather than the more traditional rationale of "art for art's sake". In this changing political climate, the Arts Council was beginning to look like a relic from a very different incarnation of Labour values, which oversaw the birth of the organisation fifty years previously.

A review set up within this framework could be expected to concentrate on industrial rather than cultural objectives, and its 1998 report, *A Bigger Picture*, fulfils such expectations. Its key aims include a doubling of the domestic market share for British films, better training provision, and a new financial framework to encourage sustained investment within the industry.[107] The one exception within this set of economic concerns is that of "a larger and more diverse audience for film in general and cinema in particular"—an objective overlapping with the BFI's agenda. By setting

---

[105] Also contributing were Daniel Battsek (Buena Vista UK); Peter Broughan (Bronco Films); Dinah Caine (Skillset); Colin Leventhal (formerly Channel 4); Wendy Palmer (MGM UK) and Richard Segal (Odeon Cinemas). See "Annex 1" of the Department of Culture Media and Sport (DCMS), *A Bigger Picture: The Report of the Film Policy Review Group* (London: DCMS, 1998), 52.

[106] DCMS, *A Bigger Picture*, 1.

[107] DCMS, *A Bigger Picture*, 9.

Wilf Stevenson to work on this particular task, the Review Group were sending a clear message to the Institute that they could not take their stewardship of the nation's film culture for granted. Indeed, the BFI had recently appointed John Woodward—an industry moderniser who pledged to rationalise and refocus the body back towards its core activities—to the position of Chief Executive. Similar changes were underway at the Arts Council of England,, where Lord Gowrie, a former arts minister for Mrs Thatcher, had been replaced as chair by Gerry Robinson, then Head of Granada Television and a known New Labour patron.[108] The only film body who appeared ready for this tide of economic reform was British Screen, whose entrepreneurial approach had been singled out for praise by the DCMS. British Screen consequently seemed to be in a strong position when they made their bid to take over the reins of Lottery funding for film development, production and distribution from the Arts Councils, with Simon Perry reportedly keen to maintain his organisation's autonomy.[109]

A Bigger Picture recommends a series of measures which should be taken to achieve the Review Group's stated objectives, including a new voluntary "all industry fund" to be spent on training, the redirection of Lottery funding towards development rather than production, and the setting up of a UK Film Office in Los Angeles to cement connections with Hollywood.[111] However, it falls short of spelling out what many felt was a likely conclusion at that point: that the current machinery for delivering film policy was riddled with competing interests and duplicated effort, and that nothing less than a complete overhaul would come close to solving the industry's problems—even those on the inside of the system were expecting radical change. Mark Dunford, officer in the Arts Council of England's Lottery Film Department, recalls that "the Film Council was mooted very early on—initially as "Organisation X", and then it finally became a reality in 1998."[112] After using the 1997 Cannes Film Festival to announce which companies had been successful in applying for Lottery franchise status, the Culture Secretary Chris Smith chose the glamorous Riviera gathering the following year to break the news that the government was planning to rationalise the separate strands of government film policy into one new "superbody". By the end of the year, *Screen International*

[108] See Richard Witts, *Artist Unknown: An Alternative History of the Arts Council* (London: Little, Brown and Co., 1998), 501–505.
[109] Louise Bateman, "Council Tips," *The PACT Magazine*, September 1998, 15.
[110] Arts Council of England (ACE), *Annual Report and Accounts 1998* (London: ACE, 1998), 3.
[111] DCMS, *A Bigger Picture*, 48-50.
[112] Interview with the author, July 2004.

reported that the embryonic organisation would have "unprecedented financial and creative influence on the industry", including an 11% share of the total National Lottery award for the arts administered by the Arts Council of England.[113] The BFI was to retain its separate identity and cultural remit, but its production facilities would transfer to the Film Council, and the entire Institute would become accountable to the new body in financial terms.

Initial concerns about the Film Council were expressed in terms of a fear of centralisation and too much power shifting into the hands of a few industry acolytes—particularly Alan Parker, Stuart Till and John Woodward, whose modernisation of the BFI had made him frontrunner to manage the new superbody. As the organisation took shape, the changing fortunes of British Screen did little to alleviate concerns. Simon Perry's hopes of taking on the management of Lottery funding began to look increasingly unrealistic, and even his organisation's autonomy came to be in doubt, prompting Perry to announce that he was "depressed and confused" by the government's actions.[114] Speculation over British Screen's future continued right until January 2000, when it was announced that it would be absorbed into the Film Council after all. The operation's private shareholders—then United Artists, Channel 4 and Granada—agreed to hand over control to the new superbody along with British Screen's staff, and also its lucrative back catalogue of film titles, said to generate a "six-figure" annual revenue.[115] Such centralisation was necessary, the Film Council argued, in order to run an efficient system of support and to speak for the industry with one clear voice. However, some commentators still valued the flexibility and diversity of approach permitted by the previous set-up: one voice can be powerful but it can also shut down debate. In an attempt to maintain some choice for producers, the new body was structured to replicate the traditional split between bigger-budget, "commercial" filmmaking, previously handled by British Screen and the low-budget, experimental ethos of BFI Production. Decision-making by committee was replaced by giving the heads of such new funds the power to "greenlight" projects as they saw fit. Successful freelance producer

113 Adam Minns, "Gov't writes British Film script," *Screen International*, 1189, December 18, 1998, 1.

114 Simon Perry cited in Erich Boehm, "Mixed review on Brit pix fund," *Variety.com*, December 15, 1998, accessed December 2005, http://www.variety.com/story.asp?l=story &a=VR1117489401&c=13,

115 Adam Minns, "British Screen to be Folded into the Film Council," *Screendaily.com*, January 20, 2000, accessed December 2005, http://www.Screen daily.com/storyid=87.

Robert Jones took on this role for the £10m per year Premiere Fund, whilst the £5m per year New Cinema Fund was to be run by Paul Trijbits.

Like their British Screen equivalents, staff from the Lottery Film department at the Arts Council of England had also been expected to transfer over to the new Film Council, but there was considerable surprise when eight out of ten of them opted for voluntary redundancy instead.[116] It is difficult not to interpret this development as evidence that the problems of working with Lottery funding for film production within the Arts Councils had eventually sapped the morale of even the most enthusiastic staff members. Nonetheless, ACE's Head of Lottery Film, Carolyn Lambert, did take up a post at the Film Council as Head of Policy, indicating that the new organisation was hoping to learn from the mistakes of its predecessors. At the Arts Council of England, the departure of the Lottery Film Unit was a part of wider institutional change instigated under the leadership of Gerry Robinson. Between 1998 and 2003, the organisation's staff numbers were cut from 322 to just 130, and the Lottery administration was integrated more closely into the Council's traditional revenue funding operations.[117] In the other home nations, similar rationalisation was occurring. Scottish Screen had been formed in 1997 from four smaller organisations, and could therefore claim to be "the UK's first integrated body for screen industry and culture", and indirectly, perhaps, the inspiration for the Film Council itself.[118] It took over the management of Lottery film funding from the Scottish Arts Council in April 2000, but with the understanding that the Film Council's remit was nationwide, and that Scottish filmmakers working with bigger budgets could therefore access the Premiere Fund directly. The same scenario had also developed in Wales, with Sgrin handling the country's smaller Lottery film projects, leaving the Arts Council of Northern Ireland as the only one of the original four distributors to hold on to its film funding responsibilities. There was evidently continued confusion surrounding these overlapping remits, which contributed towards the decision to add the prefix "UK" to the Film Council's title in 2003.

---

[116] Lottery Officer Mark Dunford, interview with the author, May 2004.

[117] Catherine Millner, "Arts Council to cut a third of its staff," *The Telegraph*, June 30, 2002, accessed March 2006, http://www.telegraph.co.uk/news/main.jhtml?xml=/news/2002/06/30/nart130.xml,.

[118] Claire Mount, "Border Aids," *The Pact Magazine*, 99, August 2000, 13.

Conclusion

The introduction of the National Lottery in 1994 instigated a chain of policy developments which radically altered the landscape of public funding for film over the following five years. The Lottery itself came into existence owing to a combination of factors, including a moral shift towards the acceptance of gambling as a means of generating revenue for "good causes", competition from the Lottery systems being set up all across Europe, and especially John Major's need for a crowd-pleasing policy, which could help to compensate for many years of under-spending in the public sector without raising taxes. Fears that the Lottery's proceeds could begin to replace taxation in the government's spending plans resulted in a major statutory check upon the system—the principle of additionality. Lottery funding was therefore to be spent on societies' "desirables" rather than its "essentials", which here encompassed the arts, sport, charities, heritage and the (then) upcoming Millennium celebrations. The system was explicitly framed by Major as "the people's Lottery"; this description combined with the element of choice involved in buying a ticket created a sense of public "ownership" over the proceeds, which is subtly different to that of general taxes. The consequent idea that Lottery funding should pay for "beds for the elderly" rather than "seats at the opera for businessmen on expense accounts" created ethical dilemmas for the distributors of the new revenue, especially for the Arts Councils with their reputations for highbrow elitism.[119]

A tension between elitism and populism was also crucial in relation to the Arts Councils' support of film production. This decision was taken as a result of discussions between the government and the film industry during the Department of National Heritage select committee, which published its results in 1995. Even at this stage, the government had difficulty favouring "large-scale direct subsidy" for the film industry, but this was exactly what was about to happen.[120] The key objective of the Arts Councils' support for cinema was "to enhance the quality, range and number of British films", and the initial procedure which attempted to achieve this goal was to treat applications for film production in exactly the same way as those for other art forms.[121] As it became clear that supporting film projects

---

[119] Anon., "Don't Tax the Poor to Amuse the Rich," *Daily Mail*, November 15, 1994, 8.

[120] Department of National Heritage (DNH), *The British Film Industry,* Cmnd. 2884 (London: HMSO, 1995), 19.

[121] Arts Council of England (ACE), "Guidelines," *National Lottery Funding for Film: Application Pack* (London: ACE, 1997), 7.

required careful handling and different skills, a separate department was set up at the Arts Council of England, and Lottery Film began to diverge from general Lottery funding for the arts. From 1997, the franchise scheme shifted funding decisions further away from the Arts Councils and into the film industry itself. At the same time, the change of political governance created a new Film Policy Review Group which incorporated, incorporating key figures from the industry at the heart of the policy-making process. This review led to the combination of several discrete film policy mechanisms within the Film Council, and ended the Arts Council of England's involvement with large-scale feature filmmaking in April 2000. The Arts Councils of the other three home nations retained a limited level of support for film, but the addition of the modifier "UK" to the Film Council in 2003 signalled greater geographical centralisation.

CHAPTER THREE

EVALUATING LOTTERY FUNDING FOR FILM

The previous chapter covered a great deal of historical ground in order to provide a coherent narrative account of the development of National Lottery funding for film between 1995 and 2000. As a result, it was necessary to introduce certain key debates and evaluative frameworks without exploring them in detail. In this chapter, I take a step back from the story of how the system developed to think more carefully about the effects of this development—and in particular to consider the problems the system encountered. This task inevitably involves an engagement with the received wisdom characterising this period; that the Arts Councils made a series of mistakes and errors of judgement which resulted in them losing the right to distribute Lottery money to filmmakers. This assumption deserves to be interrogated in-depth, and to this end, I make use of detailed statistical analysis and a series of production history accounts. The key instances of "failure" within the Lottery funding system are projects which receive awards but are not produced, films which are produced but then fail to find distribution, and those which are distributed but fail to find an audience—the notorious Lottery "turkeys". The chapter concludes with a brief account of the fortunes of Lottery funding for film after 2000, particularly the case of the Film Council's support for a film that generated an extraordinary amount of press hostility—the bawdy comedy *Sex Lives of the Potato Men* (2003).

Films, facts and figures

How can we begin to assess the impact of National Lottery funding upon the British film industry? Is it possible to state whether or not the industry became more or less "healthy" as a result? In tackling these questions, a good place to start is with a summary of the film production supported by the Lottery during the period to be discussed, 1995 to 2000.[1] The analysis

[1] To be precise, the period in question is made up of the financial years 1995–6 to 1999–2000.

that follows is based on data supplied for the purposes of this project by the four respective Arts Councils of the UK.[2] These lists, comprising every award given to the film sector, were generated directly from each Arts Council's own set of electronic records, and are therefore as complete and accurate as possible. Having said that, there were historical differences between the various local systems, which presented problems when it came to standardising and collating the information. These problems meant that it was also necessary to verify and supplement my data using secondary sources—in particular the information published annually by the British Film Institute (BFI) in their *Film and Television Handbooks*. Once collated, the information formed the foundation of my awards database, which was used to generate the following figures and tables. These tables, graphs and charts provide a detailed summary of precisely how money from the National Lottery was spent by the Arts Councils on film production between 1995 and 2000. A full list of this data is available online.[3]

Table 3-1: National Lottery awards for film production by region

Arts Council	Awards	Total Awarded	Total Project Cost[4]	Spend	UK Population[5]
ACE	288	£110,011,693	£402,882,400	81.4%	83.6%
ACNI	40	£2,186,443	£23,658,111	1.6%	2.8%
ACW	33	£3,255,796	£20,273,888	2.4%	4.9%
SAC	128	£19,640,639	£97,746,930	14.6%	8.6%
Totals:	**489**	**£135,094,571**	**£544,561,329**	**100%**	**100%**

Overall 489 awards were made to a total value of around £135 million. As some films received more than one award, this represents 425 projects with an estimated total budget of around £550 million.[6] The regional

---

[2] I am grateful to Scott Royal, Michael Clarke and Isabelle Andrews at ACE; Linzi Nelson at SAC; Lorraine McDowell at ACNI and Anneli Jones at ACW for helping me obtain this data.

[3] James Caterer, "The People's Pictures Appendices," *Google Sites*, https://sites.google.com/a/brookes.ac.uk/jamescaterer/.

[4] Estimated by applicant at point of application for Lottery funding.

[5] Office for National Statistics, "Census 2001: Population," *National Statistics Online*, accessed March 2004, http://www.statistics.gov.uk/cci/nugget.asp?id=185

[6] This is calculated from budgets submitted before production took place. However, when a sample of these estimates was compared to the budgets published by the BFI their accuracy was found to be high enough for my purposes.

breakdown in Table 3-1 indicates that the Arts Council of England (ACE) dominated the spend, with over 80% of the money going into the English region; Scotland received close to 15%; whilst Wales and Northern Ireland both received around 2%. This regional spread is broadly similar to the make-up of the UK's population, and therefore reflects the method by which the total Lottery allocation for each of the home nations is calculated. The most significant exception in this case is Scotland, which spent significantly more on film per head of population than the other regions; £3.84 compared to Northern Ireland's £1.29. This demonstrates that each of the Arts Councils was allowed a certain degree of flexibility when setting priorities, and could concentrate their allocated funds within different areas. The Scottish Arts Council (SAC) chose to place film production further up their priority list than the other councils. This focus upon film in Scotland was framed within particularly nationalistic language, and therefore directly engages with the political consequences of devolution in the late 1990s.[7]

As Table 3-2 illustrates, by far the most common type of film project funded by the Arts Councils was the commercial feature film made for the cinema, which received around 95% of the total spend. Falling within this bracket are feature-length documentaries, such as Kevin MacDonald's *Donald Cammell: Ultimate Performance*; the film franchise projects made by DNA, Pathé or the Film Consortium; and one IMAX film, *Journey to the Centre of the Brain*. This total also includes the six films made under the "Greenlight Fund" managed by British Screen, and designed to support bigger-budget films by well-established directors. Short films also received considerable support from the Lottery. Almost 200 were made, and with an average award of just £28,000 (compared to a typical £466,000 spent on features), they were an efficient means of spreading the money across the maximum number of projects. Funding the production of shorts is seen as a way to opening doors into the industry and strengthening the talent base, as such films often function as a kind of 'calling card' for new directors and producers. Specialist projects included those funded by the "Artists' Film and Video" scheme, a development of the relationship between the Arts Council of England's Visual Arts department and avant-garde filmmakers dating back to the 1970s. The strength of this relationship can be measured by ACE's ability to retain this aspect of support when all others were transferred over to the Film Council in 2000.

[7] For a production history of one of SAC's film projects see James Caterer, "Playing the Lottery Twice: The Dual Nationality of *Stella Does Tricks*," *Journal of Media Practice* 5:3 (2004): 133–143.

Table 3-2: Film production activity by region and project type

		Features	Shorts	Other
ACE	Awards	191	73	24
	Value	£107.1m	£2.1m	£0.8m
ACNI	Awards	16	16	8
	Value	£1.4m	£0.4m	£0.3m
ACW	Awards	13	19	1
	Value	£2.3m	£0.9	£0.1m
SAC	Awards	60	66	2
	Value	£18.1m	£1.5m	£0.1m

The different types of projects funded also highlight regional differences in priorities and eligibility. For example, The Arts Council of Northern Ireland (ACNI) relaxed the criteria on distribution to include projects made to be broadcast on television, thus leading to several Lottery-supported TV series such as the BBC's *Eureka Street*.[8] This experiment represents an area of further overlap between the "public benefit" criteria associated with Lottery funding, and the concept of public service broadcasting. Meanwhile, the Arts Council of Wales (ACW) took a broader line on the requirement that awards must go towards the creation of a "capital asset", allowing the Welsh Film Archive to apply successfully for £62,000 towards restoring Maurice Elvey's 1918 film *The Life Story of David Lloyd George*. The smaller Arts Councils also spent a higher proportion of their budgets on the comparatively cheaper "development" stage of their projects. Still, the vast majority of the awards overall went on supporting films during their production phase, but when this data is broken down by year, a progression towards greater diversity emerges. In 1995–1996, less than 5% of the awards went to activities outside the production stage, but by 1999–2000, this had leapt to over 26%. A significant factor in this change of emphasis was the introduction of the film franchise scheme in 1997, as the new "mini-studios" were encouraged to consider development and distribution on a more equal footing with production. This trend continued with the Film Council's policy directions, such as its prints and advertising fund, which aimed to provide

[8] Arts Council of Northern Ireland, *The National Lottery Arts Fund: Film Development and Film Production* (Belfast: ACNI, 1998), 2.

a wider release for art-house and foreign language films in the UK exhibition sector.[9]

So far, this analysis provides an insight into what happened to the £135 million of Lottery money spent on film production between 1995 and 2000. But can we decide whether the film industry really became healthier as a result? Economists Stephen Pratten and Simon Deakin's work on the British film sector provides a list of five criteria which have been used to measure the health or, in their terms, "competitiveness", of the industry:

- the balance of external trade
- the number of UK films in production
- investment in UK film production
- the percentage of UK films given a theatrical release
- the percentage of UK box office taken by UK films.[10]

The balance of external trade is a complex set of calculations concerning imports and exports, and its scope is closer to the remit of the British Film Commission than the Arts Councils during this period. More useful and far easier to quantify for the purposes of this study are the number of UK films made and the amounts invested. Figure 3-1 and Figure 3-2 provide a visual representation of these two indicators throughout the 1990s. Despite obvious fluctuations, with 1996 in particular representing an unsustainable peak, the overall trend throughout the 1990s had been for more UK films to be made, from around 60 per year at the start of the decade to around 100 per year by the end. Even adjusted for inflation, investment has grown more impressively to over double the amounts seen in 1990.[11]

Of course, these banner figures tell only part of the story. Annual levels of investment are often dominated by a few big budget American productions. For example, in 1999 *Gladiator* was made largely in the UK at a cost of £92 million, not much less than the total of £105 million spread across all 47 of the wholly British financed films that year. This is where the BFI's four-tiered system of classification can be useful, as it allows a distinction between wholly UK financed films (Category A), majority

---

[9] See "Distribution and Exhibition," *UK Film Council,* accessed April 2004, http://www.ukfilm council.org.uk/funding/distributionandexhibition/

[10] Stephen Prattten and Simon Deakin, "Competetiveness Policy and Economic Organisation: the Case of the British Film Industry," *Screen*, 41:2 (Summer 2000): 223.

[11] Inflation adjusted, investment grew from £217m in 1990 to £564m in 2000. Lawrence Officer, "What Is Its Relative Value in UK Pounds?" *Economic History Services,* accessed March 2006, http://http://www.eh.net/hmit/ukcompare/.

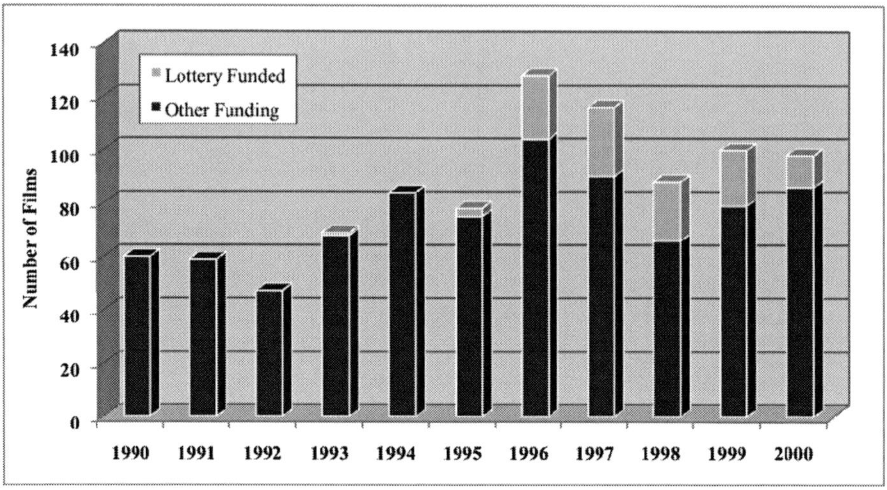

Fig. 3-1: Number of films produced in the UK, 1990–2000

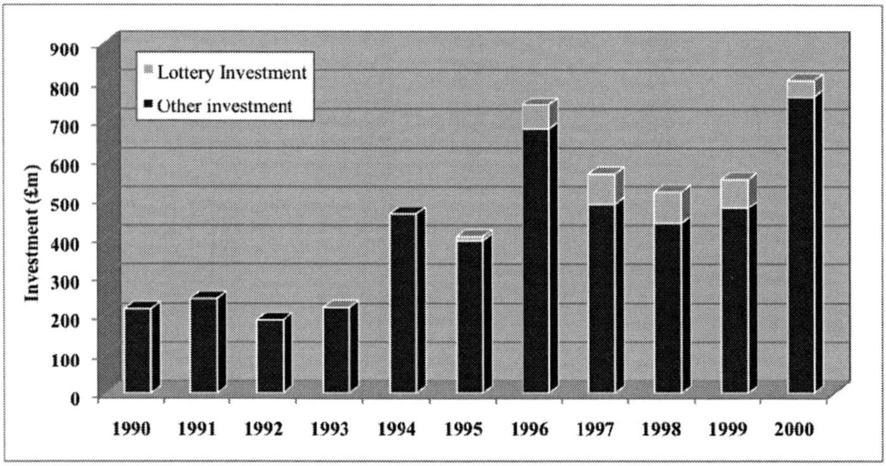

Fig. 3-2: Investment in UK film production, 1990–2000[12]

[12] Figures not adjusted for inflation.

or minority UK co-productions (Categories B & C) and international productions made in the UK (Category D).[13] Table 3-3 combines my list of Lottery-funded feature film projects with the annual "UK Film Production" tables published by the BFI, and highlights Category A production.

Table 3-3: Lottery funding for "Wholly UK-financed" features

	Lottery Funded		All	
	Number	Value (£m)	Number	Value (£m)
1994	0	0	35	53.36
1995	2	6.30	28	64.31
1996	10	18.89	53	84.88
1997	17	44.75	65	148.20
1998	12	40.34	43	107.11
1999	12	43.83	47	105.12
2000	6	10.77	45	119.73
TOTALS:	**59**	**164.89**	**316**	**682.71**

According to the BFI's records, 120 Lottery-funded feature films made it into production, with around half of these films qualified as "Category A" activity—"films where the cultural and financial impetus is from the UK and where the majority of the personnel are British."[14] The extra £40 million or so per year does seem to be reflected in an overall increase in Category A investment, which rose from £53 million in 1994 to £119 million by 2000. Whilst it is clear other factors contributed to this growth, such as the growing industry confidence following breakthrough hits like *Four Weddings and a Funeral*, it is not unreasonable to conclude that the UK production sector was given a significant boost by the influx of Lottery money.

However, the aims of Lottery funding for film production were to increase not only the number but also in the "quality" and "range" of films

[13] The BFI system developed throughout the 1990s from a two-level distinction between British and American financed production in 1992 to the 2004 version which has five groups. However as the four-tiered system was in place throughout the period of this study and so this is the one which is used throughout.

[14] Phil Wickham, *Producing the Goods? UK Film Production Since 1991: An Information Briefing* (London: BFI Information Services, 2003), 1. This publication usefully collates the annual BFI tables into one long alphabetical list.

made in the UK.[15] It is possible to make a connection between budget or, more often, "production values", and quality. The complaint that, to the consumer, low-budget British films appear to be of an inferior quality next to the polished glossiness of Hollywood product is pervasive, and dates back at least as far as the debates surrounding the quota system in the 1930s. In 1997, as part of the activity triggered by the incoming Labour government's Film Policy Review Group, the Department of Culture Media and Sport commissioned market research on cinema-going preferences in the UK. They found that:

> certain... attributes associated with British films, particularly those relating to low budgets and small-scale, gritty realism are not positive endorsements for the many younger and less educated people who prefer to see big budget films with well-known stars…[16]

Whilst it is clear that the amount of Lottery funding available would be unable to raise UK budgets even to within a fraction of the average Hollywood film, it is possible to verify that the average amount invested in each UK film produced did rise over the five-year period. This rise was especially marked for wholly UK financed films, which, in 1994, cost an average of £1.52 million, rising to £2.66 million by 2000. Of course, it does not necessarily follow that a more expensive production will, by definition, result in a higher-quality finished product. This correction may have been absorbed largely by rising salaries for crew and technicians, which were often inadequate in the lean years preceding 1995.[17]

As Table 3-4 demonstrates, the top end of the budgetary range is dominated by glossy period dramas. Mike Leigh's *Topsy Turvy* (1999), which dramatises the creation of Gilbert and Sullivan's popular operetta *The Mikado* in 1885, was a major departure for a director closely associated with contemporary social realism. The skill of its design team was duly rewarded with the film industry's ultimate accolade for high production

[15] Arts Council of England (ACE), "Guidelines," *National Lottery Funding for Film: Application Pack* (London: ACE, 1997), 7.

[16] Department of Culture, Media and Sport (DCMS), *A Bigger Picture: The Report of the Film Policy Review Group* (London: DCMS, 1998), 56.

[17] Budgetary limitations meant that previously crews on many British films had been working on a deferred payments basis. See the production history of *Clockwork Mice* in Alexandra Frearn, "Made in Britain to fit the screen," *The Times*, October 26, 1994, 14.

Table 3-4: Lottery-funded features budgeted at over £5 million.

Title	Total Awarded	Project Cost
Topsy Turvy	£2,000,000	£13,500,000
The Claim	£2,000,000	£12,500,000
Amy Foster	£2,000,000	£9,210,526
Love's Labour's Lost	£1,056,909	£8,545,545
Plunkett and Macleane	£1,000,000	£8,490,000
A Christmas Carol: The Movie	£1,242,776	£6,846,526
Esther Kahn	£700,000	£6,574,885
An Ideal Husband	£1,000,000	£6,350,000
Still Crazy	£1,890,000	£6,300,000
Mansfield Park	£1,000,000	£6,162,000
The Lost Son	£2,300,000	£6,056,250
The Land Girls	£1,500,000	£6,000,000
The Parole Officer	£2,000,000	£5,994,371
The House of Mirth	£2,000,000	£5,832,750
Whatever Happened to Harold Smith	£500,000	£5,635,842
Wilde	£1,500,000	£5,600,000
Photographing Fairies	£890,000	£5,200,000
My Life So Far	£1,000,000	£5,128,000

values: two Oscars in "technical" categories.[18] *A Christmas Carol: The Movie* (2001) was the only fully animated Lottery-funded feature film. Expensive visual spectacle was provided by *The Claim*, in which Michael Winterbottom notoriously built a detailed frontier town set in challenging mountain terrain and then proceeded to raze it to the ground for the film's climax, with more explosions found in *Plunkett and Macleane*'s loud action sequences. One surprising example in this regard is *Photographing Fairies* (1997), an otherwise modest period tale with a supernatural edge that erupts into extravagant fantasy sequences orchestrated by Ron Mueck, previously best known for the puppet-driven children's film *Labyrinth* (1986).

Another measure of quality raised by the DCMS audience research is that of the presence of "well-known stars". Again, the maximum budgetary

[18] *Topsy Turvy* won "Best Costume Design" (Linda Hemming) and "Best Make Up" (Christine Blundell and Trefor Proud) at the 72nd Annual Academy Awards in 1999. See "Awards Database," *Academy of Motion Picture Arts and Sciences*, accessed January 2005, http://www.oscars.org/awardsdatabase/.

range reached by the Lottery-funded projects (around £13 million, see Table 3-4) is still some way shy of the amounts needed to pay for major Hollywood stars, such as Julia Roberts: *Notting Hill* (1999) cost in excess of £15 million without the expense of a period setting. American actors who starred in Lottery-funded films included Kevin Spacey (*Ordinary Decent Criminal* (2000)); Nicholas Cage (*A Christmas Carol: The Movie*) and Alicia Silverstone (*Love's Labour's Lost* (2000))—all reasonably major stars of the period, but perhaps not with the ability to "open" a movie all by themselves. The most commonly featured stars were (diversely) British: Jonny Lee Miller, Peter Mullan, Kelly Macdonald, Ioan Gruffudd and Emily Woof, all of whom appeared in four of the 95 features made and released with the help of Lottery money. The exception to this pattern is the startling regularity with which Australian actress Rachel Griffiths is featured in a lead role: *My Son the Fanatic* (1997), *Among Giants* (1998), *Divorcing Jack* (1998), *Hilary and Jackie* (1998), and *Very Annie Mary* (2001), all of which see Griffiths tackling accents from Northern English to Northern Irish and even Welsh.[19] This is most likely testament to a well-respected character actress' versatility and range, rather than to her pulling power at the box office. On a similar note, it is no surprise that for several years the film which was widely reported as being the first to fully repay its Lottery investment had an impressive cast list: *An Ideal Husband* (1999) featured Rupert Everett, Julianne Moore, Minnie Driver and Cate Blanchett. However, overall, it is fair to say that the UK star system was not significantly strengthened by Lottery investment, remaining driven by character actors, television comedy stars (e.g. Steve Coogan in *The Parole Officer* (2001)) and imported American stars, wherever budgets allowed.

The idea of "quality" in the context of public funding for national cinema is demonstrably complex and difficult to quantify. To return to Pratten and Deakin's more easily measurable performance indicators, the next factor to be considered concerns the distribution sector. It has become common place to diagnose the main problem of the British film industry within this area: too many films are made, and so this line of argument goes, without a second thought, as to how they will reach an audience. This criticism is often levelled at state-supported cinema throughout

[19] Akin Ojumu notes that Griffiths could "rival Gwyneth Paltrow in the adopted Brit stakes." Ojumu, "Everyone's talking about Rachel Griffiths," *The Observer*, July 2, 2000, accessed January 2006, http://film.guardian.co.uk/Column/0,,3387 56,00.html.

Europe—and especially in Germany.[20] It is also implied in the policy development noted above, which signalled a move away from investing money solely into production in favour of development or distribution. Given this background, I was expecting my research to reveal a stack of unreleased Lottery funded films, but this is one area where the results proved to be surprising. Figure 3-3 was constructed with the help of the BFI tables which list "What happened to…?" the films produced in each year, published in the yearbook two years down the line. This reveals that the Lottery-funded films had a far higher likelihood of being distributed within two years of production than the average British film during this period: 77% achieved this compared to just 57% overall. Unfortunately this seems to have had little effect on the industry's overall performance by this indicator, as illustrated in Figure 3-4, with the proportion of all UK films left unreleased two years after production stuck stubbornly around the 30% mark. Nonetheless, the relative success of the Lottery-funded films by this benchmark is striking.

This relatively strong performance can be attributed to the process of application and selection for awards. The notion of "public benefit" is compromised if the films are not seen by a wide audience, and so each of the Arts Councils had assessment criteria in place which gave preference to those projects most likely to be distributed. The Scottish Arts Council's guidelines for example informed applicants that "You must... show that you have serious interest from a distributor in your project."[21] This strategy does seem to have paid off, although, as the following section demonstrates, there were significant regional variations within this overall success story. It was also more difficult for certain types of films to find theatrical release, notably documentaries and features made as European co-productions. The types of release achieved by each film should also be taken into consideration. There is a great deal of difference, both in terms of cost and potential reward, between the handling of a specialist art-house release, such as Lynne Ramsey's *Ratcatcher*, and the blanket international distribution provided by Universal for *Billy Elliot*.

Such issues act as a link between distribution and the factors contributing towards Pratten and Deakin's final performance indicator: domestic market share within the exhibition sector.

---

[20] Martin Blaney, "Subsidy Heaven," *Screen International,* 98, October 21, 1994, 8.

[21] Scottish Arts Council (SAC), *National Lottery Film Production Guidelines* (Edinburgh: SAC, 1998), 12.

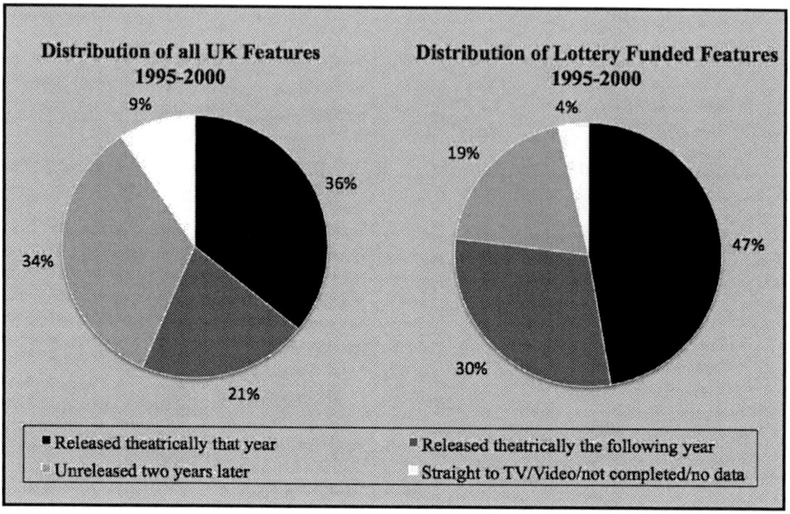

Fig. 3-3: Distribution of Lottery-funded films compared to all UK features.

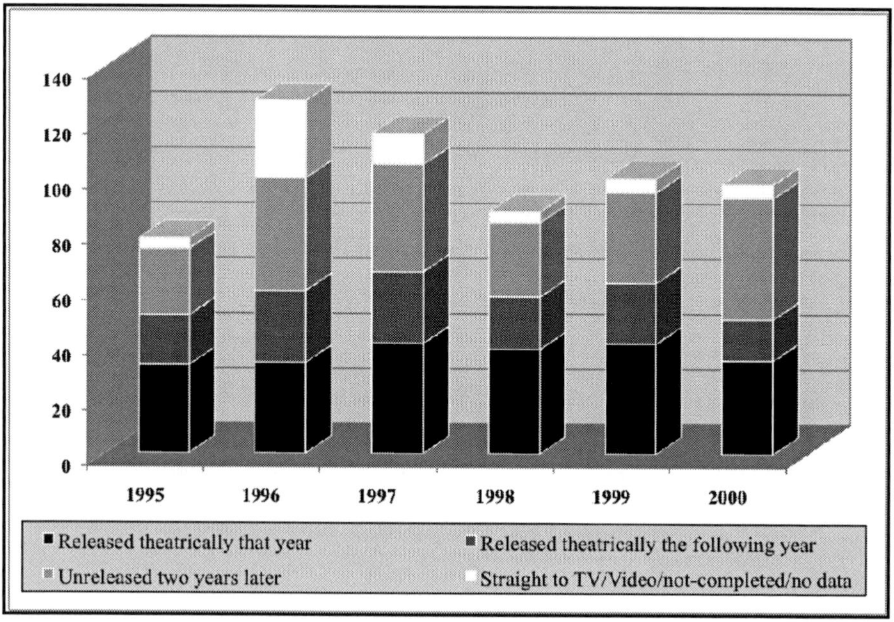

Fig. 3-4: Distribution of British feature films, 1995–2000.

This particular measure of the British film industry's health saw consistent emphasis across government film policy documents during the 1990s. Gerald Kaufman's select committee report in 1995 placed this indicator first in its list of problems for the industry, noting that "British films managed to capture just 2.5% of British box-office receipts in 1993".[22] By 1998, *A Bigger Picture* gave UK films a far more generous estimate of 23% of box-office takings in this country, but also proposed an extremely ambitious target of doubling this level of performance within an unspecified timeframe.[23] This is the same kind of patriotic, populist thinking underpinning the National Lottery as a whole: if "the people's Lottery" is to create a kind of "people's national cinema", then British audiences must be broken out of their habit of preferring American movies at their local multiplex. Unfortunately, this is also the area in which Lottery funding for film production failed to make a significant difference to the industry. Table 3-5 lists feature films that received National Lottery funding in order of UK box office as of May 2003.[24] 94 such films had been released by this point, generating a total of £57.7 million in UK cinemas. This performance failed to recoup the total lottery investment of £84.7 million, let alone their actual cost of around £315 million. As with many such figures, the total is dominated by one film, *Billy Elliot* (2000), which took over £18 million. Only 11 other films grossed more than £1 million, with 50 films taking less than £100,000.

Billy Elliot aside, approximately £8 million per year was added to the UK box office by Lottery-funded feature films over the five-year period; this is a negligible amount given a yearly total of around £500 million. On a film-by-film basis, the average box-office take for all UK films (including co-productions) was £1.4 million, so with an average take of just £614,000, the Lottery features were generally underperforming. Stripping out co-productions to leave wholly UK financed films brings the averages much closer together, but bearing in mind that the average American film took £2.3 million in the UK alone, this performance is rather dispiriting.

---

[22] Department of National Heritage (DNH), *The British Film Industry,* Cmnd. 2884 (London: HMSO, 1995), 5.

[23] Department of Culture, Media and Sport (DCMS), *A Bigger Picture: The Report of the Film Policy Review Group* (London: DCMS, 1998), 3.

[24] Box office figures are the BFI's, as collated in Wickham, *Producing the Goods?*, 22–56.

Table 3-5: UK Box Office (£m) for features funded by the National Lottery.

Film	Take (£m)	Film	Take (£m)
Billy Elliot	18.387	*The Trench*	0.086
Shooting Fish	4.024	*Pandaemonium*	0.073
This Year's Love	3.601	*Babymother*	0.062
Mike Bassett: England Manager	3.568	*The Lost Son*	0.056
The Parole Officer	3.284	*Metroland*	0.049
An Ideal Husband	2.893	*Amy Foster*	0.049
Plunkett and Macleane	2.779	*Stella Does Tricks*	0.042
Wilde	1.878	*It Was An Accident*	0.031
The Land Girls	1.574	*Gabriel and Me*	0.029
A Christmas Carol	1.462	*Miss Julie*	0.029
Topsy Turvy	1.174	*Bent*	0.028
Hilary and Jackie	1.041	*Downtime*	0.028
My Name is Joe	0.949	*My Life So Far*	0.028
Still Crazy	0.934	*Titanic Town*	0.026
Hideous Kinky	0.794	*A Midsummer Nights Dream*	0.026
The House of Mirth	0.709	*The Last Great Wilderness*	0.025
Regeneration	0.649	*House of America*	0.022
Mansfield Park	0.587	*The Wisdom of Crocodiles*	0.019
Love's Labour's Lost	0.531	*The Darkest Light*	0.018
Divorcing Jack	0.47	*Strictly Sinatra*	0.018
Ratcatcher	0.432	*Large*	0.017
Orphans	0.413	*Captain Jack*	0.017
Love And Death On Long Island	0.394	*The Slab Boys*	0.016
Ordinary Decent Criminal	0.373	*Gallivant*	0.016
There's Only One Jimmy Grimble	0.355	*Wild About Harry*	0.015
Love is the Devil	0.277	*Simon Magus*	0.013
Whatever Happened To Harold Smith?	0.254	*Crimetime*	0.013
The Winter Guest	0.251	*Another Life*	0.011
The Claim	0.245	*I Could Read the Sky*	0.011
The Tango Lesson	0.216	*The Navigators*	0.009
Beautiful Creatures	0.204	*Janice Beard 45wpm*	0.009
The Woodlanders	0.177	*Room to Rent*	0.009
Fanny and Elvis	0.162	*Hold Back the Night*	0.008
True Blue	0.152	*This Filthy Earth*	0.007
Get Real	0.151	*The Secret Laughter of Women*	0.007
Very Annie Mary	0.149	*Lighthouse*	0.006
The Governess	0.137	*Prometheus*	0.006
My Son the Fanatic	0.131	*A Kind of Hush*	0.006
Gregory's Two Girls	0.128	*The Last Yellow*	0.005
Beautiful People	0.117	*Darklands*	0.005
House!	0.114	*Dust*	0.004
Keep The Aspidistra Flying	0.111	*Esther Kahn*	0.003
Photographing Fairies	0.104	*Food of Love*	0.002
Late Night Shopping	0.104	*The Sixth Happiness*	0.002
A Room For Romeo Brass	0.098	*Glastonbury the Movie*	0.001
Complicity	0.096	*The Life of Stuff*	0.001
Among Giants	0.091	*Kin*	0.001

In some ways, this can be read as a knock-on effect of the increased likelihood of Lottery films receiving theatrical distribution: either some of the films which got into cinemas were of poor quality, thereby lowering the overall average box office, or there really is only a finite audience for UK films, and they were being spread increasingly thin. Both of these arguments have been made before within film policy debates—generally by opponents of state intervention. Another way of accounting for this under-performance is to note that UK films tend to receive far less support in terms of advertising and marketing than their US equivalents. It is important to remember that domestic theatrical box office alone is, in many ways, an inadequate indicator of a film's eventual earning potential. For example, according to admissions data recorded by the European Audiovisual Observatory, Ken Loach's *My Name Is Joe* (1998) was seen by far more cinemagoers in both France and Italy than in Britain.[25] Other films recouped significant amounts of their budgets at the US box office: *Hilary and Jackie* (1997, $4.88 million) and *The House of Mirth* (2000, $3.04 million) are two such examples.[26] In addition, the theatrical release is just the beginning of a film's extended life on video, DVD and television.

However, these complex, long-term considerations are far less attractive to policy-makers than the prospect of reversing a half century of Hollywood domination on home soil.[27] Ensuring that more British films are made and distributed are noble objectives and, as my figures demonstrate, both were achieved by the Arts Councils with a substantial degree of success between 1995 and 2000. But, without an attention-grabbing British smash-hit (*Billy Elliot* arrived too late) or even a steady level of reasonable domestic box-office successes, the system of support for film production offered by the Arts Councils was always going to be vulnerable to criticism from the press, as discussed in detail in the following section. However, as potent as this particular performance indicator appears to be, its dominant status within the debate surrounding films supported by the National Lottery should not go unquestioned. It is possible to defend the scheme even within the logic of economics. If the

[25] Total admissions were 237,901 in the UK; 441,983 in France and 311,286 in Italy. Germany and Spain were not far behind with 215,595 and 114,690 admissions respectively. See European Audiovisual Observatory, *Lumiere Database*, accessed April 2, 2004, http://lumiere.obs.coe.int/web/EN/film_stats.php?film_id=8114.

[26] US box-office figures from *Variety.com*, accessed April 2, 2004, http://www.variety.com.

[27] As Pratten and Deakin note, the last year that British films took more at the domestic box-office than American pictures was 1946.

state steps in to correct a perceived failure of the market—in this case, a failure to deliver adequate numbers of British made films—then it is unfair to judge the results purely in market-driven terms. Here, the issue of additionality again becomes relevant; money raised by the National Lottery is required to be spent on projects which would not otherwise have gone ahead. Whether or not it is possible to enforce this principle within the film industry, it suggests that riskier, less obviously "commercial" projects should have benefited, and that a failure to reap huge economic returns on such projects should not necessarily render them worthless.

As argued in Chapter One, the history of film policy interventions demonstrates that other motives have been considered just as important as pure economics. These motives are often labelled "cultural", and therefore separated neatly from economic concerns, but this need not necessarily be the case. The impulse to fund the making of short films or artists' film and video projects is often couched in cultural terms, but such activity may also be considered vital "research and development" for the wider industry as a whole, providing a source of both new talent and innovation at the formal level. Even at the elevated terrain of feature filmmaking, markets do exist outside of the multiplex strongholds. As Ben Gibson, Head of BFI Production throughout the 1990s, points out, the idea of exactly what constitutes a "commercial" strategy in filmmaking has long been associated with the blockbuster model utilised by Hollywood. However, stripped of such connotations, a "commercial" product is simply one which can repay the cost of its production and generate a profit on top. In these terms, Derek Jarman's *Wittgenstein* (1992)—which was still being exhibited at small picture houses in Paris well over a decade after its production—is just as commercial a prospect as many big budget comedies or heritage films.[28] However, not all experimental filmmakers go on to earn the reputation of Jarman, and it is equally inevitable that some such projects will fail to recoup their costs, inviting accusations of waste and elitism. But, as the budgets for these riskier ventures tend to be small, the amounts lost can perhaps be more easily justified than in the case of bigger budget, expensive "flops". This chapter documents an example of these flops, *Amy Foster*, as well as considering other types of failure amongst the Lottery funded films.

[28] Interview with the author, May 2004.

Losing the Lottery

Throughout the 1980s and early 1990s, the occasional international breakthrough hit such as *Chariots of Fire* (1981), *A Fish Called Wanda* (1988) and *The Crying Game* (1992), masked an increasingly desperate situation for many British films in their domestic market place. The end of the failing quota system and the Eady Levy had left the British industry largely unprotected against the influx of American movies, leading to a point in the early 1990s when only around 5% of domestic box office was taken by British films.[29] It became clear that this level of performance could not sustain a functioning industry, and as the various film policy reviews of the period began to publish their recommendations, there was a renewed focus on regaining box-office share in the domestic market.[30] Against this background, it was inevitable that National Lottery funding for film production would come to be judged first and foremost on the basis of how well its feature films did in UK cinemas. Not surprisingly then, much of the negative commentary surrounding Lottery funding for film focused on its "flops"—the films that failed most spectacularly at the box office. But, as Figure 3-5 shows, there were also other, less high-profile ways in which a Lottery-funded film could fail.

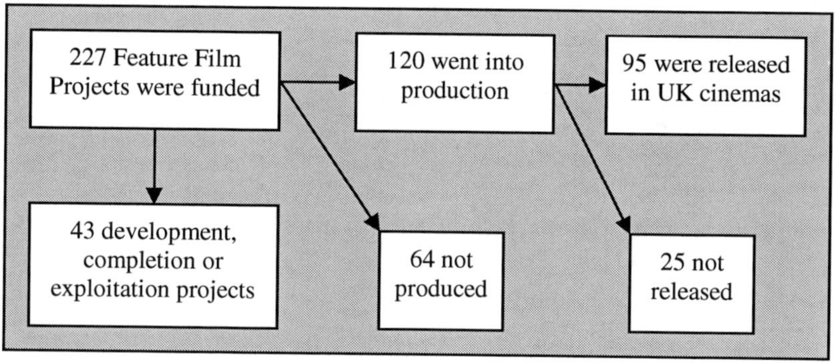

Fig. 3-5: What happened to the National Lottery-funded feature films?

---

29 Eddie Dyja, *BFI Film and Television Handbook 1996* (London: BFI, 1995), 39.
30 e.g. the Department of National Heritage (DNH) 1995 report recommends funding distribution networks to help increase the performance of British films at the UK Box office. *The British Film Industry*, Cmnd. 2884 (London: HMSO, 1995), 21–2.

Roughly speaking, approximately one-third of Lottery-funded film projects remain unproduced, and of those that were made, one-fifth failed to find theatrical distribution within the UK. There are various ways in which to interpret this information. The fact that a third of projects never reached the production stage could be read as an indication that the Arts Council's application procedures weren't tight enough, and that they were unable to weed out projects which weren't financially viable, despite this viability being one of their three key selection criteria. This is not an unreasonable criticism, and is perhaps further evidence of the Arts Council's fundamental incompatibility with the entrepreneurial structures of the film industry. On the other hand, it is important to recognise that awards for production could not be drawn down until shooting had actually begun. Accordingly, these "awards" were actually provisional soft commitments, promises of money offered in an attempt to attract further investment, which sometimes failed to materialise.

At this stage, the projects considered most likely to fail were either those with the highest budgets (>£5m) or those with the lowest (<£1m). Table 3-6 lists the larger-budget projects that fell into this unproduced category. Notably, almost all of these projects would have been period films, and most drew on existing literary sources (e.g. Neil N. Gunn's *The Silver Darlings* (1941); William Golding's *The Spire* (1964)). Probably the most unusual is the Film Consortium's *Journey to the Centre of the Brain*, a biological documentary which was to have been shot in the expensive IMAX format. Certainly the most notorious of these projects is Pathé's aborted *The Man Who Killed Don Quixote*, the failed production of which became the subject of a feature documentary in 2002; *Lost in La Mancha* charts writer-director Terry Gilliam's frustrated attempts to shoot his long cherished version of Cervantes' classic novel in the face of biblical downpours, hostile financiers, and the serious illness of his lead actor, Jean Rochefort. Whilst not all of these features failed in such spectacular fashion, it is worth taking a closer look at one example to help understand the factors which could work against such projects—even after they had secured access to Lottery funding.

Based on the history of two of eighteenth century London's most notorious criminals, *Jack Sheppard and Jonathan Wild*, was to have been the second feature film from writer-director Benjamin Ross, after the modest success of *Young Poisoner's Handbook* in 1994.[31]

---

[31] *Young Poisoner's Handbook*—Budget: £1.35m; UK gross: £0.2m; US gross: £0.45m; Germany 14,000 admissions. Sources BFI, *IMDB, Lumiere Database*.

Table 3-6: Unproduced Lottery--funded feature films costing > £3 million.

A.C.	Applicant Name	Title	Total Awarded	Project Cost
ACE	Pathé Pictures Ltd.	*The Man Who Killed Don Quixote*	£3,640,625	£21,875,000
SAC	Raging Star Films Ltd.	*Mary, Queen of Scots*	£542,386	£15,604,241
ACE	Renaissance Films Ltd.	*Daniel Deronda*	£2,000,000	£9,500,000
ACE	Picture Palace Films Ltd.	*The Spire*	£1,000,000	£9,100,000
SAC	Freeway Films Ltd.	*The Silver Darlings*	£1,000,000	£8,000,000
ACE	The Film Consortium Ltd.	*Journey to the Centre of the Brain*	£1,250,000	£7,187,500
SAC	Parallel Pictures Ltd.	*Poor Things*	£1,000,000	£6,500,000
ACE	Mass Productions Ltd.	*Cassandra at the Wedding*	£1,000,000	£5,520,000
ACE	Mass Productions Ltd.	*Jack Sheppard & Jonathan Wild*	£1,000,000	£5,500,000
ACE	Parallax Pictures Ltd.	*Days Like This*	£1,000,000	£5,100,000

The project was in development with Film on Four for three years whilst Ross researched the period and drafted the script. Ross' producer was Samantha Taylor, who had arranged the finances for his first feature, and this time was working to raise a budget of £5.5 million. This represented a significant step up from *Young Poisoner's* £1.35 million, but in retrospect seems rather modest compared to similar period productions.[32] *Jack Sheppard and Jonathan Wild* was awarded Lottery funding of £1 million in 1997, and went into production for the first time in early 1998, but the film's finances collapsed and shooting had to be abandoned. A further attempt to reconfigure the project occurred in 2001 when the script was restructured, the cast changed, and filming planned to take place in Eastern

[32] e.g. *Elizabeth* (1997) cost £13m; *Plunkett and Macleane* (1999) cost £10m.

Europe rather than the UK. However, this version was subsequently dropped by Film Four at a point when the company had ambitions to dramatically expand their international operations. The protracted nature of *Jack Sheppard and Jonathan Wild*'s production process is not uncommon in the film industry—either in the UK or internationally—and there are still hopes that the film will one day come to fruition.[33] Nonetheless the story of the film's failed attempts to make it into production provides a useful case study of the benefits and limitations of National Lottery funding for larger-budget film production.

On the application form submitted to the Arts Council of England in May 1997, *Jack Sheppard and Jonathan Wild* is summarised as:

> ...an epic, action costume drama set in the eighteenth century. Jonathan Wild, a man of no formal education, rises to the self-created role of Thief-taker General... Jack Sheppard is a thorn in his side—an ungovernable criminal. Adored and famed by the masses, he triggers Wild's ultimate downfall.[34]

Here the story is framed within the generic conventions of crime movies, which often navigate around the moral ambiguity of their anti-heroes by structuring the narrative around a distinctive "rise and fall" trajectory. Later there is a claim for authenticity based upon Wild and Sheppard's status as "real historical characters", but it is interesting to note that the application contains no reference to the characters' rich variety of fictional incarnations.[35] With a literary pedigree including John Gay, Henry Fielding and Bertolt Brecht, the producers could easily have capitalised on this source of cultural status when arguing for the film's "benefit to the public". Instead, they chose to emphasise its "originality" in dealing with London's disenfranchised, the script's "sardonic humour", and its "gruesomeness". In this sense they were following in the tradition of the earliest cinematic incarnations of Sheppard and Wild, which included a chase film from 1903 and an adaptation of Ainsworth's novel *Jack*

[33] In 2006 a revised version of the script went back into pre-production at Film Four. Benjamin Ross, interview with the author, October 2005. All subsequent quotations from this source unless otherwise attributed.

[34] Samantha Taylor, "National Lottery Application Form: Film Production for the Cinema," submitted to the Arts Council of England in May 1997. Held on file at the UK Film Council.

[35] Sheppard and Wild in fiction: John Gay, *The Beggars Opera* (1728); Henry Fielding, *Jonathan Wild the Great* (1743); William Henry Ainsworth, *Jack Sheppard: A Romance* (1839); Berthold Brecht and Kurt Weil, *The Three-Penny Opera* (1928).

Sheppard shot on-location around Manchester in 1923.[36] Another major cinematic precedent is provided by Paramount studios 1969 co-production *Where's Jack?*, an expensively mounted adventure starring Tommy Steele and Stanley Baker.

Although not a great critical or commercial success, this version established the potential for Sheppard and Wild's story to work within two normally disparate cinematic genres: the genteel costume drama and the violent gangster movie. Almost thirty years later, Benjamin Ross aimed to realise this potential in his ambitious "epic about the birth of modern England."[37] Initially at least, the company most sympathetic to Ross' hopes for *Jack Sheppard and Jonathan Wild* was Channel Four. David Aukin, then head of the broadcaster's film operations, had approached Ross in 1995 with the offer to develop his next film, and as the project took shape Aukin remained enthusiastic. However, in retrospect 1995 was a point of transition for Film on Four: its model of support for medium-budget independent filmmaking was enjoying the high-profile success of *The Crying Game* (1992), *Four Weddings and a Funeral* (1994), and *Shallow Grave* (1994), but overall its films were seen as a "loss leader" for the channel's up-market brand identity. The financial protection previously enjoyed by the innovative fourth channel had been removed in 1993 as it became responsible for selling its own advertising rather than leasing this space to ITV, and this inevitably led to increased commercial pressures right across the channel's operations. Unaware of the dangers ahead, Ross signed up with Aukin, and Samantha Taylor began to put together the film's financing. A portion of the £5.5 million would come from Channel Four, but as the company's policy during this period was to act as minority investors, this left a significant amount still to be raised. The Lottery application sent to ACE in 1997 requested £1.5 million, but was ultimately awarded £1 million—a relatively large award but a modest 18% of the budget. To put this into context, under ACE's guidelines producers could apply for between 10% and 50% of the total costs up to a maximum of £2 million. The average level of Lottery investment in each feature film project was around 30%.[38]

Jack Sheppard and Jonathan Wild's National Lottery award was approved in October 1997. Thus the producers had been able to satisfy the

[36] I am grateful to Nathalie Morris for bringing the 1923 version to my attention: Anon., "Jack Sheppard Newest Highwayman Picture," *Kinematograph Weekly*, February 8, 1923, 60. Also see Denis Gifford, *The British Film Catalogue Vol. 1: Fiction Film, 1895–1994*, 3rd ed. (London: Fitzroy Dearborn, 2000), 27, 126, 306.

[37] Ben Ross, interview with the author, October 2005.

[38] Source: awards database.

Arts Council on the three basic criteria: "public benefit", the existence of partnership funders, and, most worryingly given what happened next, the financial viability of the project. By this point, pre-production was already underway for a shoot to take place in the UK in early 1998. Sets were being built, the crew was finalised, and Ross had signed up a high-profile American actor to play Wild: Harvey Keitel. All this activity was going on despite the fact that Taylor was still attempting to finalise or "close" the film's financial arrangements. She explains that the project's difficulties were caused by one basic problem: for its investors, the budget of the film was too high for its predicted "value" in the market place.[39] Following the contributions made by Lottery and Channel Four, the remainder of the money was to have come from a tax shelter scheme, but the risk-averse nature of this deal meant that the producers had to "prove" that the film would take at least $12m in the international market place. Pre-sales were not consistent with this level of profitability, which meant that the deal was doomed to failure. The budget could not be reduced owing to the costly period trappings of the story, and at this stage production could not be moved overseas to cheaper locations because of the Lottery investment, which required that as much production work as possible be carried out in the UK.[40] These restrictions left very little room for manoeuvre and, in the short-term at least, even less hope for the project's completion.

The remarkable fragility of this deal provides a useful example of the problems inherent in the UK film economy owing to its "cottage industry" structure. Despite the support of a major broadcaster and access to a large pool of public funding, *Jack Sheppard and Jonathan Wild* was ultimately forced to rely on a complex one-off deal between various independent parties, all of which placed their own demands on the project. Another important consequence of industrial instability is that of lack of continuity in personnel. Just as *Jack Sheppard and Jonathan Wild* went into production, Ross lost his support at Channel Four with David Aukin leaving and Paul Webster coming in as his replacement.[41] This made a quick reprieve increasingly unlikely, and it took several years before the film was reconsidered by Film Four—this time without the Lottery

---

[39] Samantha Taylor, interview with the author, February 2006.

[40] ACE required that the film be registered as British under Schedule 1 of the Films Act 1995, and the value of the Lottery award must be spent on shooting in the UK. ACE, "Guidelines," *National Lottery Funding for Film: Application Pack* (London: ACE, 1997), 7.

[41] See John Hill's interview with Paul Webster, "'Changing of the Guard": Channel 4, Film Four and film policy', *Journal of Popular British Cinema*, 5 (2002): 53–63.

funding. By 2001, Film Four had implemented a "kill the middle" policy, abandoning the medium-budget films which were their traditional speciality in favour of either very low-budget experimental work or projects on a grander international scale, for which status *Jack Sheppard and Jonathan Wild* was now being reconsidered. But despite the efforts of a new producer (Robert Jones, who went on to head the premier fund at the Film Council), a script editor (author John Preston), and the addition of another American star, Tobey Maguire, who was to play Sheppard, the film once again dropped down the list of Film Four's priorities. The company went on to make the WW2 drama *Charlotte Gray* (2001) instead, which, whilst not quite the unmitigated disaster that it was widely reported to have been, was an expensive under-performer that helped contribute towards a significant downsizing of the company's ambitions.

So what can this story of frustrated creative ambitions and financial instability teach us concerning the effects of Lottery funding upon large-scale feature production—particularly in terms of the ability of these projects to reach completion? Perhaps the most obvious conclusion is nonetheless important to acknowledge: in some cases—and especially in the higher budgetary range—the inclusion of an element of Lottery funding in a film's budget was not the overriding factor in its production process. As a vivid illustration of this point, Ben Ross, whilst possibly not the most financially involved of directors, was not aware of the fact that his producers had been awarded public funding.[42] However, there are also broader issues of policy direction here: the Arts Councils, acting as distributors of the new funding stream, were not in a position to instigate and develop new projects, as the Lottery legislative framework initially ruled out the soliciting of applications, hampering strategic decision-making.[43] Instead the Arts Councils were placed in a reactive role, making decisions on projects which had already reached a certain stage of their development. As such, to some extent the essential elements of many of these projects were already firmly established before Lottery money was added into the equation, limiting its impact. *Jack Sheppard and Jonathan Wild* did not fail because it had Lottery funding, although it may not have reached the advanced stage that it did without it. On the other hand, it is

---

[42] Ben Ross, interview with the author, October 2005.

[43] See ACE, "Statement of compliance with policy and financial directions," *2nd Annual Report and Accounts 1995/6* (London: ACE, 1996), 99.

also vital to remember that many projects which applied for Lottery funding were turned down and, as a result, failed to get into production.[44]

What is more difficult to assess is whether the failure of *Jack Sheppard and Jonathan Wild* was necessarily a bad thing for the UK film industry at this point. There is a clear commercial argument to be made against the wisdom of throwing money at extravagant projects with no clear idea of their audience, and when this money belongs to the public, this argument becomes not just financial but also political. This kind of debate is often expressed in terms of having either a "production-led" or a "distribution-led" outlook. A well-known defence of the production-led philosophy was put forward by Sally Hibbin, Ken Loach's producer and, later, a participant in the Film Consortium. Reacting to the Film Policy Review Group's conclusions, which would become the strategic basis of the Film Council, Hibbin deplored the "distribution-led" approach as an "anathema", warning of the danger of "film-making by tribunal." She argues that:

> Our success had always come from being production-led, from making films that people are passionate to make, not products designed to gain the largest audience figures.[45]

From this perspective, it is possible to claim that Film Four made a mistake in preferring the pre-sold literary adaptation *Charlotte Gray* to the arguably more original *Jack Sheppard and Jonathan Wild*. Clearly, there are also problems with Hibbin's strategy—not least the potential to waste money making films which, no matter how great they may be, never get the chance to find an audience because of the problem of distribution. Securing adequate distribution for Lottery-funded films was a crucial element of the Arts Councils "public benefit" strategy: undoubtedly, the films needed to be seen by as many members of the public as possible in order to justify their Lottery-funded status.

As discussed earlier on in this chapter, the Arts Councils' attempts to increase the likelihood of Lottery-funded feature films getting into theatrical distribution saw some overall success: 77% of these films were released within two years of production, as opposed to an industry average of 57%.[46] Nonetheless, despite the Arts Councils' safeguards, 25 Lottery-

---

[44] e.g. *All American Man*, written by Craig Ferguson and to star Minnie Driver, was rejected by Scottish Screen in 2001 and has yet to go into production. Tina Dawson, "Sorry Minnie," *Daily Mail*, March 19 2001, 7.

[45] Sally Hibbin, "Britain has a new film establishment and it is leading us towards disaster," *New Statesman,* 127:4378, March 27, 1998, 40–1.

[46] See Fig. 3-3 on page 88.

funded features failed to find a place in UK cinemas (Table 3-7). Several of these were documentaries, two of which were made in association with the BBC and by filmmakers with strong reputations in the industry: Kevin Macdonald's *Total Performance*; and Isaac Julien's *Franz Fanon.* Geoffrey Macnab suggests that such collaborations tended to suffer from "a schizophrenic arrangement", which hampered distribution, as the Arts Councils requested a theatrical release but the BBC needed them to be broadcast as quickly as possible.[47] Another conclusion to draw from the list of unreleased films is that it seemed more difficult for films produced outside of England to secure distribution. The Arts Council of Northern Ireland (ACNI)'s features had a poor record in this regard, with just three of ten productions getting into cinemas. The assessment for ACNI's Lottery film-funding was managed by the Northern Ireland Film and Television Commission, whose then Chief Executive Richard Taylor confirms that checks were made on each project's distribution plan, but that these plans were occasionally "aspirational" in nature.[48] However, as John Hill describes, the special economic and political situation of Northern Ireland means that it is possible to defend film production "for its own sake" in terms of the benefits which accrue to local economies—even if these are not always easy to quantify.[49]

The list also contains a relatively high number of international co-productions. Overall there were only six Lottery-funded features classified by the BFI as "minority UK co-productions" or non-US foreign films with some UK financial involvement. Three of them appear on this list (*Aberdeen, St. Ives*, and *Bogwoman*), and the extremely low UK grosses of two others (*Dust* and *Esther Khan*) indicate that they received only a cursory cinema release in this country. Another title here, *Pornografia*, adapted from the novel by Witold Gombrowicz, appears to have had no other UK involvement whatsoever, being a Polish TV production supported by Eurimages and backed by Canal+. There is no evidence of any significant release for these productions outside their respective domestic markets.

---

47 Geoffrey Macnab, "Unseen British Cinema" in *British Cinema of the 90s*, ed. Robert Murphy (London: BFI, 2000), 141.

48 Richard Taylor, interview with the author, February 2006.

49 John Hill, *Cinema and Northern Ireland: Film, Culture and Politics* (London: BFI, 2006), 183–187.

Table 3-7: Lottery-funded features unreleased in UK cinemas.

A.C.	Applicant	Title	Budget	Type
ACE	Jezebel Films	*Erica und Klaus Mann*	£400,663	Documentary
ACE	Kismet Films	*Doctor Sleep*	£3,600,000	Feature
ACE	Wildgaze Films	*Five Seconds to Spare*	£3,145,000	Feature
ACE	Normal Films	*Frantz Fanon*	£268,593	Documentary
ACE	Dan Films	*LA Without a Map*	£4,917,305	Feature
ACE	Antelope (UK)	*Mozart in Turkey*	£4,100,000	Documentary
ACE	RAG Films Intl	*Nana*	£340,000	Documentary
ACE	Peggy Su Deco.	*Peggy Su!*	£1,091,766	Feature
ACE	Intrinsica Films	*Pornografia*	£3,400,000	Feature
ACE	Leda Serene	*Speak Like a Child*	£933,996	Feature
ACE	DNA Films	*The Final Curtain*	£3,992,352	Franchises
ACE	Artisan Films	*The Revenger's Comedies*	£4,302,836	Feature
ACNI	De Facto Films	*Bogwoman*	£1,035,500	Feature
ACNI	Lexington Films	*Crossmaheart*	£515,000	Feature
ACNI	First City Features	*Mad About Mambo*	£5,000,000	Feature
ACNI	Little Bird	*St Ives*	£3,000,000	Feature
ACNI	Northlands Films	*Sunset Heights*	£1,300,000	Feature
ACNI	Bandit Films	*The Mapmaker*	£2,000,000	Feature
ACNI	Igloo Productions	*Us Boys*	£100,948	Documentary
ACW	Bloom Street Prods	*One of the Hollywood Ten*	£3,162,000	Feature
ACW	CF1 Cyf	*Testimony of Taliesin Jones*	£2,700,000	Feature
SAC	Freeway Films	*Aberdeen*	£2,500,000	Feature
SAC	Daybreak Films	*Daybreak*	£750,000	Feature
SAC	Pelicula Films	*Follow the Moonstone*	£180,000	Feature
SAC	Figment Films	*Total Performance*	£223,673	Documentary

Aberdeen was shot by a Norwegian crew, partly in Scotland, and with an international cast including Stellan Skarsgård and Charlotte Rampling; it was fairly successful in Norway and Sweden, but made little impact elsewhere.[50] *Pornografia* was only released in Poland, although it attracted critical acclaim at international film festivals. These somewhat mysterious projects could be used as evidence to support the critics of subsidy for European cinema, who imply that some such productions are merely opportunistic scams designed to exploit international public funds. If this is really the case, then the limited number of these projects in the context of Lottery funding as a whole could equally be read as a success for the Arts Councils' vetting systems.

On a different note, it reflects badly upon the Arts Councils' claims surrounding cultural diversity that two of the most interesting Lottery-funded films in these terms did not manage to secure UK distribution.[51] *Peggy Su!* is set amongst Liverpool's Chinese community in the 1960s.[52] It was developed at the BBC as a project for playwright Kevin Wong, and is a light romantic comedy with colourful production design and a cast led by veteran Chinese actor Burt Kwouk. The film's director was Trinidadian Frances-Ann Solomon, who went on to head Leda Serene, a Canadian production company with a portfolio of culturally diverse projects.[53] *Peggy Su!* had been taken on by The Sales Company through their arrangement with BBC Films, but a change in management at the Sales Company left the film with uncertain support.[54] In contrast, the project was very well-supported by the local community in Liverpool where it was made; a showcase screening held in the city's Chinese district was attended by over 700 people, but not by agents from the Sales Company. A much smaller private screening in Soho resulted in two distributors seeing the film, one of which, Metrodome, showed interest for a time but later pulled out, leaving it without the chance to be seen in UK cinemas. This story illustrates one of the major characteristics of the film industry in England, which often draws on regional settings and narratives but is

---

[50] *Aberdeen* admissions—Norway: 43,301; Sweden: 11,556. Source: *Lumiere Database.*

[51] "Diversity and inclusion" was designated one of five "key priorities" for the Arts Council of England in 1998. Gerry Robinson, "Achieving a New Era for the Arts," *The Arts Council of England Annual Review 1999* (London: ACE, 1999), 2.

[52] Michael Brooke, "Peggy Su!" *Screenonline*, accessed January 2006, http://www.screenonline.org.uk /film /id/588353/

[53] "Company Info," *Leda Serene*, accessed December 2005, http://www.leda serene.com/mt3/content/ company_info .as

[54] Frances-Anne Solomon, email interview with the author, January 2006.

largely managed from London. During this period, the Arts Council of England was no exception in this regard, although more recent developments have tended to devolve funding streams, such as those administered by the Regional Screen Agencies.[55] Greater involvement at the local level could have helped *Peggy Su!*'s chances of establishing an audience across the UK.

Another unreleased project, *Speak Like a Child*, was the debut feature film from the African filmmaker John Akomfrah. Akomfrah was a founding member of the Black Audio Film Collective which produced politically engaged and formally experimental documentaries throughout the 1980s and early 1990s, most notably *Handsworth Songs* (1986). By the late 1990s, the collective had been dissolved, but Akomfrah remained a distinctive figure in UK film culture, combining his own work with critical practice and advisory roles.[56] His move into low-budget feature production was a natural project for the culturally diverse development slate at BFI Production, and he was backed up with Lottery funds of £433,000 in May 1997. This was the same month that Ben Gibson ended his tenure as Head of Production at the BFI in response to the decision to freeze its funding.[57] Akomfrah's film, an introspective drama concerning three troubled teenagers in an isolated children's home, was completed in just over a year and was selected for the Venice Film Festival in September 1998. By this point the news that BFI Production was to close its doors had been widely circulated, and the outspoken Akomfrah used the film's premiere press conference to launch a public attack on the Institute.[58] The director was furious at what he saw as the dumping of his project at the point when it most needed the organisation's help in promotion and publicity. The BFI responded with a promise to honour their commitment to all the projects affected by the shutdown, but it seems Akomfrah's fears for his film were justified as it was not picked up for theatrical or video distribution in any territory, its audience restricted to television screenings.[59] Akomfrah's rift

[55] From the perspective of 2011, the future of the Regional Screen Agencies seems increasingly insecure in the face of spending cuts.
[56] e.g. John Akomfrah, "Wishful Filming," *Black Film Bulletin* (Summer 1993): 14.
[57] See Ben Gibson, "Lights, Camera, Axe Man," *The Guardian*, March 13, 1998, 10–11.
[58] Dalya Alberge, "Director attacks film institute," *The Times*, September 8, 1998, 9.
[59] In the UK it was screened on Channel Four, and found a place on a specialist black movie channel in the US. Richard Katz, "BET Movies Fest to Bow 7 Pix," *Variety.com*, June 24, 1999, accessed February 2006, http://www.variety.com/article/VR1117503413.

with the Institute has since been healed to the extent that he was appointed as one of its panel of governors in 2002.

Between them, *Peggy Su!* and *Speak Like a Child* suffered from a combination of regional disparity and institutional instability; however, it is also noteworthy to highlight the possibility that these types of projects are the most likely casualties of the disjuncture between the production and distribution sectors of the UK film industry. Distribution is, in many ways, more conservative in outlook than production—especially the kind of production stimulated by cultural subsidies. It is a sector strongly controlled by international conglomerates: for example, in 1994, five major distributors (UIP, Buena Vista, Fox, Warner Bros, Columbia TriStar) accounted for 78% of UK box-office revenues—a not untypical figure.[60] The only independents of any size at this point were Rank and Entertainment, who were both releasing bigger-budget British films or American independents. Art-house releases were handled almost exclusively by Artificial Eye, Metro Tartan and the BFI themselves, three small set-ups with a limited capacity. As the 1990s progressed and Lottery-funded films began to appear in large numbers, the distribution picture became even less differentiated, with both Rank and the BFI's stepping down distribution facilities. Exhibitors have traditionally maintained a higher percentage of returns from less successful films to cover fixed costs; so, when a film fails theatrically, it is the distributor who loses the most.[61] Faced with these market conditions, it is not surprising that many British films lose out, receiving cursory releases with little or no advertising, or no release at all.

When accused of granting unfair advantage to Hollywood films, the traditional response of the UK's film distributors is to argue that they are only giving audiences what they want, as there is actually little demand for British product.[62] Using this logic, in the late 1990s the market was unbalanced by the Lottery investment in production, resulting in too many British films being made. The problem with this argument stems from the notion of "demand" itself and, in particular, its unproblematic application to a complex creative sector such as the film industry. For the majority of today's mainstream cinemagoers in the UK who have no particular preference about the types of film which they will go to see, "demand" is

---

[60] Dyja, *BFI Film and Television Handbook 1996*, 43.

[61] See the comments of Richard Segal, managing director of Odeon Cinemas in Macnab, "Unseen British Cinema," 138.

[62] e.g. the arguments against the introduction of the quota system in the 1920s. Margaret Dickinson and Sarah Street, *Cinema and State* (London: BFI, 1985), 5–33.

surely less of an issue than "choice". In a period when the multiplex was becoming the UK's dominant exhibition environment, consumers should have had a wider choice of options available to them, including space for more British films than had been previously available. In reality, however, increasing numbers of screens has tended to mean more screenings for the biggest blockbusters rather than a wider range of films.[63] Of those UK films to have made it onto the list of available options behind the multiplex ticket office, it is those which had the marketing muscle of large international companies behind them that tended to succeed, as *Trainspotting* (1996), *The Full Monty* (1997) , and *Billy Elliot* (2000) all demonstrate. The sizeable success of these films would seem to suggest that there is indeed "demand" for British films amongst British cinema audiences, provided they are given equal opportunities in the market place.

The invisibility of the unreleased films supported by the National Lottery meant that they were not a great concern for most sectors of the press. The same could not be said for the notorious Lottery-funded "flops", and still the most familiar and unchallenged criticism of the system is that it tended to produce terrible films which nobody wanted to see. Julian Petley has usefully summarised the progression of this discourse in the British press between 1995 and 2000,[64] noting that, aside from Alexander Walker's hostility and the odd piece in the *Daily Mail*, early reporting surrounding Lottery funding for film was largely factual and editorially neutral. It wasn't until early 2000 that the story was promoted to the top of the news agenda. Walker then began to be cited in publications other than the *Evening Standard*, such as *The Spectator* and a *News of The World* "exclusive", which claimed that "a staggering £90 million of Lottery money has been pumped into hopeless new films that have sunk without trace at the box office."[65] However, Petley also describes with concern the way in which this story was then taken up by the traditionally more even-handed broadsheet press, such as *The Independent*[66] and *The Observer*.[67] Vanessa Thorpe and Antony Barnett's

[63] See Stuart Hanson, "Spoilt for Choice? Multiplexes in the 90s" in *British Cinema of the 90s*, ed. Robert Murphy (London: BFI, 2000), 48–59.
[64] Julian Petley, "From Brit-flicks to shit-flicks: The cost of public subsidy," *Journal of Popular British Cinema*, 5 (2000): 37–52.
[65] Anon., "£90m of Lottery cash blown on film flops," *News of the World*, March 12, 2000, cited in Petley, "From Brit-flicks," 44.
[66] Louise Jury, "Millions spent on British films no one wants to see," *Independent on Sunday*, April 9, 2000, 14.

piece, "Lottery movies: 9 hits, 121 misses" cites government figures, stating that, of 130 feature films funded since 1996, only nine could be counted as successes.[68] The successes are not listed, but the feature ends by highlighting four of the failures: *The Lost Son* (Lottery grant: £2,300,000; UK takings: £49,302); *Downtime* (Lottery grant: £768,898; UK takings: £28,135); *Beautiful People* (Lottery grant: £553,823; UK takings £116,966) and *Amy Foster* (Lottery grant: £2,000,000; UK takings: £48,711).

The range of films chosen here to make the point of the Lottery's failure is interesting and, when examined more closely, actually illustrates several of the problems with this basic argument. *The Lost Son* was a medium-budget European co-production with a French star, Daniel Auteuil, which was handled by the Film Consortium with contributions from Film Four, Canal+ and French broadcaster TF1. It was able to benefit from distribution support under the European MEDIA II scheme, and performed noticeably better in Italy, Spain, and especially in France than it had done in the UK.[69] Accordingly, when considered in the broader international market for which it was clearly made, *The Lost Son* was not quite the complete disaster it may appear to be at first glance. By comparison, *Downtime* was a low-budget thriller costing just over £1.5 million, with other investors including BSkyB and Channel Four. It did not achieve a wide theatrical release, and its production companies, budgetary restrictions and cast (Paul McGann and Susan Lynch) suggest that it may have been designed primarily for the video rental and television market. Therefore, in order to assess fully the success of an audiovisual product such as *Downtime*, it would be necessary not only to look at its performance in cinemas but also its video rentals and television viewing figures.[70] At the other end of the cultural spectrum is *Beautiful People*, an

---

[67] Vanessa Thorpe and Antony Barnett, "Lottery Movies: 9 Hits, 121 Misses," *Guardian Unlimited*, March 12, 2000, accessed December 2005, http://film.guardian.co.uk/News _Story/Observer/0,,145977,00.html.

[68] This figure of 130 Lottery funded features is significantly higher than my own tally of 120 made, 95 released, but as the government source is unnamed it is not possible to investigate this inconsistency.

[69] *The Lost Son* admissions—UK: 10,120; Italy: 14,208; Spain: 14,190; France: 22,288. Source: *Lumiere Database*. *IMDB* notes that it was also released in Japan, Australia and Argentina, although it did not receive a US release.

[70] Although television viewing figures are freely available from the Broadcasters' Audience Research Board (BARB), figures for video rentals are particularly difficult to obtain as the trade journals which publish them are priced out of the reach of public resources such as the BFI National Library.

art-house film developed by BFI Production under Ben Gibson. Its UK box-office haul becomes more impressive when the nature of its release is taken into account: it earned £101,465, with just ten prints in circulation—a per-print average of £10,146.[71] This means that, on a print by print basis, it outperformed a film which *The Observer* article referred to as a box-office success: *Plunkett and Macleane* made £2,222,820 on a 346 print release, averaging £6,424 per print.[72]

Probably the most deserving of the description "Lottery-funded flop" from *The Observer*'s list is *Amy Foster,* which was released in the US under the title *Swept From the Sea*. Adapted from a short story by Joseph Conrad, this expensive production was budgeted at £9.2 million, of which £2 million was provided by the Lottery under the Greenlight Fund. This funding stream was aimed at attracting directors "of international repute" to make bigger budget films in the UK.[73] The international director in question was Beeban Kidron, who had started her career with the BBC before moving to Hollywood to make *Used People* (1992), and the cross-dressing comedy *To Wong Foo* (1995). Crucially, *Amy Foster* also had major Hollywood support from Columbia-TriStar/Sony Pictures, and could therefore rely upon a wide international release. Working with producers Polly Tapson and Charles Steel, Kidron assembled an impressive supporting cast, including Ian McKellan, Kathy Bates and Joss Ackland; however, the two starring roles went to relative unknowns Vincent Perez and Rachel Weisz. Perez was an established leading man of French cinema (e.g. *La Reine Margot* (1996)) but had yet to prove himself a draw in Anglophone cinema, and this was Weisz's first lead role. The film's "production notes", released as part of its publicity concede that:

Weisz was not necessarily the first choice of the filmmakers. "There were thoughts of going for a more established name," says producer Charles Steel, "but once we saw Rachel, we all said 'Yes. This is Amy Foster.'"[74] This sounds like an attempt to put a positive gloss on what the producers felt was a possible weakness in the film's appeal. *Amy Foster*'s theatrical trailer begins with the titles: "From Joseph Conrad...", "...comes a timeless tale of passion", emphasising both its literary pedigree and its

---

71 Anon, "Films of 1998," *Screen Finance*, 13:8, May 11, 2000, 5.

72 Anon, "Low budget films clog overloaded Brit distribution chain," *Screen Finance*, 12:9, May 13, 1999, 1, 6.

73 ACE, "National Lottery: The Greenlight Fund," *National Lottery Pack for Film Production Applicants* (London: ACE, 1997), separate note.

74 Columbia-TriStar, "*Amy Foster*: Production Notes," held at the BFI Library, London.

accessible (or even universal) romantic narrative.[75] The key elements of this "timeless tale" are introduced: the Slavic Yanko (Perez) leaves his home country for America, but is shipwrecked on the Cornish shore. Only the mysterious outcast Amy (Weisz) offers him kindness, and they fall in love, but their relationship is tested by the ignorance and barbarism of their local community. There is a suggestion of the story's tragic outcome in Amy's final tearful words: "I will love him till the end of the world." Other central pleasures of the film are also showcased: the careful period authenticity set against spectacular Cornish cliffs and seascapes; the lush romantic scoring by John Barry; and the quality British supporting cast augmented by the "Academy award winner, Kathy Bates." Bates' presence provides a further link to what must have been an irresistible and apparently fortuitous point of reference for the publicity team: the surprise smash hit still in cinemas as *Amy Foster* was released in early 1998, *Titanic* (1997). Both films are of a similar period, feature doomed sea voyages to America, and centre upon love stories crossing contemporary boundaries of respectability. It also seems possible that the alternative title for the film, *Swept from the Sea,* was preferred internationally because of its closer correlation with *Titanic*, whilst in the British market, the more restrained *Amy Foster* was selected to indicate deference to the source material. Perhaps the application of the weightier, literary moniker was even a conscious strategy for securing access to UK public funding. Application material submitted by the producers to British Screen and the Arts Council would seem to confirm this suspicion, as the project is summarised as "an adaptation by Tim Willocks of a short story written by Joseph Conrad."[76]

Swept from the Sea was released in the US with a modest 55 prints on January 23, 1998.[77] *Variety*, one of the few publications to give the film a positive review, also noted that this strategy was "a platform release to capitalize on [its] pedigree."[78] Despite the endorsement from the leading US trade journal, generally, reviews were negative. The *New York Times* warned that:

---

[75] Here I am referring to the trailer packaged with the UK DVD release published by Columbia-TriStar.

[76] Source: ACE electronic records.

[77] Release and box office data from *www.variety.com*, accessed January 2006.

[78] Leonard Kledy, "Quality doesn't always been B.O. quantity," *Variety.com*, September 24, 1997, accessed January 2006, http://www.variety.com/article/VR111662671?categoryid =13&cs=1.

> The story is told in a blunt, utterly humorless style with portentously lumpy language and broad acting that puts a permanent scowl on the faces of most of its characters.[79]

Roger Ebert called it "a plodding retelling of 'Amy Foster,' not one of Joseph Conrad's best short stories."[80] The lead actors were singled out for particular criticism: Weisz was referred to as "impassive" and even "bovine", whilst Perez was widely perceived to have failed in his struggle with both the English dialogue and a Slavic accent.[81] Furthermore, takings were not impressive: the film averaged just $4,107 per screen, ranking 30th in a box-office chart still dominated by *Titanic*, and the following week's drop in revenue of 66% spelt the end for hopes that the film could gradually build an audience. It was removed from cinemas with a total gross of just $303,686. This poor performance was repeated in the UK a few months later. Hostile reviews ("overwrought and unintentionally comic", "a turgid melodramatic mess", "a rather cumbersome cross between *Lorna Doone* and *The Archers*")[82] were followed by disappointing box-office returns (39 prints earning an average of just £458), resulting in a short, three-week run and a gross of £48,711. The film fared little better in other territories, although Perez proved a slightly more attractive asset in his home market of France.[83]

So why did *Amy Foster* fail? And to what extent was its publicly-funded status relevant in this regard? Of course, it is notoriously difficult to answer this type of question with any degree of certainty, but it is possible to identify several factors that may have been significant in this case. Certain influences would appear to be purely down to chance, such

---

[79] Stephen Holden, "Romance in the Rain," *New York Times*, January 23, 1998, accessed January 2006, http://www.nytimes.com/library/film/012398swept-film-review.html.

[80] Roger Ebert, *Chicago Sun-Times*, January 23, 1998, accessed January 2006, http://rogerebert.suntimes.com/apps/pbcs.dll/article?AID=/19980123/REVIEWS/801230304/1023,.

[81] Edward Guthmann, "Swept from the Sea" is Lush and Moody, but heavy handed plot is predictable," *San Francisco Chronicle*, January 23, 1998, accessed January 2006, http://www.sfgate.com/cgibin/article.cgi?f=/c/a/1998/01/23 /DD49151.DTL.

[82] David Gutten, "Amy Foster," *Daily Telegraph*, May 8, 1998, 24; Charlotte O'Sullivan, "Amy Foster," *Time Out*, May 6, 1998, 78; Richard Williams, "Amy Foster," *The Guardian*, May 8, 1998, 7.

[83] French admissions were almost three times those in the UK, and the Spanish gross was almost as high as that of the US. Sources: *Lumiere Database*; *Variety.com*.

as the unusual market circumstances surrounding *Titanic*'s release.[84] *Titanic* witnessed many audience members returning for repeat viewings, which clearly had the potential to effectively soak up the audience for *Amy Foster*. There is little evidence that the bad reputation of Lottery-funded films was a factor in this case, as there was no mention of the film's public contribution in any of the negative reviews. But other choices were made which clearly could have been influenced by financial imperatives. The producers' fear that the unknown status of both its leads would harm its chances with a mainstream audience seems to have been born out, particularly with regard to Weisz, as Perez at least had a fan base in mainland Europe. Equally, the marketing's attempt to attract two different and potentially incompatible audiences—that for the prestige heritage adaptation and that of the mainstream "weepie"—may have simply turned both types of viewer off the film. Both dilemmas—the need to cast stars and the desire to have as broad an appeal as possible—became more important as the budget for a film rises.[85] £9 million was a big risk for a "British" film, and yet still did not enable it to compete on anything like equal terms with its competition; in this case, unfortunately one of the most expensive and successful films of all time.

If *Amy Foster* was both too expensive to be confidently pitched at a more specialist audience and too cheap to compete with Hollywood, it is then possible to conclude that the Greenlight Fund was fundamentally misconceived. Perhaps the Arts Council and British Screen should have made more medium- or low-budget films rather than gambling larger amounts on a few international productions. But in fact *Amy Foster* was by far the lowest performing of the Greenlight Fund's features.[86] Overall, the case of *Amy Foster* is perhaps most important as evidence that the complexity of film production, with its many and diverse creative inputs and stakeholders sometimes producing a product which is somehow less than the sum of its parts, with or without the presence of public funding. As Richard Caves describes, the process of filmmaking is unusual in economic terms, in that information as to the likely success or failure of

---

[84] Peter Kramer, "Women First: *Titanic*, action-adventure films, and Hollywood's female audience," *Historical Journal of Film, Radio and Television*, 18:4 (1998): 599–618.

[85] See the difficulties faced during the production of *Jack Sheppard and Jonathan Wild* for more detail on this point.

[86] *Ordinary Decent Criminal* didn't do much better, but *Wilde*, *The Land Girls* and *Topsy Turvy*, all grossed between £1 and £2 million in the UK, and were also relatively strong competitors internationally, e.g. *Topsy Turvy* took $6.2m in the US. Source: *Variety.com*.

the product only becomes available after a significant amount of costs have already been "sunk".[87] It may only become clear that a film is likely to fail after it is shot and effectively "finished". At this point, an important decision has to be made: either to write off the losses sustained so far and proceed no further with the project, leading to its languishing on a studio shelf for eternity; or to risk further investment in the form of paying for prints, advertising and distribution. Sometimes, this logic suggests the right economic decision is *not* to make or to distribute a project, irrespective of how unpopular this course of action may be with the various creative talents involved.

The textual focus of most academic film studies means that paying serious attention to films which were unproduced may appear perverse, whilst unreleased films lack a reception context and therefore feel strangely unfixed. However, the film industry has always worked by *not making* far more films than it ever actually *makes*. This is especially true of Hollywood, where, during the early 1990s, around $500 million a year was spent on script development, with only 1 in 20 going into production.[88] The ratio of scripts to finished films in the UK is not as dramatic due to the lower sums of money available to spend on development, but even within the context of a Lottery-supported production sector, less than half of the applications to the Arts Councils were granted funding, of which only half made it into cinemas.[89] In terms of researching film history, this means that, by limiting investigations to those films that completed the production process, a potential wealth of information, anecdotal or otherwise, could be missed. Indeed the histories of projects which encounter difficulties during production or in distribution are likely to be the most useful if the concern is to identify problems within the industry or, as with policy-based research, how state-sponsored institutions have attempted to solve such problems. Therefore the Lottery mechanism's apparent "failures" (64 unproduced projects and 25 unreleased films) may both be seen as natural "wastage" for sound economic reasons, and also as evidence for the development of future film policy directions.

---

[87] Richard E. Caves, *Creative Industries: Contracts between Art and Commerce* (Cambridge: Harvard University Press, 2000), 15.

[88] Arts Council of England (ACE), "The Spectrum Report," *Lottery Film Franchising: A Feasibility Study* (London: ACE, 1996).

[89] According to Lottery Film Officer Mark Dunford, application success rate for film projects was lower than the 50% average across all other arts sectors. Interview with the author, July 2004.

What happened next?

The Film Council opened the doors of its glamorous West End offices in April 2000. Its aims had been outlined in a speech by Chairman Alan Parker entitled "Towards a Sustainable Film Industry":

> Essentially our intention is to use public money to make better, more popular and more profitable films in real partnership with the private sector, which drives our industry and largely creates our film culture. The overall aim is well-targeted assistance rather than scattergun subsidy.[90]

Parker's rhetoric is far more industry-focused and populist than that which accompanied the Arts Council's first forays into film production five years before. The nakedly ambitious word "profitable" would have been unthinkable previously, buried as it was under the legal jargon of "recoupment". It is notable that Parker chooses to shift the idea of "film culture" from its broad and inclusive BFI definition to something closer to "the market", which is largely attributable to the private sector. The rejection of "scattergun subsidy" creates clear distance from the Arts Councils' more reactive approach, but the aim of "well-targeted assistance" was only made possible by a gradual relaxation of the initial guidelines on using the proceeds of the National Lottery. The direct soliciting of applications—once considered a dangerous step towards "croney-ism"—was now considered vital in order to make strategic use of the funding, and the whole issue of additionality had become less politically charged five years into the system's operation. In 1998, the Labour party had introduced a new Lottery "good cause" known as the New Opportunities Fund, which had significantly blurred the line between society's "desirables" and its "essentials" by funding projects which took place in schools and hospitals. If industry reporting is to be believed, the Film Council were openly discussing "scrapping the additionality clause governing Lottery funding", although it would not have been within their power to do so.[91]

Statements such as these have contributed towards a growing unease surrounding the Film Council's wide-ranging powers and limited statutory controls. As Margaret Dickinson and Sylvia Harvey point out, unlike

---

[90] Alan Parker, "Towards a Sustainable Film Industry," *UK Film Council*, accessed January 2006, http://www.ukfilmcouncil.org.uk/aboutus/towards/.

[91] Adam Minns, "UK's Film Council sets aside $16m for bigger films," *Screendaily.com*, May 2, 2000, accessed December 2005, http://www.screendaily.com/storyid=1229.

previous government bodies dealing with the film industry (such as the NFFC), the Film Council was created by ministerial decision and not by an Act of Parliament.[92] It remains a private company overseen by a board appointed by the Department of Culture, Media and Sport, but in 2004 this board had very limited representation from the educational or cultural sectors. This seems to suggest a lack of balance between the Film Council's twin primary aims: developing a sustainable industry whilst also promoting an accessible and diverse film culture, although exactly what constitutes "film culture" in this business-driven context was clearly being renegotiated. All of which leads Dickinson and Harvey to this pointed question: "If business leaders were working effectively and in the public interest why interfere, and if they were not why trust them to direct government policy?"[93] This mistrust forms the background to the controversy over another high profile Film Council initiative—the Digital Screens Network.[94] This policy was designed to broaden the range of films available in UK cinemas by funding new digital projection technology. In return for the subsidised equipment, the cinemas must agree to show a percentage of "specialised films"; however, in addition to smaller venues, many large multiplexes have been able to access this funding, leading to concern that Lottery money is being used to enhance the business of private exhibitors with potentially little benefit in terms of increased diversity of programming.

The Film Council enjoyed a honeymoon period when several high-profile successes appeared to have found the correct balance between commerce and culture. In 2001, *Gosford Park* saw the veteran American director Robert Altman earn his best reviews for many years, featured a large ensemble cast which showcased many of the best-known British character actors, and won an Academy Award for "Best Original Screenplay". It was expensive to make, costing £13.5 million, of which £2 million came from the Premiere Fund, but it had a hugely successful run in UK cinemas, which generated £12.6 million, with a further $40 million following from the US.[95] Meanwhile, *Bend it like Beckham* and *28 Days*

92 Margaret Dickinson and Sylvia Harvey, "Public policy and public funding for film: some recent policy developments in the UK," *Screen,* 46:1 (Spring 2005): 87–95.

93 Dickinson and Harvey, "Public policy," 91.

94 See UK Film Council, "Digital Screen Network," *UKFC*, accessed March 2006, http://www.ukfilm council.org.uk/ funding/distributionandexhibition/dsn/.

95 Budget and UK box office figures from Phil Wickham, *Producing the Goods? UK Film Production since 1991* (London: BFI, 2003), 33. US box office from *IMDB.com.*

Later, both released in 2002, seemed to suggest that the UK film industry was now producing low-budget independent films which could compete internationally.[96] The "barrage of vitriol" directed towards Lottery funding for film subsided just as the Arts Councils ended their five-year tenure as gatekeepers for the film industry, suggesting that the organisations' critics had been right all along: perhaps the tired traditionalists of the Arts Councils were not capable of dealing with an entrepreneurial industry like filmmaking. The Film Council, by contrast, appeared dynamic and in touch with what both the industry and the public wanted. In 2002, the Council proudly announced that it was investing £750,000 in "a hilariously clever and absurd sex comedy", which had already received £35,000 of funding at script-development stage and was to star three of television's most popular and credible comedy performers.[97] The resulting film, released two years later, caused a startlingly strident reaction from the British press, including *The Times*, whose front page carried the banner headline "Is this the worst film ever made?"[98]

Sex Lives of the Potato Men (2004) stars comic Johnny Vegas, Mackenzie Crook (*The Office*) and Mark Gatiss (*The League of Gentlemen*), and its plot revolves around a string of sexual misadventures. It is bawdy in the tradition of the *Carry On* films, but also graphic in its engagement with the "gross-out" comedy of disgust found in many hit American movies of the 1990s. As such, its mode of address is determinedly adolescent and scatological; its intended audience would be made up of the young male fans of *Loaded* magazine or the "adult" comic *Viz*; therefore it was always going to antagonise the largely older and middlebrow contingent of film critics for the national newspapers; indeed James Christopher of *The Times* describes the screening for the broadsheet press as characterised by "a genuine atmosphere of shock."[99] This shock fed through into a set of reviews so scathing that they turned the film into a news story in itself. The front cover of the *Daily Mail* trumpeted "Fury as Lottery Money Funds Vile Sex Film", citing reviews which dubbed it "one of the most nauseating films ever made", and promoting a "furious

---

[96] Worldwide box office grosses - *Bend it like Beckham*: $76,580,371; *28 Days Later*: $82,719,885. Source: *IMDB*.

[97] UKFC, "UK FILM COUNCIL exposes Sex Lives of the Potato Men," *UK Film Council*, October 28, 2002, accessed March 2006, http://www.ukfilmcouncil.org.uk/news/?p= 1035885317451&skip=240.

[98] Anon., "Is this the worst film ever made?", *The Times*, February 20, 2004, 1.

[99] James Christopher, "Masterclass in nauseous ineptitude," *The Times*, February 20, 2004, 3.

backlash" against the Film Council's investment.[100] Inside the paper, Christopher Tookey's review describes the film as an "abomination" and "perniciously anti-social garbage" before calling for the Head of the Premiere Fund, Robert Jones to be fired. Significantly, the *Mail* uses the controversy surrounding the new film to revive a favourite old news story—that of the "Lottery-funded film flops", digging out a list of failures all released between 1998 and 2000. If the Film Council had hoped that this discourse had disappeared, they must have been sorely disappointed.

The furore caused by the Film Council's decision to support this otherwise unremarkable film demonstrates that the old arguments and tensions underlying public funding for British cinema could not be resolved by a few years of relative success. The language used to savage *Sex Lives of the Potato Men* is indicative of several long-running concerns, particularly the dislike of Americanisation ("If you like *Jackass*, you'll still hate it."[101]); the belief that the movies are a force for moral degradation and the decline of social values ("it is symptomatic of a new national culture of instant self-gratification and yobbishness"[102]); and a general disdain for popular culture from those who consider themselves above it (Tookey openly refers to the film's potential audience as the "lumpen proletariat"). The *Daily Mail* article also cites a series of right-wing commentators who repeat the familiar arguments against Lottery funding for filmmaking: the money should be spent on hospitals and sports centres instead; it should support great art, not puerile trash; it's wasteful to invest in films which could be funded elsewhere. *The Times* is better informed on film financing, but nevertheless concludes that "films are being financed simply because of the attractive tax regime available rather than the quality of the movie."[103]

Around the same time as the fuss over *Sex Lives of the Potato Men*, the "attractive tax regime", cited by *The Times* was also in crisis. As described in Chapter One, film producers had been benefitting from tax relief under Section 48 of the Finance Act of 1997. This effectively meant that 15% of the budget of a film produced in the UK for less than £15m could be made available up-front in order to help with production costs. In February 2004, a loophole associated with this scheme was unexpectedly closed by

[100] Michael Seamark and Tom Kelly, "Fury as Lottery money funds vile sex film," *Daily Mail*, February 21, 2004, 1, 5.
[101] Will Self cited in Xan Rice and Dalya Alberge, "Investors laugh at their unfunny film," *The Times*, February 20, 2004, 3.
[102] Christopher Tookey, "Vile beyond belief, and we paid for it," *Daily Mail*, February 21, 2004, 5.
[103] Rice and Alberge, "Investors laugh," 3.

the Treasury, catching the industry and the Film Council unawares and subsequently jeopardising the completion of several high-profile projects, including *The Constant Gardener* (2005). The following review of film policy instigated by the DCMS reinstated a form of tax relief, but also significantly refined the system by which films could qualify as British. Hence the narrowly defined economic criteria set in place by the Films Act of 1985 were replaced by a much broader set of benchmarks known as the "Cultural Test".[104] This new points system is heavily weighted in favour of its first section, "Cultural Content", meaning that any film based on British subject matter, set in the UK and with British lead characters and English dialogue, is almost certain to score enough points to pass.[105] An obvious consequence of this change was that high-profile international productions, such as the *Harry Potter* series, could qualify for tax breaks on cultural grounds, side-stepping issues surrounding the origin of their finance and the direction of their profits, and substantially boosting the figures of inward investment in UK film production.

As the industry "superbody" matured, it tended to divert its Lottery funding towards schemes where less money could be spent in a more strategic fashion. The "Super Slates" which replaced the Franchises were indicative in this regard, being focused entirely upon development rather than production, as was the Council's introduction of support for the distribution of films in the UK. Its Prints and Advertising Fund allocated £2m a year, and helped to increase the reach of British and foreign language titles such as *This is England* (2006), *The Lives of Others* (2006) and *A Prophet* (2009). The Film Council also experimented with a screen quota of sorts, as cinemas which benefited from the subsidised Digital Screens Network projectors were required to show a certain percentage of "Specialised Films" with the new equipment. The exact level of this quota varied depending upon what was already being shown in the cinema, and increased annually, so that after a few years an "independent" cinema like The Phoenix in Oxford (programmed by City Screen) could *only* show films approved as specialised on their digital screen.[106] The problem with this system was that the Film Council's definition of "specialised film" was broad and flexible, and decisions sometimes felt inconsistent to

[104] UKFC, "Cultural Test Points," *UK Film Council*, accessed May 2011, http://www.ukfilmcouncil. org.uk/culturaltestpoints.

[105] Although this was not the case for the first version of the test which was rejected by the European Commission in 2006. Maggie Magor and Philip Schlesinger, "'For this relief much thanks.' Taxation, film policy and the UK government," *Screen* 50:3 (2009): 310–313.

[106] Interview with Deborah Allison, Programmer for City Screen, July 2011.

exhibitors. For example Joe Wright's Oscar-nominated *Atonement* (2007) *did* qualify as specialised, whilst apparently similar period dramas like *The Duchess* (2008) and *Young Victoria* (2009) did not.[107] Whilst these irregularities could be easily absorbed by multiplexes with their large number of screens, it meant that a policy designed to broaden the range of films available to UK audiences sometimes ended up restricting what smaller cinemas could show.

As the decade progressed it became clear that the UK Film Council was beginning to benefit from a critical mass of successful film projects. By the end of 2004, the trade journal *Screen Finance* reported that recoupment from investments in film productions was now bringing in up to 20% of the UKFC's annual income. Revenue continued to be generated by the portfolio of projects inherited from the Arts Council of England: for example *The Parole Officer* (2001) paid back £514,000 in 2003–2004, whilst more recent hits *Gosford Park* (2001) and *Bend it like Beckham* (2002), were recouping up to £2m a year.[108] This improved financial performance was coupled with a more effective publicity machine to help counter public relations disasters like *Sex Lives of the Potato Men*. For example, in 2007 the Council published a bold claim that the film industry was worth £4.3 billion towards GDP.[109] This headline-grabbing strategy would become essential, as the financial climate changed dramatically over the next few years. In 2009 *Screen International* reported that the body was facing a 15% reduction in its Lottery income owing to the cost of the London Olympics, and was seen as vulnerable to further cuts should the Conservatives win the upcoming election.[110] The UKFC's overheads were higher than other comparable organisations, and the salaries it paid to its top executives were also attracting criticism. Later the same year, to the surprise of industry onlookers, the Film Council entered into talks with the BFI around a proposed merger.[111] The antipathy between the two bodies was no secret, stemming partly from arrangements which placed the older organisation within the financial power of the newer, but also from a fundamental difference in approach familiar from the history of film

[107] Hannah Patterson, "Dealer's Choice," *Sight and Sound* 18:4 (2008): 30.
[108] Tim Adler, "Lottery recouping accounts for 15% of UKFC Income," *Screen Finance*, December 2004, 4.
[109] Tim Adler, "Film Industry worth £4.3 bil. To UK GDP," *Screen Finance*, July 2007, 2.
[110] Geoffrey Macnab, "Film Council at the Crossroads," *Screen International*, April 24, 2009, 6–7.
[111] Geoffrey Macnab, "When will two become one?" *Screen International*, September 11, 2009, 10–11.

policy discussed in Chapter One; put simply, the UKFC was focused on industrial initiatives, whilst the BFI had deep-seated cultural concerns.

Following the Conservative and Liberal Democrat coalition taking over government from Labour in May 2010, the impact upon the UK Film Council was even more dramatic than had been feared. There was to be an immediate "bonfire of the quangos", and the UKFC was placed firmly on the pyre. A high-profile campaign was launched to save the body, which was joined enthusiastically by British actors, producers and even a few Hollywood directors, including Clint Eastwood. Incoming Minster for Film Ed Vaizey went on the counter attack, openly criticising the body for spending public money to promote itself in an attempt to secure its own future.[112] Meanwhile the Culture Secretary Jeremy Hunt was unyielding and unapologetic on the decision, stating that it was "simply not acceptable in these times to fund an organisation where no fewer than eight of the top executives are paid more than £100,000."[113] Hunt promised to channel the money saved back into film and to raise the level of Lottery funding available by £3m a year, but it was clearly disingenuous to suggest that this support could continue entirely without overheads. As discussed in Chapter Two, Lottery funding is, by design, a selective mechanism aimed at societies "desirables" rather than its "essentials". Even putting aside the strategic planning necessary to make effective use of this type of subsidy, it is therefore obvious that *somebody* has to call for bids, administer applications, make funding decisions, provide payments, and monitor the results. The question now was: who would carry out this work after the Film Council was taken out of service?

Ed Vaizey had already been instrumental in abandoning the proposed merger between the Film Council and the BFI, citing their mutually incompatible remits.[114] Clearly this predisposed the Minister to consider other options before recanting, and for a while it was even mooted that the Arts Council of England would regain its responsibility for distributing Lottery funds to the film industry—despite the largely ignominious nature of its previous experience. However within six months, Vaizey bowed to

---

[112] Diana Lodderhouse, "U.K. Gov't tells UKFC to stop lobbying," *Variety*, August 17, 2010, accessed June 2011, http://www.variety.com/article/VR111802 3001?refCatId=3599.

[113] Jeremy Hunt, "I've cut the UK Film Council so that the money goes to the industry," *The Observer*, August 8, 2010, 5.

[114] Adam Dawtry, "How is the BFI suddenly able to take over from the UK Film Council?" *The Guardian*, November 29, 2010, accessed June 2011, http://www. guardian.co.uk/film/filmblog/2010/nov/29/uk-film-council-bfi-ed-vaizey?INTCMP =ILCNETTXT3487.

the inevitable—albeit creating an outcome that would have been almost unthinkable only a year prior. Rather than the UKFC swallowing up the BFI, as had been feared during merger talks, in fact, the opposite occurred: the BFI took on the Lottery distributing powers of the Film Council and, with it, a large number of the defunct bodies' staff. As of April 2011, the British Film Institute's new responsibilities included:

> funding film development and production; training; distribution and exhibition; supporting film UK-wide; film certification, the Cultural Test and co-production; strategic development; industry research and statistics; and the MEDIA Desk UK.[115]

Meanwhile the British Film Commission's role in attracting inward investment was transferred to Film London. Industry commentators such as *Variety*'s Adam Dawtry reacted with barely concealed incredulity to the news that the BFI was now charged with building a "sustainable" British film industry, when that lofty (and some would say unreachable) aim had been quietly dropped from the Film Council's mandate.[116] The BFI's educational remit has historically seen it working alongside the Higher Education sector, but its new hegemonic position should not be immune to academic scrutiny. If the Film Council attracted criticism over its lack of accountability, it should then not go unnoticed that the BFI is a charity with a Royal Charter, that it elects its own Board and that its accounts are not subject to the same level of public scrutiny as those of the previous incumbents.

Conclusion

The introduction of National Lottery funding for film in 1995 offered the first opportunity for a generation of British filmmakers to receive significant help from the state. As a result, overall investment in the industry rose significantly, far more films were made, and some headway was made on the problem of distribution. Many first-time filmmakers were given opportunities to make short films, and artists' film and video projects flourished. However, the system was clearly not without its problems. Under the Arts Councils, it is difficult to defend the box-office record of the majority of the feature films, and the franchise scheme proved

---

[115] UKFC, "Closure of the UK Film Council," *UK Film Council*, accessed June 2011, http://www.ukfilmcouncil.org.uk/.

[116] Dawtry, "How?" http://www. guardian.co.uk/film/filmblog/2010/nov/29/uk-film-council-bfi-ed-vaizey?INTCMP=ILCNETTXT3487.

disappointing in terms of the numbers of films each consortium produced. As the Film Council took over, the situation appeared to rapidly improve, but it is worth noting that several of their early successes were actually the fruit of longer term developments. *Bend it like Beckham*, for example, had previously been in development with British Screen before it was folded into the new superbody, and *28 Days Later* was made by the Lottery franchise company DNA Films which, along with the other two franchises, continued to operate under the auspices of the Film Council. *The Magdalene Sisters* was a considerable critical and commercial success for Peter Mullan, but Mullan's development from actor to auteur had been financed by the Lottery through the Scottish Arts Council for several years. On the other hand, the vitriolic reaction to *Sex Lives of the Potato Men* demonstrates the dangers of the body's new populist ethos, and the episode certainly did nothing to improve the Council's relations with the cultural filmmaking sector. How the current transfer of powers from the Film Council to the BFI will work out remains to be seen, but it is somewhat ironic that, fifteen years down the line, Lottery funding for film is back in the hands of a body with a predominantly cultural remit and little experience of dealing with the commercial film industry.

With National Lottery funding for film production, the relationship between the government and the film industry took on a set of ideological contradictions. The concept of additionality seemed to encourage innovative, risk-taking British cinema which would not otherwise be provided by market forces, but many Lottery-funded films were condemned as wasteful when they failed to recoup their public investment. Applicants had to demonstrate that their project would be "of benefit to the public", building on the rhetoric of "the people's Lottery", but this often meant balancing the opposing impulses of pluralism and populism. The initial strict controls on the use of Lottery money put the Arts Councils into a reactive role, as applications could not be solicited, and projects must already have reached an advanced stage of their development. This meant that the structural problems of the industry were unlikely to be solved by such "scattergun subsidy", but the Lottery-funded attempt to increase vertical integration and provide "the advantages of continuity", the franchise scheme, faced under-funding and overly high expectations. Overall, despite the very significant scale of the investment, National Lottery funding for film production was not a panacea for all the difficulties of UK film industry. Nonetheless, in its first five years it helped over 400 moving image projects at some stage in their development, assisted the careers of many thousands of directors, actors and crew, and left a legacy of several hundred completed films. These films deserve to be considered not only as footnotes in a broad history of British cinema and the state, but as texts in their own right, each with its own specific contexts, modes of address, formal strategies, and ideological frameworks. The National Lottery enabled them, but it does not, in the final analysis, define them.

CHAPTER FOUR

MAINTAINING THE MAINSTREAM

The first three chapters of this book have followed the precedents set by the majority of writing on film policy by concentrating upon historical context, statistical analysis, and institutional change.[1] This empirical approach is vital in documenting and illuminating the period in question—a time of rapid change for the UK film industry which has been much misrepresented and misunderstood. One of the most important consequences of this misrepresentation is a lack of serious attention paid to the "end products" of these policy tensions and debates: the films themselves.[2] All film projects applying for National Lottery funding had to satisfy the Arts Councils in terms of "public benefit". These "benefits" included raising the production values of commercial feature films, broadening the audience for artists' film and video work by developing innovative exhibition strategies, and increasing access to the important training functions of the short film. As these examples suggest, it is through the films that the public was brought back into the circuit of funding as cinemagoers, visitors to art galleries, or consumers of home entertainment media. In order to investigate the system of public funding for filmmaking as a meaningful whole, it is therefore essential to consider the films produced in detail in order to understand their production histories and their impact at the level of reception. The aim is not to construct a simplistic model of direct causal influence, but rather to examine the complex networks of film policy in practice. Political rhetoric, institutional procedures, individual decision-making, filmmakers, the press and audiences all belong to these networks, and all find a common focus at the level of individual texts. These texts are therefore both the most challenging and the most rewarding objects of film policy analysis.

---

[1] e.g. the essays collected in Albert Moran (ed.), *Film Policy: International, National and Regional Perspectives* (London: Routledge, 1996).

[2] This point has been made forcefully by Julian Petley in "From Brit-flicks to Shit-flicks: The Cost of Public Subsidy," *Journal of Popular British Cinema,* 5 (2002): 37–52.

As detailed in Chapter One, the history of public funding for filmmaking in the UK can be characterised in terms of two major driving forces. Firstly, and most commonly, the goal of this financial support has been to strengthen and enhance the commercial film business in the face of Hollywood's domination of the international movie industry. Secondly, many smaller initiatives have been motivated by a range of factors that can be grouped loosely (if not unproblematically) under the heading of "cultural" film policy. There are significant points of contact between these two areas; broadly speaking, however, they have been tackled in different ways by different institutions. A defining characteristic of National Lottery Funding for film production is that it attempted to bring these two impulses together under one broad remit. Thus the budgets of the projects supported by the Arts Council of England ranged from less than £5,000 to over £20,000,000,[3] encompassing short films, artists' film and video, low-budget features aimed at niche markets, medium-budget comedies, and costly period dramas. This is a continuous spectrum of activity where cultural and economic goals are often intertwined. However, for the purposes of this analysis, it has been necessary to select and classify similar types of projects in order to identify trends and patterns. Therefore this chapter is concerned with popular cinema, particularly the Lottery-funded romantic comedies which worked with one of the most successful generic forms of 1990s UK cinema, other comedies which deal with the pregnant concept of "community", and the scheme's biggest runaway hit, *Billy Elliot*.

Stephen Crofts has described a range of strategies taken by different national cinemas in response to—or in despite of—Hollywood's hegemonic status.[4] Two of these strategies are of particular interest here: firstly that of European commercial cinema, which targets similar audiences to Hollywood's populist product. Crofts notes that France offers the most convincing example of this tendency, but it should be remembered that this level of domestic success is founded upon economic protectionism—including strict quotas and production subsidies. The genres which survive best under these circumstances tend to be those with higher levels of culturally specific reference points, particularly comedies. European film industries have also traditionally benefited from their linguistic separation

---

[3] Terry Gilliam's aborted *The Man Who Killed Don Quixote* was budgeted at £21m when it was provisionally allocated two Lottery awards totalling £3.6m in 1999–2000.

[4] Stephen Crofts, "Reconceptualizing National Cinema/s" in *Film and Nationalism*, ed. Alan Williams (New Brunswick: Rutgers University Press, 2002), 25–67.

from Hollywood, whereas their Anglophone equivalents have often been tempted, in Crofts' terms, to try to "imitate" Hollywood. Thus production bases already weakened by the inroads of English-speaking Hollywood companies are further confounded by often ill-advised attempts to conquer the American market. This strategy is unlikely to be successful, and can also compromise the national specificity of indigenous cinema. A further possibility, as recently exemplified by Working Title, is to forge direct ties with Hollywood, thereby producing international cinema with British cultural content. These different strategies provide a useful starting point from which to consider the romantic comedies funded by the National Lottery. Some worked in the same manner as economically protected European commercial cinema by appealing to less translatable aspects of British culture, whilst others emulated models with proven international appeal. In this sense, such films can be seen to embody many of the dilemmas facing producers of popular cinema outside of Hollywood: competition or collaboration, subversion or submission, resistance or surrender.

Romantic Comedy

In terms of popular appeal, comedy is the dominant genre of 1990s British cinema. As demonstrated in Table 4-1, British comedy films have a record of significant domestic success. Of the top-twenty highest-grossing releases, at least half can be classified as comedies, and many of the remainder have strong comedic elements. An interesting case here is *The Full Monty*, which was marketed as a family-friendly comedy despite its generally downbeat tone, strong language and eponymous nudity. Its extremely wide appeal, along with other comedy-drama hybrids such as the gangster films directed by Guy Ritchie, indicate that successful popular texts do not need to restrict themselves to one set of generic conventions; indeed the most successful often combine different attractions for different audiences. When these domestic returns are compared with those from the United States some interesting differences emerge. Relatively speaking, the Bond films performed more strongly across the Atlantic, whilst those films with lower budgets and no major stars did less well (e.g. *The Full Monty* and *Billy Elliot*). Probably the clearest exception to this trend was *Four Weddings and a Funeral*, which performed very well in the US without big stars or action sequences. This surprise hit, produced by Working Title and Channel Four instigated a cycle of romantic comedies strongly British in flavour, if increasingly international in terms of finance. Working Title went on to produce

Notting Hill and *Bridget Jones' Diary*, and Miramax made *Shakespeare in Love*—all films featuring high-profile female American stars, with sizeable budgets co-financed by Hollywood.

Table 4-1: Top-twenty highest-earning UK films at the domestic box office.

Rank	*Title*	Year	UK Gross[5]	US Gross[6]
1	*The Full Monty*	1997	£52.2m	$45.9m
2	*Bridget Jones' Diary*	2001	£41.4m	$71.5m
3	*Notting Hill*	1999	£31.0m	$116.0m
4	*Chicken Run*	2000	£29.5m	$106.8m
5	*The World is Not Enough*	1999	£28.6m	$127.0m
6	*Four Weddings and a Funeral*	1994	£27.8m	$52.7m
7	*Shakespeare in Love*	1999	£20.8m	$100.2m
8	*Tomorrow Never Dies*	1997	£19.9m	$125.3m
9	*Goldeneye*	1995	£18.2m	$106.6m
10	*Billy Elliot*	2000	£18.2m	$22.0m
11	*Bean*	1997	£18.0m	$45.3m
12	*Sliding Doors*	1998	£12.5m	$11.9m
13	*Trainspotting*	1996	£12.4m	$16.5m
14	*Snatch*	2000	£12.3m	$30.1m
15	*A Fish Called Wanda*	1988	£12.0m	$63.5m
16	*Lock, Stock and Two Smoking Barrels*	1998	£11.8m	$3.6m
17	*Shirley Valentine*	1990	£11.6m	$6.3m
18	*Moonraker*	1979	£10.6m	$38.0m*
19	*East is East*	2000	£10.3m	$4.2m
20	*Kevin and Perry Go Large*	2000	£10.3m	N/A

* Indicates figure for theatrical rentals rather than gross.

These confident and glossy romantic comedies seemed to encapsulate much of the potential of British popular cinema during the 1990s, and offered a template for other producers keen to compete with Working Title's status as leaders of this lucrative market. Miramax achieved this successfully with *Sliding Doors*, whilst other attempts, such as Film Four's *Martha meet Frank, Daniel and Laurence* (1998), made less of an impact. Given this production context, it was not surprising that a good many filmmakers sought to produce romantic comedies with the help of

[5] UK figures at 16 August 2001, not adjusted for inflation; Source: BFI Handbook 2002, p. 50.

[6] US figures on July 1, 2006, not adjusted for inflation; Source: IMDB.com.

National Lottery funding after it was made available to them in 1995. As the system was being designed, the impact of *Four Weddings and a Funeral* was still fresh in the minds of UK film producers and politicians alike: Gerald Kaufman's report on the health of the industry in 1995 considers it the primary reason for guarded optimism.[7] Whilst responding to press concerns that the Arts Councils would spend Lottery funding on "elitist" art cinema, its National Lottery director Jeremy Newton argued that "many commercial films do serve the public good by virtue of their high artistic quality", whilst *The Financial Times* stated that *Four Weddings and a Funeral* "promoted the public good by making people happy."[8] In this sense, the Arts Council and some sections of the press were arguing that high artistic quality and broad popular appeal were not mutually exclusive options for UK cinema; in fact, quite the reverse. If Lottery-funded popular cinema could succeed on both of these fronts then many of the scheme's economic objectives would be met without sacrificing the "quality", which is central to notions of public benefit.

However, the eventual box office fortunes of Lottery-funded romantic comedies were decidedly mixed.[9] *Shooting Fish* (1997) and *This Year's Love* (1999) were amongst the most successful of all Lottery-funded films with UK audiences. At the other end of the scale, Bill Forsyth's sequel *Gregory's Two Girls* (1998) and the "slacker" comedy *Late Night Shopping* (2000) were both financial failures for Film Four and the Scottish Arts Council. Those films which attempted to crossover between romantic comedy and heritage cinema were no more consistent: Pathé's *An Ideal Husband* (1999) was a hit, whilst Miramax's *Mansfield Park* (1999) was a notable disappointment. These crossover films raise the issue of how romantic comedy should be defined for the purposes of this chapter. I have opted to focus here upon contemporary, urban-set films which have a strong comedic tone, an emphasis on romance, and which end with the union of the central couple or couples. Almost inevitably, setting such rigid generic boundaries brings attention to the ways in which even the most apparently clear-cut examples deviate from this formula. *Shooting Fish* arguably places as much importance upon the homosocial bond between its two male protagonists as it does upon heterosexual

---

7 Department of National Heritage, *The British Film Industry*, Cmnd. 2884 (London: HMSO, 1995), 39.

8 Jeremy Newton, "Films that Serve the Public Good," *The Independent*, April 7, 1995, 18; Antony Thorncroft, "Movies Cash In on the Lottery," *Financial Times*, April 15, 1995, 10.

9 For a full list of the box office returns for Lottery-funded films, see Table 3–5 on page 90.

romance, and of *This Year's Love*'s multiple couplings some have happy endings and others rather the opposite. Another important factor in generic identification is how the film is packaged and sold, and to which audiences. Much romantic comedy is marketed towards female audiences, or as "date movies" for mixed-gender crowds. In this regard, *Fanny and Elvis* (1998) is an interesting example which attempted to reconfigure the star persona of Ray Winstone for female audiences. Other Lottery-funded romantic comedies complicated the generic formula by replacing heterosexuality with homosexuality, and one such film, *Get Real* (1998), is an illustration of how popular cinema can succeed with niche audiences, resulting in greater longevity and different kinds of public benefits.

The increasing visibility of gay characters within romantic comedy is noted by Frank Krutnik, who argues that the genre has transformed itself in recent decades as a result of social changes such as the gay rights movement, second-wave feminism, and the breakdown of the nuclear family. This transformation is evidenced by a concentration of elements which foreground artifice and irony—either within the film's narratives or in their aesthetic strategies:

> False presences do not necessarily signify the decay of the sexual dialectic, of romantic comedy. Post-liberationist new romancers... must learn to love, learn to lie, learn to love the lie.[10]

It is important to remember that Krutnik's conclusions are based upon a sample of successful romantic comedies produced by Hollywood and therefore inflected by an American vernacular. The question of whether there are equivalent tropes to be found within popular cinema produced in different national settings is a complex and important one. Can the success of recent British romantic comedy be ascribed to its intrinsic Britishness, or most often Englishness? Or is this a kind of "false presence" in itself—a Hollywood genre incorporating national identity as a form of product differentiation? These types of questions can be fruitfully considered in relation to the Lottery-funded production sector's first moderate success: the romantic comedy *Shooting Fish*. This was the second film made by the production team known as the Gruber Brothers: the British director Stefan Schwartz and his American producer Richard Holmes. Their first project, *Soft Top, Hard Shoulder* (1992) had a budget of just £180,000 but generated

[10] Frank Krutnik, "Love Lies: Romantic Fabrications in Contemporary Romantic Comedy," in *Terms of Endearment: Hollywood Romantic Comedy of the 1980s and 1990s*, eds. Peter Williams Evans and Celestino Deleyto (Edinburgh: Edinburgh University Press, 1998), 33.

significant critical acclaim, winning two Scottish BAFTAs and the audience award at the London Film Festival, and was also notable for its appropriation of a distinctively American genre, —the road movie.

The Gruber Brothers were therefore well-placed to win Lottery support for their next venture, *Shooting Fish*, and in November 1995 they received £980,000 towards its budget of £2.9 million.[11] This was one of the first awards for film production to be announced by the Arts Council of England. Alongside the Oxford-Cambridge boat race drama *True Blue* (1996) and the thriller *Crimetime* (1996), *Shooting Fish* was clearly one of the Council's more populist choices. Director Schwartz's interviews reinforced this impression:

> ...we just thought Britain isn't making fun, light, energetic pieces any more. Wouldn't it be great fun just to do that and not worry about an agenda, not worry about teaching the audience anything, just write a pure piece of entertainment?[12]

This description of the team's lack of guile has to be taken with a pinch of salt given that, in order to secure Lottery funding, they would have had no choice but to spend time worrying about the Arts Council of England's "agenda". However the funder's guidelines stated that projects should be likely to make a contribution to "a vibrant and successful British film culture", suggesting that they would not be immune to the kind of breezy optimism espoused by the Gruber Brothers.[13] *Shooting Fish* is the story of a pair of ingenious con men—one British and one American—whose joint ambition is to accumulate enough money to buy a stately home. Bearing in mind its production history, the temptation to read the film as a parable of how to succeed in the impoverished British film industry is almost irresistible. Its transatlantic protagonists echo the filmmakers themselves, and the process of attracting finance to an independent film project is not dissimilar to the confidence tricks which make up the film's narrative. The protagonists' shared fantasy of success is one which is informed by the heritage iconography found in most period dramas and many romantic comedies. This fantasy may be, as one critic described it, entirely "ersatz",

[11] Source: awards database.
[12] Stefan Schwartz cited in Wally Hammond, "Fishy Business," *Time Out*, October 15, 1997, 75.
[13] Arts Council of England, *National Lottery Funding for Film: Application Pack* (London: ACE, 1997), 7.

but it is nonetheless an image of national identity which has been successful in attracting international audiences to British cinema.[14]

Returning to Krutnik's discussion of recent Hollywood romantic comedies, *Shooting Fish*'s two male protagonists would seem to make ideal "post-liberationist new romancers" as they have built their lives around lying. The film's US publicity tagline emphasises this possibility: "As con artists they were hard to beat. But they were easy targets for love."[15] However, this is to overplay the romantic content within the film itself. The strongest relationship of *Shooting Fish* is a homosocial one: Dylan (Dan Futterman) and Jez (Stuart Townsend) live, work and play together; when newcomer Georgie (Kate Beckinsale) enters their lives the potential for a classic romantic triangle which would upset the men's friendship is largely unfulfilled. The confident Dylan makes an initial pass at Georgie and is rejected, leaving the field open for Jez to overcome his shyness and gradually win her over. But this plotline remains secondary to the male characters' primary economic drive, as Jez and Dylan are rewarded for their lasciviousness with the genteel lifestyle which they crave. Dylan then pairs off with Georgie's sister, a conclusion which neatly avoids separating the two men despite their move from overgrown children into fully fledged manhood. This ending also side-steps difficult issues of class distinction, leaving an earlier scene to reverberate uncomfortably. Two of the conmen's victims—a posh business man and a cockney wideboy—get their revenge by smashing up Jez and Dylan's home. They wreak their violence in the name of "the Britain we loved", with each upper class signifier being answered by a working class one: "Here's to warm beer... Lager!", "Waterloo!... Vindaloo!" The one British icon on which they both agree is "Margaret Thatcher!", perhaps fitting for a film in which romance plays second-fiddle to entrepreneurialism.

The box-office performance of *Shooting Fish* suggested that this aspirational view of British society struck a chord with domestic audiences, as it grossed over £4 million in the UK. Only three wholly UK financed films performed better than this in domestic theatrical runs in 1997, including *Bean*, which took over £17 million.[16] The Arts Council was happy to take some of the credit for *Shooting Fish* at a point when it seemed that Lottery funding for film had the potential to transform the

---

[14] Wally Hammond, "Shooting Fish: review," *Time Out*, October 15, 1997, 76.

[15] "Shooting Fish (1997)," *Internet Movie Database*, accessed July 2006, http://uk.imdb.com/title/ tt0120122/.

[16] Source: BFI, "UK Box Office for UK Feature Films 1997," in *BFI Film and Television Handbook 1999*, ed. Eddie Dyja (London: BFI, 1998), 32.

industry's fortunes. Reporting on the film's pre-release success at festivals, *The Guardian* concluded that "*Shooting Fish* goes some way towards vindicating the Arts Council's much criticised policy of subsidising films with National Lottery money."[17] A similar article in the *Daily Telegraph* was more equivocal, pointing out that whilst *Shooting Fish* may have allowed the Arts Council to recoup its investment it was the first of 66 films funded to date to do so. *The Telegraph* also cited an unnamed Arts Council spokesman who attempted to play down the importance of recoupment: "the prime reason for doing this is to make good quality British films."[18] Nevertheless, it remained clear that this story was beginning to set an agenda for future reporting on Lottery funding for film production, which would often focus upon less satisfying box-office returns. In fact, early hopes that *Shooting Fish* would go on to repeat the international success of *Four Weddings and a Funeral* proved unfounded. It was picked up for distribution in the US by Fox Searchlight, but was unlucky in coinciding with *The Full Monty*, which had also been co-financed by Fox. This pushed its American release back into the middle of 1998, by which point another small British romantic comedy was attracting attention thanks to its inventive plot and Hollywood lead actress: *Sliding Doors*. Possibly as a result of this competition, *Shooting Fish* was unable to find an audience in the US, meaning that a Lottery-funded international cross-over hit remained an elusive goal.

The transatlantic feel and "ersatz", heritage-friendly Englishness of *Shooting Fish* suggest that its producers were aiming for international success, yet it also seems likely that this international approach made the film attractive to UK audiences, who are generally more attuned to mainstream Hollywood cinema. The strategy of *This Year's Love* is clearly rather different. This is a self-consciously unconventional romantic comedy which repeatedly invokes the tropes of the genre in order to subvert them with cynicism and dark humour. Like a mirror image of *Four Weddings and a Funeral*, the film begins with a bride and groom leaping out of bed on their wedding day and rushing to get ready, but a rapid discovery of infidelity means that the couple's nuptial bliss lasts no longer than the film's opening credits. The film's colourful but downbeat setting in Camden Town is very different to the clean and prosperous London found in *Sliding Doors* (1998) and especially *Notting Hill* (1999). This setting also licences a British version of the "grunge" or "slacker" aesthetic

[17] Dan Glaister, "Fast fade into the black by feelgood comedy," *The Guardian*, May 29, 1997, 12.
[18] Nigel Reynolds, "Lottery's film cash nets a flying fish," *Daily Telegraph*, May 29, 1997, 10

found in several American independent romantic comedies of the 1990s.[19] This is signified visually—particularly through costume and hairstyling, and also narratively—with the film's six central characters lacking careers, ambition, and any clear sense of where their lives are heading. The grunge aesthetic is most striking in relation to the casting of Jennifer Ehle, still recognisable from her role as Elizabeth Bennett in the Andrew Davies' BBC adaptation of *Pride and Prejudice* (1995), but here playing a blonde dreadlocked "trustafarian".[20] With her public school background, Ehle's Sophie is the only character deriving from the upper-middle-class world of *Four Weddings*, but she has left it behind and is now an embittered single mother living on a canal boat.

This Year's Love therefore aims to represent life in London with a degree of realism, particularly when compared with the view of the city found in many British romantic comedies of the late 1990s. It may then seem surprising that the film was funded not through the Arts Council of England,, based in London, but rather by the Scottish Arts Council based in Edinburgh. The Scottish Arts Council and its institutional partners, such as the Scottish Film Production Fund tended to use more strongly nationalistic language when inviting applications for Lottery funding than the other home nations.[21] Projects needed "a strong Scottish element" in order to be successful, including consideration of where the project would be based, the Scottishness of key creative personnel such as the director and actors, and how the project might be seen as "culturally relevant to Scotland."[22] Despite its London setting, the writer and director of *This Year's Love*, David Kane, is a Scot who had previously been a writer of drama and television plays for BBC Scotland. In addition, Kane's script is an ensemble piece comprising three key Scottish roles, although one was eventually filled by an English actress, Catherine McCormack. The film's plot sees its characters swap romantic partners over the course of several years, and therefore relies upon the narrative possibilities of a busy community like Camden where much of the population originates from elsewhere. In this sense, the film could be said to be "culturally relevant" to Scotland in terms of representing a Scottish diaspora, through the experience of young "ex-patriot" Scots living in a diverse English metropolis.

---

[19] e.g. *Singles* (1992); *Reality Bites* (1994); *Before Sunrise* (1995).

[20] The 1990s slang term "trustafarian" is a combination of "trust fund" and "rastafarian", and refers to an upper middle-class person who funds a counter-cultural lifestyle with money from their wealthy background.

[21] See James Caterer, "Playing the Lottery Twice: The Dual-Nationality of *Stella Does Tricks*," *Journal of Media Practice* 5:3 (2004): 133–143.

Like David Kane and his Scottish characters, *This Year's Love* can, to a certain extent, be viewed as an outsider, fascinated by—but not infatuated with—the nostalgic Englishness of many British romantic comedies. Its central conceit is that people need to try many different relationships before they get it right, but the revolving structure of the film's entanglements—and especially its equivocal ending—suggests that this searching can become endless, resulting in loneliness and despair. This is felt most sharply in the fate of the fragile scouser Liam (Ian Hart), whose childlike innocence is initially attractive to both Sophie and Marey (Kathy Burke), but who falls apart in the face of adult betrayals, eventually attempting suicide. Liam's sad end severely tempers the apparently happy reunion of the couple briefly married at the film's opening, who have, in Krutnik's terms "learned to love the lie." This darkness of tone sets the film apart from much popular cinema and would appear to align it more closely with art-house drama. Nonetheless, it was heavily promoted upon its wide UK release of 265 prints, handled by distributors Entertainment.[23] The simplest of explanations for the confidence placed in this film is that it was in a position to exploit two normally exclusive sections of the domestic cinema audience, as the quotation from *The Sun* review used on its poster put it: *This Year's Love* is "*Trainspotting* meets *Four Weddings*".[24] This is a classic populist marketing ploy applied to a film which in some senses did not seem an obvious commercial proposition, and the film went on to generate £3.6 million in the UK, making *This Year's Love* the Scottish Arts Council's most successful Lottery-funded film.

However, it is also notable that this moderate success was not repeated in the international marketplace. *This Year's Love* was released across Europe, but of its eventual admissions total, only 16% were from countries outside of the UK.[25] It was not distributed at all in the other biggest Anglophone markets of Australia and the US. This failure to reap significant rewards across the global film market could be ascribed to a range of factors, perhaps the film's dark sense of humour, and almost certainly its lack of international stars. Kathy Burke and Jennifer Ehle are both highly regarded television performers domestically, but almost unknown abroad. Another Lottery-funded romantic comedy which relied heavily upon television for its creative inputs was *Fanny and Elvis* (1999), which was the debut feature film for female writer-director Kay Mellor, who was a well-respected presence in British television, having written

[23] Source: *Variety.com*.
[24] Nick Fisher, "This Year's Loser," *The Sun*, February 20, 1999, 24.
[25] *This Year's Love* total admissions: 985,396. UK admissions: 827,474. Source: *Lumiere Database*.

several popular and acclaimed drama series including *Band of Gold* for Granada in 1995. Her script for *Fanny and Elvis* came to fruition thanks to a Script Factory event held by the BFI, where Mellor directed a rehearsed reading with a cast that included Dawn French.[26] The project impressed Nik Powell of Scala Films, who was able to raise the £3.2 million budget thanks partly to Granada's relationship with Mellor, but more significantly through Scala's position as part of the Lottery franchise company, The Film Consortium. The pattern of Lottery awards for *Fanny and Elvis* is indicative of the franchises' ability to access funding for the different stages of a project's progress. An initial award of £30,000 was made in February 1998 to support pre-production, followed by the main production award of £1.1m in July of the same year. Two smaller awards were also made during production, followed later by an "exploitation" award of £400,000 to help finance prints and advertising.[27]

This indicates a high degree of confidence in the project on the part of both the Film Consortium and the Arts Council of England, both of which continued to oversee Lottery spending by the franchises. This confidence would have been based on Mellor's reputation as a talented writer, Powell's experience as producer, and the casting of a British star, Ray Winstone, as the male lead. A prolific actor who has worked in both British television and film for over twenty years, Ray Winstone's persona as a violent hard-man is firmly established, making him a surprising choice for romantic comedy. Winstone's character, Dave, begins the film on familiar ground as a second hand-car dealer with a raging temper. Mellor's script is fascinated by the sexual appeal of the bad boy; her heroine Kate (Kerry Fox) is a writer of romantic fiction who dreams of being swept off her feet by a succession of Heathcliff-like men in period costume. However the plot is driven not only by Kate's romantic fantasies, but also by her biological clock: abandoned by her husband in her mid-thirties, she becomes desperate to have a baby. This means that Dave must become potential father material—a transformation achieved both narratively (he already has children whom he dotes on from a previous marriage) and through performance, with Winstone turning on the charm, smiling, dancing and even breaking into song. However, whilst Winstone may be a draw within the crime and gangster genres of UK cinema, with hindsight it seems unlikely that the audience for these films could be attracted to such

[26] Sue Summers, "Why the film crew call her Sir," *Daily Telegraph*, November 14, 1998, Arts, 7.

[27] In total, *Fanny and Elvis* received five National Lottery awards totalling £1,577,850. Source: awards database.

a female-orientated romantic comedy. The film was a financial failure, generating just £162,000 at the UK box office and little more overseas.

It is easy to blame the failure of a film such as *Fanny and Elvis* on its stars. If the respected character actress Kerry Fox had been replaced in the lead role by Kate Winslet or even Gwyneth Paltrow its commercial prospects would surely have improved; however, there is also a wider problem here connected with the perceived lack of cinematic qualities in such low-budget, small-scale British cinema. Kay Mellor's background reinforces the impression that such material is easily available as prime time television drama, reducing the domestic audience's inclination to seek it out on the big screen. The critique of British cinema as being limited by a televisual aesthetic was famously argued by the future head of the Film Council, Alan Parker, in his documentary *A Turnip-Head's Guide to the British Cinema* (1986), and is present in many critical dismissals of British films.[28] *Fanny and Elvis* received its television premiere in one of the most prestigious slots in the ITV schedule, at 9pm in the week running up to Christmas 2001. Its audience peaked at 5.22 million, which represented a 22% share of terrestrial viewers.[29] As such, it was rated only slightly lower than editions of popular ITV dramas such as *The Bill* (5.58 million) and *A Touch of Frost* (5.60 million) screened that week. In contrast, in UK cinemas, *Fanny and Elvis* recorded just 36,344 admissions.[30] Whilst it is true to state that all but the biggest blockbuster films reach a majority of their audience through television, the fate of *Fanny and Elvis* poses uncomfortable questions surrounding the status of "popular cinema" in UK film culture. Primarily, if films made in the popular idiom fail to reach a broad swathe of the cinema audience, then what is their purpose or, in terms of the Lottery film debate, what is their "public benefit"?

On the one hand, in terms of accessibility, it is difficult to object to the prospect of even the less-popular Lottery-funded films reaching over 5 million members of the UK general public. The cultural value of these films is arguably unaffected by the means in which they are viewed; indeed it is often easier to feel part of a genuinely national audience when watching a film on television. On the other hand, funding films which may

---

[28] e.g. Mark Kermode's assertion that Stephen Frears' *The Queen* (2006) is "profoundly uncinematic". Kermode, "Sorry Ma'am, but you don't belong in a picture palace," *Guardian Unlimited*, September 24, 2006, accessed October 2006, http://arts.guardian. co.uk/comment/story/0,, 1879500,00.html.

[29] Sources: *BARB*: *Weekly TV Audience Network Report* (December 23, 2001); BARB, "Weekly Viewing Summary: Terrestrial Top 30," *BARB*, accessed January 2007, http://www.barb.co.uk/ viewingsummary/weekreports.

[30] Source: *Lumiere Database*.

be regarded as little more than glorified television drama will hardly help to improve the economic prospects of the film industry—especially in the international arena. One possible way round these dilemmas surrounding the "popular" is offered by the idea of "niche" marketing, which claims that genuinely mass entertainment is a thing of the past. Nonetheless, the increased variety, specialist appeal and, in particular, the longevity of digital media products will continue to ensure their profitability.[31] An example of a Lottery-funded romantic comedy with strong "niche" appeal is *Get Real* (1998), which replaces the traditional heterosexual union of the romantic comedy formula with a gay love story between two male pupils in a middle-class secondary school. Both *This Year's Love* and *Fanny and Elvis* contain gay characters in secondary roles—either as added romantic complications or as narrative facilitators. However, as Vitto Russo observes, the presence of implicit gayness in classical Hollywood cinema was often associated with the conventions of melodrama rather than comedy, and this association arguably remains a potent one.[32] Even more recent and more liberal representations of gay characters, such as those in social problem films or soap operas, tend to focus upon the psychological challenges of becoming socialised as a homosexual—an emphasis which tends to exclude successful, stable relationships.

As its title implies, *Get Real* fits into a tradition of "coming out" narratives which valorise a version of emotional truth-telling informed by American therapy culture. However, it mostly avoids the melodramatic tendencies of such narratives, being comedic in tone and focusing upon the relationship between two schoolmates rather than their individual psychologies. Its project is therefore both pluralist, in its representation of minority experience, and populist as it works within an accessible generic form: the high school romantic comedy. *Get Real* began life in 1992 as a stage play with the confrontational title of *What's Wrong with Angry?* Its playwright, Patrick Wilde, considered it as a protest piece designed to stimulate debate around two of the biggest issues for British gay activists in the early 1990s: the lowering of the age of consent for gay men, then set at 21, and the removal of Clause 28 which outlawed the discussion of

---

[31] e.g. the idea of "the long tail" where infinite shelf-space in digital retail offers the possibility of generating small amounts of revenue almost indefinitely. See Chris Anderson, *The Long Tail: How Endless Choice is Creating Unlimited Demand* (London: Random House, 2006).

[32] Vitto Russo, *The Celluloid Closet: Homosexuality in the Movies* (New York: Harper and Row, 1987).

homosexuality in schools.[33] It was first performed in a small local fringe theatre in London, but proved popular enough to be transferred to the West End in September 1995. By this stage, Wilde's profile as a writer had been boosted by his involvement with the BBC2 drama *This Life* (1996–1997), and he began to work on a film script based on his play with director Simon Shore and producer Stephen Taylor.[34] The team received development support from British Screen, but the project only became financially viable after the Arts Council of England approved an award of £800,000 in February 1997. This represented almost half of the film's projected budget—close to the maximum amount available under the Arts Council's guidelines—with the remainder coming from private sources.

Several title changes occurred during its production process, with the provocative *Sweet Sixteen* eventually being dropped in favour of the Americanism *Get Real*. The film was completed by early 1998 and played the international festival circuit before becoming one of the first titles picked up for distribution by the newly-formed Paramount Classics division. This suggested that *Get Real* was destined to play in art-houses rather than multiplexes, but a review in *Variety* emphasised the film's crossover potential: "pic[ture] could catch on locally and internationally in a moderate way among mainstream aud[ience]s, its true market."[35] How did a Hollywood trade journal such as *Variety* come to the conclusion that this low-budget British film about schoolboy homosexuality belonged in the cinematic mainstream? Its generic identity and comedic tone are both vital factors in this equation, as *Variety* directly compares the film to John Hughes' high school romantic comedies of the 1980s (e.g. *The Breakfast Club* (1985)). The suburban milieu of Basingstoke is considered to be the parallel of Hughes' Chicago, and the script is commended for its "warm and funny portrait of British teen angst", with the more challenging content almost entirely overlooked. From this populist perspective, *Get Real* is little more than an entertaining twist on a standard high school romance narrative: this time, the shy outsider who attracts the most popular boy in school just happens to be a boy himself. Clearly this is some distance from the political context of Patrick Wilde's original play;

---

[33] Patrick Wilde, "Author's Introduction to *What's Wrong With Angry?*" in *Staging Gay Lives: An Anthology of Gay Theater*, ed. John N. Clum (Boulder, Colorado: Westview, 1996), 64–65.

[34] Patrick Wilde, "Patrick Wilde's History of *Get Real*," *BenSilverstone.net*, accessed October 2006, http://www. bensilverstone.net/bsgetreal.

[35] Derek Elley, "*Get Real* review," *Variety.com*, September 21, 1998, accessed October 2006, http://www.variety.com/review/VE1117913335.html?categoryID =31&cs=1,.

partly as a result, readings informed by this context tended to find the film unsatisfying.

Writing for *Sight and Sound*, José Arroyo found Wilde's script "complex and compelling", but remained unconvinced by its cinematic qualities or its performances.[36] Compared with the inner-city gay romance of *Beautiful Thing* (1995), with its fairy tale happy ending, or the confrontational and sexually explicit Channel Four series *Queer as Folk* (1999–2000), Arroyo felt *Get Real* to be "rather quaint" and a product of an earlier period. In defence of recent British queer cinema, Ros Jennings has identified a strategy of "positive unoriginality" in films such as *Beautiful Thing*. She uses this notion to explain the contradiction between the prosaic quality of these films and their potentially subversive gender content.[37] *Get Real* could be defended in the same way, although the film's reception in the US illustrates how easily subversive content can be overlooked or ignored. *Variety*'s hope that *Get Real* would find a mainstream audience was over-optimistic. Essentially, it received a limited release worldwide and performed adequately, but did not crossover into the multiplexes;[38] however, the film shows signs of having found a wider audience on video or television, as it has subsequently built up a considerable fan community on the internet.[39] Many members of *Get Real*'s internet-based fan community are gay teenagers for whom the film's subversive gender content is meaningful and important. Amongst its fans, one key area for debate is the film's ambivalent ending, which sees its protagonist Steven (Ben Silverstone) coming out in spectacular fashion during a school assembly, but only at the cost of his relationship with the Head Boy John (Brad Gorton), whose fate is unresolved. The biggest fan-site contains a large "slash fiction" section where devotees can continue the story or modify its ending, and many contributors imagine a more positive future for the film's gay couple. For its international supporters, the film's ordinary Englishness becomes a source of exotic appeal, with pages devoted to translating British slang terms into their more widely known American equivalents.

As a multi-media text, *Get Real* eventually came full-circle, moving from political fringe theatre to the West End, becoming a potential cross-

---

[36] José Arroyo, "*Get Real,*" *Sight and Sound*, 9:5, May 1999, 48.

[37] Ros Jennings "*Beautiful Thing*: British queer cinema, positive unoriginality and the everyday" in *British Queer Cinema*, ed. Robin Griffiths (London: Routledge, 2006), 183–194.

[38] UK box office: £151,000; US box office: $1,152,411. Sources: BFI, *IMDB*.

[39] See *BenSilverstone.net*, accessed July 2006, http://www.bensilverstone.net/bsgetreal.

over hit movie which became a cult success. For its small but widely dispersed fan-base, it combines the pleasures of exotic Englishness with a positive representation of gay experience. Such a journey could not have been fully predicted by the Arts Council and British Screen, whose funding decisions were influenced by commercial considerations. However, neither is it an outcome which is out of tune with their remits as public organisations. As with *This Year's Love*, the longevity of *Get Real* illustrates that a useful strategy for Lottery-funded British popular cinema was to exist on the boundaries of what is generally considered as popular cinema in order to attract different kinds of audiences. The biggest American stars and the most spectacular production values were out of their budgetary reach, and so instead they opted to focus on several of the often-cited strengths of the contemporary UK cinema "brand", such as ensemble acting, and distinctive scripts dealing with taboo topics. Such elements may more often be associated with the international art-house circuit than the multiplex chains, but when combined with a popular generic form, such as the romantic comedy they offer a level of product differentiation which has the potential to connect with wider audiences.

These modest objectives may fall a long way short of the boldest ambitions for Lottery-funded popular cinema; when taken individually, such films are unlikely to present a serious challenge to Hollywood's hold over the UK's cinematic imagination. *Shooting Fish* may be considered as an attempt to imitate Hollywood in terms of tone and ideological stance, but this imitation could have weakened its impact in the international market place, as it was compared with more expensive and starrier competition. By contrast, *Fanny and Elvis* seems to have been designed primarily with the domestic market in mind, building upon the reputation of Kay Mellor and the attractions (or otherwise) of Ray Winstone playing against type, but in doing so, it effectively appeared to have restricted itself to the status of a television film. Above all, the range of Lottery-funded romantic comedies discussed in this chapter illustrates that repeating the Working Title formula of international success is not as easy as it may appear; indeed, this may not be a possible or a necessary outcome for Lottery-funded filmmaking. Perhaps a more realistic—and defendable—goal is to make films which are designed for success in the UK market, and which draw upon elements of cultural specificity to create pictures for the people.

Comedies of Community

The notion of "community" forms one half of the most influential modernist theory of nationality, Benedict Anderson's idea of "imagined communities". Anderson defines the term as "a deep, horizontal comradeship" which must be imagined on a national basis due to the differences in scale and meaning between community and nation.[40] The former is small, intimate and natural; the latter large, impersonal and constructed. Reinforcing the generally positive usage of the term, Raymond Williams notes that:

> unlike all other terms of social organisation (*state, nation, society* etc.)... ["community"] seems never to be used unfavourably, and never to be given any positive opposing or distinguishing term.[41]

To a large extent, this meaning continued to prevail in 1990s political discourse. Major proposed that the strength of the National Lottery would lay in its emphasis on the "grassroots", where "new ideas and projects would come from local communities".[42] However, there was a possible "positive opposing" term to community within the rhetoric of Lottery funding: the notion of "diversity".[43] The idea that the nation is an imagined community with shared social values exists uneasily alongside a pluralist concern for diversity. The insistence upon similarity within communities of any size—imagined or otherwise—can act to stifle the voices of minority groups defined by race, ethnicity, sexuality, and so on. Several Lottery-funded films dealt with explicitly nationalist subject matter, such as the England football team, or terrorism in Northern Ireland, whilst others created symbolic communities of hapless thieves or Welsh bingo players to reflect upon the commonalities of culture across the nations constituting the United Kingdom.

---

[40] Benedict Anderson, *Imagined communities: Reflections on the Origin and Spread of Nationalism* (London: Verso, 1983), 7.

[41] Raymond Williams, *Keywords: A Vocabulary of Culture and Society* (London: Fontana, 1976), 76.

[42] Major cites the statistic that almost 80% of Lottery awards were for £100,000 or less. John Major, *John Major: The Autobiography* (London: Harper Collins, 1999), 405, 410.

[43] e.g. "Diversity and inclusion" was designated one of five 'key priorities' for the Arts Council of England in 1998. Gerry Robinson, 'Achieving a New Era for the Arts', *The Arts Council of England Annual Review 1999* (London: ACE, 1999), 2.

Towards the end of *Mike Bassett: England Manager* (2001), the film's eponymous anti-hero makes a speech which encapsulates the film's view of its subject, football:

> For a lot of people the England team is more important than their work, more important than their marriage, more important than the telly! When we win, take a look out of your window. People are going to work with smiles on their faces, they're talking to each other at the bus stop, in the pub, on the bus itself...

Here England's national sport is depicted as a mundane but potent source of cohesion, which is to be both celebrated and gently ridiculed. The English football team is a powerful example of what Michael Billig refers to as "banal nationalism"—the referents of national identity which, he argues, are latent and omnipresent, rather than removed from everyday life to the realm of Politics.[44] These signs or "habits" may be omnipresent, but they are not universal in their meaning, and different referents may be invoked to very different ends. Billig cites John Major's famous speech from 1993 as an interesting example in this regard, with its description of Britain as "the country of long shadows on county grounds, warm beer, invincible green suburbs, dog lovers and pools fillers".[45] This list is clearly exclusive as well as inclusive; in particular, the choice of cricket "county grounds" rather than football stadiums is revealing. Major was, and still is, a football fan himself, but he implicitly recognises the problems inherent in allowing football to stand in for the nation as a whole. To begin with there is no British football (or cricket) team, although football is far more important outside of England than cricket. What is more, football has been identified historically with the working class, whilst cricket was played by the ruling elite. But perhaps most problematically, fans of national football teams—and those of England, in particular—seem to represent the dangers of nationalism as well as its benefits: unity but hostility towards difference; pride and affirmation in victory, but more often the ignominy of defeat; communal celebrations or ugly outbreaks of violence.

Both the positive and the negative nationalist connotations of football are to found in *Mike Bassett: England Manager.* However, this is not a hard-hitting exposé of violence on the terraces; it is a comedy, and as such, tempers these dangers with humour. All of the films selected for discussion in this section are comedies of one type or another: *Mike Bassett: England Manager* is a spoof television documentary, whilst the

---

[44] Michael Billig, *Banal Nationalism* (London: Sage, 1995).
[45] John Major cited in Billig, *Banal Nationalism*, 102.

Welsh comedy *House!* (2000) and Steve Coogan's star vehicle *The Parole Officer* (2001) both draw on the traditions of Ealing Studios. This focus on comedy is motivated by its place within discourses of national cinema, where comedy films are often described as the least "translatable", and the most locally, regionally or nationally specific. Comedy is a common genre within low- to medium-budget popular cinema of national film industries outside of Hollywood, and indeed comedies constituted the largest generic grouping within the Lottery-funded feature films, making up around a third of releases.[46] The idea of comedy as untranslatable is connected to the belief that there is such a thing as a British sense of humour, or a Welsh one, or a Northern Irish one. When the producers of a Lottery-funded comedy about the Troubles in Northern Ireland, *Divorcing Jack* (1998), were faced with the decision of whether it should be released in the wake of the Omagh bombings, they used the following justification:

> The black wit of Northern Irish writers... is one of the few ways we have of dealing with the wounds of a divided society. It is part of a "normalising" process that helps restore a sense of dignity and control eroded by the events of the last 30 years.[47]

This argument claims that humour can have a profound effect upon a community's sense of itself, and whilst "black wit" is a particularly spiky example, the idea that comedy functions as an important element of shared cultural expression is much less contentious.

Mike Bassett: England Manager emerged from an era in English football when the national squad was conspicuously failing to keep up with the glamourous internationalism of teams like Manchester United. Writers John Smith and Rob Sprackling were particularly inspired by the 1994 Channel Four documentary *Graham Taylor: An Impossible Job*, which revealed that the apparently placid England manager was prone to violent mood swings and uncharacteristic dressing room outbursts.[48] Their resulting script was picked up by producer Neil Peplow, who had also been involved in the first significant commercial success amongst Lottery-funded films, *Shooting Fish* (1997). The initial development of *Mike Bassett: England Manager* was supported by DNA, the Lottery franchise set up by Duncan Kenworthy and Andrew Macdonald, who successfully

---

[46] Of the 95 Lottery-funded features released 1995–2000, at least 30 were identifiable as comedies of one sort or another.

[47] Robert Cooper, 'All right Jack', *The Guardian*, October 1, 1998, 23.

[48] Martyn Palmer, 'We Can Laugh About It Now', *The Times*, September 15, 2001, 36.

negotiated a production award of £2m towards a budget of £4m in 1997. However DNA later decided not to proceed with the project, meaning that its production award would have been revoked under the standard conditions attached to a National Lottery award.[49] The production was rescued by Entertainment, an independent film distributor in the UK, and Hallmark, a producer of international TV movies. A further application to the Film Council was successful, albeit for a smaller amount of £1.2m towards a revised budget of £3.5m.[50] This is therefore a film with a rocky production history, which illustrates how rapidly the film industry was changing during this period, partly owing to alterations in the method of distributing National Lottery money to filmmakers.[51] Nonetheless, when it finally reached UK cinemas in September 2001 it performed relatively strongly, returning more than its budget in theatrical receipts alone.[52] This popularity resulted in a spin-off television series for ITV, *Mike Bassett: Manager* (2005), making it one of the very few British film properties to receive this treatment.

The ability of *Mike Bassett: England Manager* to cross over into television is not too surprising given that the film draws heavily upon televisual forms and modes of address. It begins with a fictional local news programme which introduces second-rate football manager Mike Bassett (Ricky Tomlinson), and afterwards utilises a mock "fly-on-the-wall" documentary style. The film therefore capitalises on a general shift towards realist techniques in British television sitcom of the period—particularly BBC2's *The Royle Family* (1998), which also starred Tomlinson, and *The Office* (2001). In terms of narrative, this faux documentary approach creates comedic tension between situations according to their relationship to the public sphere: for example, direct-to-camera interviews with characters giving information which is often

---

[49] National Lottery awards were non-transferable and had to be repaid in full should the applicant fail to complete the specified project. See Arts Council of England, *National Lottery Funding for Film: Application Pack* (London: ACE, 1997), 11.

[50] Details of National Lottery awards made by the UK Film Council are available through their website: www.ukfilmcouncil.org.uk.

[51] In terms of the time period of my thesis *Mike Bassett: England Manager* is therefore a borderline case, but its place on the list of awards made by the Arts Council of England between 1995 and 2000 means its inclusion can be justified.

[52] *Mike Bassett: England Manager* (2001) UK gross: £3.6m. 7th highest grossing UK film at the UK box office in 2001. BFI, 'Top 20 UK Films at UK Box Office 2001', accessed October 2006, http://www.bfi.org.uk/filmtvinfo/stats/boxoffice/20ukfilms-01.html.

contradicted by "behind the scenes" footage. The film aims for a naturalistic visual texture and the camera is often handheld. Even the games themselves are partially rendered using split-screen editing, which replicates the familiar squarish shape of the traditional TV image and repeats it across the widescreen cinematic frame. All of this feels natural, even comforting, for modern audiences for whom the aesthetics of football are strongly televisual: liveness, the improvised commentary by expert commentators, and the sense of witnessing an event of national significance are all vital for the sport's media appeal and its subsequent economic survival. By filtering its representation of international football through a secondary medium, television, the film invokes one of the most potent communal experiences within the modern media landscape.

Despite this investment in the game's modern media appeal, the imagined national community of *Mike Bassett: England Manager* is based around nostalgic notions of Englishness. Bassett is a working class underdog, passionate rather than talented, optimistic but fallible; and his mediocre career and contingent arrival at the top of the game are treated humorously. However, certain moments are coded as serious: at his inaugural press conference, Bassett reacts to cynical journalists by reeling off a list of English achievements—Parliament, the industrial revolution, the literary canon, defeating Hitler, and inventing football itself—subsequently prompting a spontaneous round of applause. This moment prefigures the film's climax, when a beleaguered Bassett is interviewed on international television and recites Rudyard Kipling's "If"—a poem eulogising the hard-working, self-effacing colonial Englishman.[53] He then reverts to his old-fashioned strategic system, and his faith in the team's troubled genius striker is repaid with a winning goal. At this point, it is notable that the film abandons its televisual aesthetic and renders the final game with cinematic sweeps and slow-motion close ups. Comic failure may be the stuff of British TV, but triumph over adversity requires the Hollywood treatment. England is knocked out in the semi-finals, but the true reward for Bassett and for the film's audience are the celebratory scenes upon his return to the UK. He leaves the plane to a rapturous reception and is plunged into a crowd of cheering fans, accompanied by a jubilant song from Robbie Williams—the foremost "new lad" of late

[53] Even in his day, Rudyard Kipling was referred to by the press as "the voice of Empire". Niall Ferguson, *Empire*: *How Britain Made the Modern World* (London: Penguin 2003), 258.

1990s British pop music.[54] This emotive conclusion visualises a nation united by sport but, like all examples of mainstream culture, football is as exclusive to certain members of society as it is accessible to others: if you are not male, white and apparently working-class, you then go uninvited to this party.

Another vital aspect of this film's exclusiveness is almost too obvious to mention: its Englishness. Amongst the feature films funded through the Arts Council of England, *Mike Bassett: England Manager* is unusually partisan, although it is easy to observe a more understated and hence possibly more pervasive Englishness at work in many of the heritage films and romantic comedies. As Richard Dyer has observed of whiteness within racial discourse, in the context of Britishness, Englishness, is often the invisible norm against which Scottishness, Welshness and Irishness are defined.[55] This clearly cannot be the case in a film about the England football team. This differentiation is illustrated in one striking sequence when the England team arrive in Brazil for the World Cup finals and run into their Scottish and Irish equivalents at the airport. Initial good-natured banter prompted by and directed towards the England players quickly turns into nasty sectarian insults between the Irish and the Scots ("Proddy bollocks!", "Fenian twat!"), and then all three teams dive into a brawl. This scene seems intended as a kind of "Englishman, Irishman, Scotsman" joke, but there is no witty punch line or attempt to deflate the macho posturing. The film cuts away in the middle of the fight and does not refer to the incident again, thus reinforcing the impression that this is a brief glimpse of the dark side of intra-national tribalism. In this sense, *Mike Bassett: England Manager* attempts to revive an English triumphalism by drawing upon a history which is not always particularly funny.

Mike Bassett: England Manager is unusual in terms of its explicit discussion of national identity. A more common narrative strategy for film comedy is to focus upon a small cohesive community, which is often placed under threat by the forces of big business or centralised national government. This is the classic populist trope identified by Jeffrey Richards in the films of Frank Capra, and is a staple of popular cinema more broadly.[56] *House!* is set in South Wales, but localises its community further through a particular physical setting. The film is set in and around

---

[54] On the 'new lad', see Claire Monk, 'Men in the 90s' in *British Cinema of the 90s*, ed. Robert Murphy (London: BFI, 2000), 162–3.
[55] Richard Dyer, *White* (London: Routledge, 1997).
[56] Jeffrey Richards, 'Frank Capra and the Cinema of Populism', in *Movies and Methods, Volume One,* ed. Bill Nicholls, (Berkeley: University of California Press, 1976), 65–77.

La Scala, a spectacular but decrepit art deco building which has served as a music hall, a cinema and most recently a bingo hall, whose old-lady customers and young staff are impoverished but loyal. The narrative begins as this cosy, old-fashioned world is attacked by the forces of big business: a modern "Mega Bingo" complex opening in the same town. In contrast to La Scala, the Mega Bingo is characterised by bland architecture, an impersonal atmosphere, and poor service. The fight to save La Scala kicks off a plot which, to begin with, at least, is strongly reminiscent of the Ealing comedy paradigm summed up by Charles Barr with the phrase "Small is beautiful."[57] Barr suggests ways in which this paradigm can be related to Ealing Studio's production circumstances and more broadly to notions of Englishness. In a similar way, *House!* can be read as emblematic of the "cottage industry" structure of British cinema and the dispersal of national identities in the Lottery-funded era.

The credits for *House!* provide some indication of the complexity of its production circumstances:

> A Pathé Distribution release of a Wire Films presentation, in association with CF1 Cyf and the South Wales Film Commission, of a Victor Film Co. production, with the participation of British Screen and the Arts Council of England.[58]

The private production companies Wire Films and CF1 Cyf, based near Cardiff, worked in conjunction with the London sales agents Victor Film Co. to put together the £2m budget for the film. They received financial assistance from both local and national public sources, including the Arts Council of England, but not, interestingly, from the Arts Council of Wales. It is difficult to identify the "English characteristic" within the project which entitled it to its Lottery investment of £350,000.[59] The film's director, Julian Kemp, is English, but the film was written by a Welsh writer, produced with a largely Welsh production team, and has an international cast, including the Scottish Kelly Macdonald and the English Miriam Margoyles. Both Margoyles and Macdonald work hard to produce Welsh accents, matching the rest of the cast, but this poses the question: if the accents were switched for Northern Irish, Glaswegian or even Geordie,

[57] Charles Barr, *Ealing Studios*, 2nd ed. (London: Studio Vista, 1993, orig. pub. 1977), 5.
[58] Taken from Derek Elley, 'Reviews - *House!*', *Variety.com*, May 8, 2000, accessed August 2006, http://www.variety.com/review/VE1117915760.html?categoryid=31&cs=1,.
[59] Source: awards database.

would the film have held the same meaning? The film's spatial location is not particularly precise: after its opening credits sequence, there are very few establishing shots; place names are elusive and the characters have little relation to a larger national framework. As such, the Welshness of the film feels strangely arbitrary and possibly even clichéd.

Stuart Hall has observed that national stereotypes are also strongly gendered, such that we tend think of an English*man* rather than an English*woman*.[60] In this light, it is significant that the community of *House!* largely comprises women, and that the only young man—bingo-caller Gavin (Jason Hughes)—is also the only character with a sense of social mobility and the means to escape. This focus on the feminine perhaps makes it more difficult to interpret the film in terms of Welshness. It also licences the film's principal narrative conceit, which shifts *House!* away from the naturalism of the Ealing comedies and more towards fantasy. As her place of work is threatened, the film's heroine Linda (Kelly Macdonald) discovers that she has psychic powers which allow her to predict which number will come out of the bingo machine next, offering the opportunity to cheat the bingo system out of a large prize and save La Scala. This ability is coded as both feminine (it is inherited from her late mother), and spiritually benevolent, as it will only work to the benefit of others: Linda's aunt calls it "a gift to the community." Thus, the power of the community unit takes a mystical turn which builds upon the pre-modern connotations of this intimate social structure, and suggests that it has the ability to renew itself indefinitely. However, this turns out to be an illusory solution, as the film's actual resolution is far more ambivalent. Linda's abilities *do* save La Scala but only indirectly with the assistance of its owner, while its bingo business proves to be beyond salvation. Instead it is transformed once more into a glitzy restaurant, which re-trains its original staff, but inevitably caters to a different, more affluent and dispersed set of customers.

This is a smart, pragmatic solution echoing the ways in which many old buildings are utilised by modern commerce in a superficial, ahistorical fashion. However, it betrays the primary source of the community's cohesion and the film's energy—the game of bingo itself. One early sequence typifies the film's kitsch investment in the game with stylised camerawork and heightened sound design. As he is introduced to the film, the bingo-caller Gavin (Jason Hughes) looks directly into the camera and

---

[60] Stuart Hall, 'The Local and the Global: Globalization and Ethnicity' in *Culture, Globalization and the World-System*, ed. Anthony D. King (Binghampton: Macmillan, 1991), 21.

winks. To the popular operatic strains of "Nessun Dorma", he then runs in slow motion down through the contestants and takes his place on the stage, telling jokes to warm-up the crowd. As he reaches the punch line of one joke, the camera performs a rapid zoom into extreme close-up, accompanied by a non-diegetic swooping noise. This indicator of directorial performativity is used frequently throughout the film, often to indicate comic surprise. According to one disparaging review, this agile camera "keeps reminding us, as if it were a Butlins Redcoat, of just how much *fun* we are having."[61] Although intended negatively, this Redcoat analogy is fitting for a film, which celebrates a type of British entertainment steadfastly parochial and which looks to the past with affection. As an audience, we are positioned to enjoy its nostalgia and yet to remain ironically distanced—much like Linda as she watches from the back of the hall, wincing at Gavin's bad jokes, but laughing all the same. By the end of the film, Linda is the manager of a thriving restaurant, but her magical powers are only useful for guessing customer's wine choices, and her old lady customers look increasingly out of place.

Mike Bassett: England Manager attempts to construct a national community whilst *House!* explores the small-scale local level, but other Lottery-funded comedies work with notions of symbolic community. Whilst most film narratives place their protagonists in the larger context of social relations, *The Parole Officer* (2001) places special emphasis upon the formation of a group, which enables particular goals to be reached. This is interesting within the context of a film which was intended as a star vehicle for Steve Coogan in the national arena and a star-making project internationally. Coogan's star persona is strongly associated with the comedy of failure, as illustrated by his most famous creation Alan Partridge, the failed television talk-show host demoted to local radio. This creates problems for his placement as a believable hero within a mainstream action-comedy such as this one, and sharing the hero's responsibilities across a team of equally incompetent thieves is one solution to such difficulties. In this film, Coogan plays Simon, a failing probation officer, who witnesses a murder carried out by a corrupt police chief. He is then forced to break into a bank vault in order to secure the evidence which will clear his name. He enlists his former clients to help with the task: Jeff (Steven Waddington) provides working-class brawn, Colin (Ben Miller) is a computer geek, George (Om Puri), an electrical engineer and the fourteen-year old delinquent Kirsty (Emma Williams) is a

---

[61] Antonia Quirke, '*House* review', *Independent on Sunday*, May 7, 2000, Culture Section, 4.

talented thief. They initially bicker, but the task brings them together, as illustrated when they toast their preparations. Colin suggests that they drink to "the most audacious crime of the century", but Simon corrects this to "having friends", an emotive moment which is played entirely straight, without comedic undercutting, bringing home the sense of community central to the film.

The Parole Officer was produced by the Lottery franchise DNA, who again secured £2 million of Lottery money towards its budget of £6 million.[62] Further investment came from Universal Studios, and the film therefore illustrates DNA's strategy of cooperation with Hollywood which was later formalised through its acquisition by Fox Searchlight.[63] DNA's collaborative strategy raised a few eyebrows within the British film industry, with some concerned that Lottery money was intended to enable the British to compete with Hollywood rather than to help finance Hollywood films. *The Parole Officer* has clear designs on the international market—most obviously indicated by the Americanisation of the title: within the film itself Coogan's character Simon is more accurately referred to as a "probation officer". The film blends Coogan's familiar TV persona of social incompetence and physical slapstick with more spectacular elements, including car chases, explosions, and its major narrative element—the unlikely heist caper plot. Despite these additions, critical response to the film tended to focus on the suitability or otherwise of Coogan's persona for the big screen.[64] This psychological barrier between television and film always seems to be a major issue for British critics in a way which would seem strange in Hollywood. But critical hostility towards this leap tends not to be reflected in box office, as the recent successes of Rowan Atkinson and Sacha Baron Cohen have made clear. *The Parole Officer* was also a reasonable sized hit with the public in the UK, generating £3.3 million upon its release in 2001.[65] However, it is vital to note that, despite the involvement of Universal Studios, *The Parole Officer* was not distributed at all in the US. The reasons for this are

---

[62] Source: awards database.

[63] Adam Dawtry, 'Searchlight to Shine for British DNA', *Variety.com* (4 September 2003), accessed December 2006, http://www.variety.com/article/VR1117891965.html? categoryid=1236&cs=1

[64] e.g. Jonathan Romney, 'Don't give up the day job, Steve', *Independent on Sunday*, August 12, 2001, 9.

[65] This places it in the ten highest-grossing UK films in the UK in 2001, including international co-productions, although it did not make the top twenty overall. See BFI, 'Top 20 UK films at UK box office 2001', *BFI,* accessed December 2000, http://www.bfi.org.uk/filmtvinfo/stats/boxoffice/20ukfilms-01.html.

unclear, but this situation may be read as further evidence of the perceived "inexportability" of comedy produced outside of Hollywood

A contemporary article in *The Times* about the transition between television and film for British comedy stars refers to *The Parole Officer* as "nouveau Ealing."[66] Is this a meaningful comparison or simply journalistic shorthand? There are certainly comparisons to be drawn between this film and *The Lavender Hill Mob* (1951), with both featuring mild-mannered white-collar workers attempting audacious robberies with the help of their apparently unsuitable gangs. Cited in the same article, Coogan highlights production strategies which fit with the artisanal image of Michael Balcon's Ealing: the well-crafted original script, and the careful choice of character actors rather than comedians to make up the supporting cast.[67] However, there are also significant differences between the films which make the evocation of Ealing more problematic. Although *The Lavender Hill Mob* is considered by Charles Barr to be amongst the least subversive of the Ealing canon, the motivations of its hero Henry Holland (Alec Guinness) are nakedly avaricious and therefore potentially disturbing for the capitalist system which exploits him. In *The Parole Officer*, Simon only robs a bank to clear his name and oust a crooked police officer, a noble motive reinforcing the social status quo. *The Lavender Hill Mob* hermetically seals its fantasy of crime and wealth within a framing device, whilst the more recent film completely ruptures its own narrative logic during its end credits sequence.[68] Here the main actors appear on stage, apparently spontaneously dropping out of character to dance along with the music, David Bowie's "Heroes". This becomes a stage-managed "number" in its own right as the actors' audience join in with a choreographed dance routine, as if they were holiday campers responding to Redcoats.

Much like *Mike Bassett: England Manager*'s celebratory end credits or the bingo sequences in *House!,* the finale of *The Parole Officer* draws the cinematic audience into the diegetic world of the film, invoking the populist pleasures of communal entertainment experiences. Each film adopts strategies associated with post-modernist play: *Mike Bassett...*'s pastiche of televisual form, *House!*'s over-determined visual style, and

[66] James Christopher, 'More than a bit of a laugh', *The Times*, August 10, 2001, 8.

[67] Michael Balcon, *Michael Balcon Presents... A Lifetime of Films* (London: Hutchinson, 1969).

[68] According to Ian Green, this device is used by Ealing comedies as a signal that their ideological bite is merely playful. Ian Green, 'Ealing: In the Comedy Frame', in *British Cinema History*, eds. James Curran and Vincent Porter (London: Weidenfeld and Nicholson, 1983), 294–302.

The Parole Officer's dissolution of the fourth wall between audience and performers. Nevertheless, such moments of direct appeal to the audience can also be taken at face value, and enjoyment of these spectacles may be licensed by the irony of their presentation. Each spectacle is also drawn from a history of working class entertainment, including football, bingo, and "end of the pier" cabaret. In this sense, the air of nostalgia surrounding these films invokes a perception that the era of public mass entertainment has slipped into the past. This perception also extends to British cinema itself—particularly given the way that these films engage with the legacy of Ealing. During *House!*, La Scala's owner shows Linda around the building's old projection box; a room crammed with movie memorabilia, film posters (several for Ealing films), and a large art deco sign that reads "Cinema". When the building is converted into a restaurant at the film's conclusion, this emblem is displayed in the main dining hall as an apt visual metaphor for the lost glory days of the British film industry. By engaging with notions of community at different scales, the Lottery-funded comedies discussed in this section endeavoured to recreate these past successes. But the scheme's biggest hit would come from a small film which struck the difficult balance between domestic reference points and international reach.

The Runaway Success: *Billy Elliot*

This chapter on Lottery-funded popular cinema takes its cue from the words of John Major, spoken as he launched the National Lottery in 1994. But any account of the British public sphere during the period between 1995 and 2000 must naturally consider the political sea change which occurred in 1997, when New Labour overturned eighteen years of Conservative Government with a landslide election victory. By definition, achieving such a victory meant that Tony Blair had shifted the Labour party in a populist direction, but the particular terms of this populist project were different to those of previous political generations. The Old Labour emphasis on overcoming poverty and injustice through collective responsibility was repackaged as tackling "social exclusion", a far less loaded concept in terms of the history of class conflict.[69] The Department of National Heritage, which had established and controlled the National Lottery, became the Department of Culture, Media and Sport. Chris Smith,

---

[69] A Social Exclusion Unit was established in 1997 to rethink government policy on these issues. See Cabinet Office, *Social Exclusion Unit*, accessed August 2006, http://www. socialexclusion.gov.uk/.

the department's first Minister for Culture, began, on the one hand, to espouse the regenerative potential of cultural activity, and on the other hand, to reconceptualise the arts -funding sector in terms of supporting "creative industries".[70] Under the new leadership of Gerry Robinson, the Arts Council of England began a process of radical restructuring. Meanwhile, a new Film Policy Review Group had been set up to rationalise the provision of funding to the film sector. Therefore, amidst all this ideological and institutional change, it would be very surprising if the decisions made by the Arts Council did not also shift in emphasis, and this was particularly relevant to an activity which epitomised the Blairite public-private partnership ideal: Lottery-funded popular cinema.

As the previous Prime Minister Major's rhetoric had often been nostalgic or even reactionary, by contrast, Blair was a forward-looking moderniser, attempting explicitly to rebrand the nation as youthful, innovative and creative. His agenda was expressed in terms such as the following:

> Radical politics... is about giving many more people the opportunity to share in the nation's wealth and power. In John Smith's words, it is about developing "the extraordinary potential of ordinary people."[71]

Blair's language here is collective but aspirational, economically-driven but emotively expressed. The key phrase (or sound bite) here could easily have dropped from the lips of a Hollywood producer or even a star during an award acceptance speech. It is affirmative and class-less, and therefore feels rather American. In this sense it resonates neatly with Jeffrey Richards' work on Frank Capra's films, which places these much-loved works of classical Hollywood in relation to the political doctrine of Populism.[72] The central tenets of the strain of Populism developed in the United States of the late-nineteenth century are the primacy of the individual, and the notion that all citizens are created equal. This is embodied within national mythology and storytelling—most notably within the "Log Cabin to White House" tale, which maintains that any US citizen, irrespective of how humble their beginnings, could become the

---

[70] See Chris Smith, *Creative Britain* (London: Faber and Faber, 1998).

[71] John Smith was Blair's predecessor as leader of the Labour party. Tony Blair, "Introduction: My Vision for Britain," in Giles Radice (ed.), *What Needs to Change: New Visions for Britain* (London: Harper Collins, 1996), 6.

[72] Jeffrey Richards, "Frank Capra and the Cinema of Populism," in *Movies and Methods, Volume One,* ed. Bill Nicholls (Berkeley: University of California Press, 1976), 65–77.

country's President. Richards' focus here is on the mythmaking of American culture of the early- to mid-twentieth century, but his discussion of Populism within Hollywood narrative structure is arguably just as relevant well over fifty years later. It is also well worth considering in relation to popular cinema produced in different national and historical contexts, especially in British cinema, which has been, to a large extent defined by its relationship with Hollywood.

Whilst all Lottery-funded popular cinema was engaged in negotiating a path between the public sphere and private enterprise, *Billy Elliot* perhaps represents the most successful marriage between the two. Its writer, Lee Hall, honed his dramatic skills writing radio plays for the BBC, and it was under the auspices of the public service broadcaster in 1996 that his debut film script began to be nurtured.[73] Looking for partners to develop Hall's script, the BBC approached Tiger Aspect, an independent production company best known for making hit comedy shows such as BBC1's *The Vicar of Dibley* (1994–2005). Tiger Aspect also brought with them an enviable list of industry contacts through their joint development deal with Working Title. By 1998, Working Title had signed up acclaimed theatre director Stephen Daldry to direct Hall's script, and the film was selected as the first to be produced under the company's new low-budget arm, WT2. Aimed at attracting younger audiences than their trademark romantic comedies or heritage films, producer Jon Finn described WT2's motto as "heart, humour and horror"; in the same article *Variety* extrapolated that "The budgets may be low, the talent may be new, but that doesn't mean art-house."[74] Then known as *Dancer*, the film was therefore something of an experiment for Working Title, and was hardly conceived as a blockbuster in the Hollywood sense. However, of the three elements of the WT2 motto, it was clearly a project which appealed to the "heart" in a manner more commonly found in mainstream Hollywood cinema. Its narrative of a young working-class lad who overcomes severe "social exclusion" during the 1984 miners' strike through an unexpected talent for ballet is deeply emotive and also profoundly Populist in a manner not unlike Capra's American mythology.

The script which subsequently became *Billy Elliot* recasts the central Populist success myth into a recent British context, and has several parallels with the New Labour project. Here the humble point of origin is not the log

[73] Patricia Dobson, "Case Study: *Billy Elliot*," *Screen International*, 1268, July 21, 2000, 15.
[74] Adam Minns, "VNews: Jon Finn and Natascha Wharton on WT2," *Variety.com*, May 3, 2001, accessed September 2006, http://www.variety.com/article/VR1117798516.html.

cabin, with its associations drawn from the wilderness/civilisation dynamic central to American culture, but the Northern coal-mining pit face—a location equally rich in symbolic meaning. The pit face represents the engine room of the industrial revolution and the foundation of modern Englishness; in 1937, George Orwell wrote that "In the metabolism of the Western world the coal-miner is second in importance only to the man who ploughs the soil."[75] After the dramatic conflict of the 1980s, coal-miners also came to stand for the passing of the industrial age, and with it the collapse of Old Labour trade unionism. The last gasp of socialist collectivism is dramatised in Hall's script with considerable sympathy towards the miners' suffering. However it is the "extraordinary potential" within the "ordinary" *Billy Elliot* which comes to take centre stage. This is not a "star-driven" film in the usual sense of featuring a well-known performer in the lead role, but rather capitalises upon its "star-making" potential, both textually and extra-textually, with the actor playing Billy, Jamie Bell, also enjoying a sudden rise to fame. The destination of Billy's upward trajectory is also significant. The final shot of the film holds the 25 year-old Billy suspended in mid-air and bathed in the London spotlight, the epitome of success and freedom from constraint. This is a fitting replacement for the Presidential goal of the original Populist myth during an era when celebrity and politics openly collided, most famously when Tony Blair held a reception at Number 10 Downing Street in July 1997, which was attended by actors, artists and rock stars.[76]

Billy Elliot was produced during 1999 and 2000 with a budget of £2.8 million, of which just over £900,000 was Lottery funding awarded by the Arts Council of England. It premiered in Directors' Fortnight at the Cannes Film Festival in May 2000 to critical acclaim, but unlike many other low-budget films at Cannes, it already had a major distributor waiting in the wings to give it a global theatrical release. Working Title owed their development into a significant concern during the early and mid-1990s to the European company PolyGram Film Entertainment, but when PolyGram was sold to Seagrams in 1999, these connections passed to their subsidiary, Universal.[77] Since this point, Universal has given the Hollywood treatment to all of Working Title's international successes, ensuring generous marketing and promotion, as well as access to an

---

[75] George Orwell, *The Road to Wigan Pier* (London: Secker and Warburg, 1983; first published 1937), 18.

[76] See John Harris, *The Last Party: Britpop, Blair and the Demise of English Rock* (London: Fourth Estate, 2003).

[77] For an account of PolyGram's rise and fall see Michael Kuhn, *One Hundred Films and a Funeral* (London: Thorogood, 2002).

efficient world-wide distribution network. With *Billy Elliot*, there were problems to address, such as the thick regional accents, some of which were overdubbed in post-production, and especially its frequent bad language, which led to it receiving a restrictive "R" rating in the US.[78] However Fox had made a hit of *The Full Monty* with the same rating a few years prior, and Universal was confident that this could be repeated. *Billy Elliot* opened first in the UK on 335 screens—a wide release comparable to many Hollywood films—and stayed in the top-five of the UK box office charts for ten weeks. In the US, a more gradual platform release was preferred, starting with just 10 screens and building to a peak of over 500 after eight weeks. When *Billy Elliot*'s international theatrical run was over, it was estimated to have earned over $100 million, and continues to generate revenue from DVD and TV sales.[79] In 2003, according to UK Film Council research, *Billy Elliot* was the most watched film on British terrestrial television.[80]

Billy Elliot's success can be used as evidence to support different arguments concerning what is best for the British film industry—particularly regarding the use of Lottery funds. The optimistic team at Working Title, who had significant influence within the Film Policy Review Group in 1998,[81] argue that high-quality UK films made in the populist mode will always be in demand, both at home and abroad, and that it makes sense to work with Hollywood rather than compete against it. Co-founder of the company Tim Bevan is known for provocative statements, such as, "I can't stand people who whinge and say they can't find distribution. They should make better films."[82] For other producers, the film demonstrates the systematic unfairness of the structure of the industry in the UK, where only a few high-profile companies can gain access both to public funding resources and to international distribution networks. Under this logic, *Billy*

---

78 The MPAA insisted that over 40 uses of "fuck", gave *Billy Elliot* an automatic "R" rating despite its family-friendly potential. Lori L. Tharps, "Foul Plié," *Entertainment Weekly*, 566, October 27, 2000, 24. A "PG-13" edited version now exists for television.

79 Distribution and box office data from www.variety.com, accessed June 2003.

80 UK Film Council, "Home grown success Billy Elliot tops TV movie ratings for 2003," *UK Film Council*, June 4, 2004, accessed June 2004, http://www.ukfilmcouncil.org.uk/information/news/?p=D4A157250ebf42C008yMs1B3B2E8,.

81 As part of the FPRG, Tim Bevan and Eric Fellner sat on panels dedicated to broadening the audience and film exports. DCMS, *A Bigger Picture: The Report of the Film Policy Review Group* (London: DCMS, 1998), 52.

82 Tim Bevan cited in Louise Tutt, "Greater Expectations," *Screen International*, 1142, January 23, 1998, 24–26.

Elliot is, in itself, no better a film than those made by less well-connected filmmakers; it just had far more money available to spend on prints and advertising. The fact that such a film received Lottery money in the first place is controversial as it seems likely that Working Title could have financed it entirely by themselves.[83] However, at the point when the Arts Council of England awarded Lottery money to *Billy Elliot*, they were under pressure to deliver a hit which could save the scheme from rising criticisms and recoup some of the money invested and lost. Mark Dunford was the Lottery Officer who recommended the application for an award, and he summarises the competing interests under which he and his team were working in the following terms: "You are damned if you succeed for putting money into something which didn't need public support, and damned if you fail for waste."[84] Nonetheless, Dunford remains proud of the Lottery Film unit's support of *Billy Elliot*.

It is also important to remember that *Billy Elliot* was by no means an obvious sure-fire hit at the point when the Arts Council chose to support it. In particular, its combination of two disparate genres—the musical and the kitchen sink social realist drama—might have been considered a risky strategy for a mainstream film. These two genres would appear to be incompatible as social realism has a strong ideological mistrust of the kind of fantasy and escapism which is central to the musical.[85] The potential for a clash between these two cinematic modes is illustrated with a striking moment which occurs early in the film. Fired up by his first experience of ballet, Billy (Jamie Bell) races home through an environment of overgrown weeds and steeply terraced housing when he is stopped by his dance teacher Mrs Wilkinson (Julie Walters) in her dilapidated Volvo. There is a brief exchange of abrasive dialogue before the car pulls away down the hill, past more terraces and an allotment. Up until this point, the scene would not be out of place within any realist British film or television drama. Many of the familiar elements of the social realist mode are present: the Northern, working-class setting; the explicitly socialist connotations of the ever-present strike; and the dialogue, which is often surprisingly gritty considering the film's family-friendly image. But as the car moves away, incongruous music begins on the soundtrack as Fred Astaire croons the signature song from *Top Hat* (1935). The music

---

[83] The decisions to fund similar projects such as PolyGram's £10m highwayman action movie *Plunkett and Macleane* had already attracted criticism.

[84] Mark Dunford, interview with the author, July 16, 2004.

[85] e.g. Lindsay Anderson, "Get Out and Push," in *Declaration*, ed. Tom Maschler (St Albans: MacGibbon and Kee, 1957), 158.

continues over the next shot of Billy on top of the hill, with the same urban scenery as before now transformed by diffused sunlight against a bright blue sky. A dirty stick picked up from the street becomes a metaphorical cane as Billy raps it on the ground before kicking it back up to his shoulders in a graceful arch.

This represents a shift away from the objective conventions of social realism towards a more subjective psychological realism; this is reality as Billy is experiencing it at that moment. This is licensed in narrative terms by Billy's powerful urge to escape his environment, which for the moment is frustrated, driving him to fantasy. Nevertheless, what follows is surprising: a cut to a few seconds of original footage from the classic musical with Astaire singing, dancing and grinning at the camera. This use of direct quotation from another film is startling for several reasons. There is no attempt to contain the footage by placing it within the diegesis, such as on a television in the corner of Billy's sitting room, for example. Neither is this a complete surrender to fantasy in the style of *Billy Liar* (1963). There is no equivalent cut to Billy Elliot's mindscreen as he imagines tap dancing down the Durham street in full evening dress. Another potential precedent here is Dennis Potter's influential television drama *The Singing Detective* (1986), but *Billy Elliot* certainly displays none of Potter's interest in Brechtian distanciation and audience discomfort; it is far too populist a project for that.[86] Rather this moment invokes a pleasurable recognition or, as is more likely for younger audiences, a demonstration of what film musicals used to connote: glamour, confidence, and awe-inspiring performances. Whilst the film frustrates the expectations of glamour by remaining in its working-class milieu until just before the conclusion, Billy's growing confidence and skill place further stress upon the film's realist façade, motivating sequences qualifying as "numbers" within the classical tradition.[87]

A good example of this is the section during which Billy dances to The Jam's "A Town Called Malice". The music begins as Billy's brother and Mrs Wilkinson clash over the boy's future. There is a cut to the backyard, where Billy has apparently escaped, and he begins movements motivated by anger and frustration, slapping walls and kicking down doors. Next he is shown on the wall around the other side of the house, defiantly sticking two fingers up at his brother whilst performing choreography inspired by lad culture: a mixture of the exaggerated arm movements of rock guitar

---

[86] David Jays argues that Potter's work fits into a European tradition of "anti-musicals". "Blues in the Night," *Sight and Sound,* 10:9, September 2000, 18–20.
[87] See John E. Mueller, "Fred Astaire and the Integrated Musical," *Cinema Journal*, 24:1 (Fall 1984): 28–40.

players and the aerial acrobatics of footballers. He then leaps down to ground level and tap dances all the way up a steep cobbled street where he finally collapses, exhausted. It starts to snow, and the next scene is Christmas. This section displays many characteristics of the "number" as posited by classic musicals. Most obviously, it expresses emotion which Billy is unable to give voice to, acting as narration as well as entertainment. It tests narrative credibility by the fact that it is based on a mastery of tap dancing, not ballet. It is also placed in an ambiguous relationship with the realistic action preceding it; the first few seconds of dancing are intercut with the argument in the house where Billy's legs are still clearly in shot. As with the *Top Hat* moment, this suggests the dancing may be taking place in Billy's imagination, thus shifting from social to psychological realism. The number also disrupts the spatial and temporal realism of the film, firstly by allowing Billy to move in unlikely ways around his house and the streets, and secondly by acting as a narrative ellipsis between two distinctive stages, or "acts" of the film's story.

If *Billy Elliot* is actually a musical masquerading as social realist drama (or vice versa), then what does this say about the functions of genre within popular cinema? The musical is often cited as an example of a genre which has somehow dissipated, no longer retaining its hold over audiences. This idea corresponds to what Steve Neale calls an "evolutionary" approach to genre history: initial growth is followed by flowering and finally by decay.[88] According to this model, the coming of sound sparked off experiments in the musical form, which later stabilised into the integrated musical. The 1960s saw the genre bloat to an epic scale, with *The Sound of Music* (1965) representing the peak of its global success. As Hollywood attempted and failed to produce more blockbuster musicals, audiences tired of the genre's artificiality, and it was eventually consigned to cinema history; however, other interpretations of this pattern are also possible. An anthropological approach could interpret the film musical as one instance of a universal form of human entertainment. From folk ritual to theatrical entertainment, the pleasures of watching musical performance coincided with film whilst it was the primary medium of popular entertainment, and then splintered off elsewhere, particularly into television (e.g. pop music performance shows, MTV, reality TV). According to other genre historians (including Steve Neale), the idea of generic purity is a fallacy, and all films are multi-generic. Hence the particular generic blend represented by the musicals of the 1950s and

[88] Steve Neale, "Questions of Genre," *Screen,* 31:1 (Spring 1990): 45–66.

1960s may have gone out of fashion, but elements of the genre will always persist, intermingled with other types of cinema: in Disney animation, such as *The Lion King* (1994); in teen films, such as *Dirty Dancing* (1987); and in conjunction with realist aesthetics in *Saturday Night Fever* (1978) and Eminem's *8 Mile* (2002). The influence of the musical also extends beyond films featuring singing and dancing. The "high concept" aesthetic of 1980s action cinema relies heavily on pop songs to do narrative work, and "post-liberationist" romantic comedies frequently feature songs from classic musicals to connote old-fashioned romance.

Placed in this context, *Billy Elliot* does not seem so different from much contemporary popular cinema, which draws on a range of attractions to appeal to different audience sectors. In fact, its major difference from most mainstream cinema is in its national and regional references, simultaneously making it exotic for international audiences and familiar and comforting for domestic ones. However, even within England, *Billy Elliot*'s positioning in the North East of County Durham makes it alien and strange for many audiences, the "Northern" arguably having a source of symbolic power equivalent to the Western for American audiences.[89] The North is the birthplace of the industrial revolution and where its decline hit hardest; a place where the landscape is rugged and the people are thought to be similarly raw and authentic. This discourse can be observed most clearly in *Billy Elliot* when Billy and his dad (Gary Lewis) travel down to London for his audition at the Royal Ballet School. The pair are instantly dwarfed by the enormous neo-classical building and awed by its size and wealthy sheen. Billy misinterprets eloquent friendliness on behalf of another auditioning boy as sexual advances and resorts to violence. The panel of interviewers are lofty and patronising; as the pair leave the room, they wish Billy's dad "good luck" with the strike, as if it was an amateur dramatic stage show. Nonetheless, Billy does get his place, and this is due to his naturalness and emotive immediacy as much as his talent. The stuttered speech he makes in response to one interviewer's question, "what does it feel like when you're dancing?" is a key turning point, displaying his potential to transform himself from Northern yob to ballet dancer.[90]

The language of naturalness and rawness recurs in the film's publicity, which consistently emphasised the discovery of Jamie Bell as a diamond in the rough, a new child star with incredible talent. The casting process

[89] See Paul Marris, "Northern Realism: An Exhausted Tradition," *Cineaste*, 26:4 (Autumn 2001): Contemporary British Cinema Supplement, 47–50.

[90] This is emphasised by its conversion into a show-stopping song "Electricity" written by Elton John for *Billy Elliot: The Musical.*

saw 2,000 boys audition as the role's demands were very specific: the child must be from the North East, have enough dancing ability to be a convincing candidate for the Royal Ballet School, and have the acting ability and charisma to carry the film, despite being an unknown.[91] This last point was crucial as to use a child from drama school could have been damaging for the film's claims surrounding authenticity. Eventually, the 13 year old Jamie Bell from Billingham in Teeside was selected; although not completely untrained—he had been taking tap lessons since the age of six—Jamie had kept his dancing a secret from his school mates to avoid bullying, echoing Billy's early clandestine attempts at ballet. This story therefore provides a complementary meta-narrative to the film itself. After the film's success, the young Jamie was thrust into the public sphere and began to be associated with a series of mentoring figures. The first was Daldry himself, who reportedly opened up his home in London to the lad. Bell has since spoken of an intense "paternal" bond between the two: "I bring out the child in him and he brings out the adult in me."[92] When Bell met Russell Crowe at the 2001 BAFTA Award ceremony, the Australian star took a shine to the newcomer despite losing to him in the Best Actor category. Crowe subsequently mentioned Bell in several award acceptance speeches, and the pair were photographed together in Los Angeles and London.[93] For a time, these adopted father figures were a potent element of Bell's star image, partly because the actor's widely circulated biography includes the fact that he grew up not knowing his own dad. But it is also possible to read Bell's connection to masculine role models, such as Crowe, as an attempt to neutralise the disturbingly ambivalent sexuality of Bell's star-making role.

Conclusion

When considered in terms of its unusual combination of generic conventions and its tempering of stardom with discourses of authenticity, *Billy Elliot* may not be as straight-forwardly commercial as its huge success might

[91] Edward Lawrenson, "Cosmic Dancer," *Sight and Sound,* 10:10, October 2000, 12–13.

[92] Chrissey Iley, "Bell de Jour," *Guardian Unlimited*, November 27, 2005, accessed July 2006, http://film.guardian.co.uk/interview/interviewpages/0,,1651459,0.html.

[93] e.g. Crowe invited Bell to attend the London premier of *Proof of Life* (2001) as his main escort in the absence of co-star Meg Ryan. Anon., "Crowe and Ryan romance damaged film," *BBC Online*, February 22, 2001, accessed July 2006, http://news.bbc.co. uk/1/hi/entertainment/1183758.stm.

suggest. In this light, its support by the National Lottery through the Arts Council of England becomes easier to justify under the principle of additionality. Of course, Working Title and the other companies involved in its production (including the Arts Council) were hoping for a hit, and maybe even a runaway success, but when this happened, it was still something of a surprise. This is indicated by this anecdote related upon its release by director Stephen Daldry:

> [Daldry] recounts with glee a story about Billy Elliot's test screenings in the US, in mall-multiplex country. The distributors told him they'd be happy with a 40-average scorecard. The Full Monty got something in the 70s. Billy Elliot, in the end, got 86.[94]

This "glee" could be interpreted as the shameful selling out of a previously credible theatre director, but it seems unlikely that such a consummate publicist as Daldry would have intended this inference. Perhaps he is simply thrilled that what he had considered to be a small-scale, low-key project was proving to be accessible to audiences across the world. The use of Lottery money to make pictures *by* the people and *for* the people was always going to be a strongly contested issue. For those who disagree with this strategy, the Arts Councils would forever be damned if they succeeded and damned if they didn't. But what neither funding bodies nor industry professionals can predict is what will happen to their cherished projects once they are released into the world.

In theory at least, any of the romantic comedies discussed in this chapter could have been as successful as *Billy Elliot*. *Shooting Fish* could have sold its elaborate con-trick across the Atlantic; *This Year's Love* might have attracted and combined the international audiences for *Trainspotting* and *Four Weddings and a Funeral*; *Get Real* was expected to crossover into the mainstream by the industry's most powerful trade paper; and Ray Winstone might even have become a global sex symbol as a result of *Fanny and Elvis*. It is perhaps harder to imagine any of the "comedies of community" discussed above breaking out internationally, as each attempts to root itself in a nostalgic notion of English (or Welsh) culture. But what none of these films had was a cultural resonance, which is hard to define and almost impossible to emulate. *Billy Elliot*'s continued popularity with UK audiences is demonstrated by its television screenings, which included the largest audience for any film on terrestrial television in

[94] Andrew Pulver, "The Hit Man," *Guardian Unlimited*, October 3, 2000, accessed June 3, 2003, http://www.guardian.co.uk/friday_review/story/0,3605,594001,00.html.

2003, and by its blockbusting stage adaptation, which has played to packed West End auditoriums for several years. This ability to resonate within British popular culture is founded upon deep currents of political ideology, from the populism of classical Hollywood to the aspirational collectivism of New Labour. The film's mythology even fed back into political discourse: a news story from February 2001 referred to a government scheme to give working-class children piano lessons and ballet classes, referred to as "the *Billy Elliot* revolution".[95] It was partly these resonances which led Tom Ryall to describe *Billy Elliot* as "the emblematic New Labour film", both in terms of its production circumstances and its narrative, which effectively dramatises the political shift between Old and New Labour.[96] In this light, even though they generally failed to emulate the international success of films such as *Four Weddings and a Funeral*, "the people's pictures" funded by the National Lottery vividly illustrate both the benefits and the risks of public support for popular cinema.

[95] Gaby Hinsliff, "'Billy Elliot' payout for poor pupils," *The Guardian*, February 11, 2001, accessed June 14, 2003, http://society.guardian.co.uk/childreninpoverty /story/0,8150, 436869,00.html.

[96] Tom Ryall, "New Labour and the cinema: Culture, politics and economics," *Journal of Popular British Cinema*, 5 (2002): 18.

CHAPTER FIVE

ARTS COUNCIL/ART CINEMA

For the first five years of National Lottery funding for film production, the cheques were signed by organisations without the word "film" in their titles. To what extent did the "art" of the Arts Councils influence the agenda of UK cinema during this period? This chapter builds upon the history of state involvement with British art cinema, as detailed in Chapter One, to investigate those Lottery-funded film projects which took place on the margins of mainstream film culture, often explicitly defining themselves in relation to discourses of "art". Before this wide-ranging material is described and categorised, it is worth remembering precisely how the Arts Councils' responsibility for the nation's artistic well-being is expressed through its Royal Charter. At the broadest scale, the Arts Councils' objectives are twofold: firstly, "to develop and improve the knowledge, understanding and practice of the arts", and secondly, "to increase the accessibility of the arts to the public".[1] This bifurcated *raison d'être* contains an implicit tension between its two halves. The first point speaks of improving practice within a separate realm of "the arts", following in a long tradition of Royal artistic patronage.[2] This logic privileges an elite group of artists whose motives and needs are held to be separate from the rest of society. The second objective of increasing accessibility is more democratic, but essential to justifying the allocation of funds from general taxation. However, there is further ambiguity in the term "accessibility": on the one hand, it simply means increasing audiences for established cultural artefacts, or in the case of cinema, the improvement of distribution and exhibition opportunities. On the other hand, however, it can also be

---

[1] This remit was originally defined by the first Royal Charter for the Arts Council of Great Britain in 1946, and was renewed in 1993 when the organisation was split to cover the three home nations of Britain. The Arts Council of England, *1st Annual Report and Accounts 1994/5* (London: ACE, 1995), 1.

[2] John Pick, *The Arts in a State: A Study of Government Arts Policies from Ancient Greece to the Present* (Bristol: Bristol Classical Press, 1988).

interpreted as leading towards the support of popular culture, or even of modifying artistic intention to suit public taste.

It was an attempt to bridge these two competing drives which first led the Arts Council of Great Britain towards filmmaking in the 1950s. During this period, the Council's Visual Arts department began to tour filmed documentaries of artists at work and key exhibitions as an efficient means of increasing public access to paintings and sculpture, particularly outside the major metropolitan areas. This activity later developed into support and active encouragement for artists who were engaged with film as an art form in its own right, and it was within this sector of avant-garde artists' film practice that the Arts Council's Film and Television department specialised from its inception in 1986. By this point, public funding for feature-length films intended for exhibition on the international art cinema circuit was the province of the British Film Institute's Production Board. The BFI also provided support for short films, as did the BBC and Channel Four. Unlike British Screen—or the various tax incentive schemes which came and went during the 1990s—all of these smaller initiatives were driven by cultural objectives rather than economic goals. The BFI's policy aimed "to encourage challenging and different approaches to cinema in the UK", whilst Channel Four's charter compelled them towards "innovation and experiment".[3] This joint emphasis on newness may separate both institutions from the Arts Councils' sense of history and heritage, but all three bodies navigate the terrain between high art and popular culture in their own particular way. The development of National Lottery funding for film production in 1995 radically altered this production ecology in ways that it was perhaps unable to achieve within the larger film industry as a whole.

To begin to explore these developments, it is first necessary to be precise about the types of filmmaking activity to be discussed. "Art cinema" is most commonly conceived of in terms of a middle-ground between radical avant-garde filmmaking on the one side and commercial movies on the other. The boundaries between these categories often feel relatively fixed and immovable;[4] however, in this chapter I want to propose a much broader definition, allowing for a full discussion of the

---

[3] Eddie Dyja, *BFI Film and Television Handbook 1996* (London: BFI, 1995), 18; Great Britain, *Broadcasting Act 1980* (London: HMSO, 1980).

[4] e.g. Michael O'Pray on the 1970s delineation between the avant-garde, oppositional or independent cinema, low-budget subsidised art cinema and its more mainstream incarnation. O'Pray, "The British Avant-Garde and Art Cinema from the 1970s to the 1990s" in *Dissolving Views*, ed. Andrew Higson (London: Cassell, 1996), 179.

points of contact and overlap between these modes, as well as their specificities. My model includes those films most frequently labelled as "art cinema": independently-produced, auteur-driven features, which distance themselves from mainstream narrative cinema by employing particular aesthetic or narrative strategies, and which tend to be exhibited as "art-house" films. For the purposes of my thesis, however, I intend to locate these films within a wider field of activity that also accommodates avant-garde artists' film and video, short films—and even conventional biopics, which take artists and art as their subject. By widening out the definition of art cinema in this manner, it is hoped that it will be possible to observe a greater richness and variety of connections between the processes of arts funding and the products which they generate.

The bulk of this chapter is taken up with a survey of representative examples of the films produced within each of these subgroupings. The desire to provide a comprehensive overview inevitably means I cannot devote much space to each individual text, but this lack of detail is balanced by the closer attention paid to the main case study: John Maybury's art cinema biopic about Francis Bacon, *Love is the Devil* (1998).

I will argue that, perhaps contrary to expectations, the broadly populist intervention of the National Lottery produced a surprisingly fertile crop of art cinema projects in the UK between 1995 and 2000. This was due, in no small part, to the Arts Councils' pre-existing expertise in this area, and also to its natural inclination towards the esoteric and experimental rather than the straight-forwardly populist. My use of an unusually wide categorisation in this chapter should not suggest that the term "art cinema" will be emptied of the wide range of meanings with which it has been associated previously. On the contrary, these rich levels of meaning inform my discussion. To begin with, art cinemas have a central place in film history, with a succession of moments or movements advancing a teleological view of the medium.[5] These movements tend to have strong national orientations—even if their eventual circulation is decidedly international. European film history is especially rich in such privileged sub-groupings, which have played an important role in legitimising filmmaking as an art form in its own right, as well as distancing art cinema, in particular, from Hollywood's populist product. Both of these beneficial effects have continued relevance within the context of state-supported national cinema. The cultural legitimacy of art cinema can be

---

[5] See Jamie Sexton, "The Film Society and the Creation of an Alternative Film Culture in Britain" in *Young and Innocent: The Cinema in Britain 1896–1930*, ed. Andrew Higson (Exeter: University of Exeter Press, 2002), 291–305.

used as an important justification for film's special protected status, whilst this protection is fundamentally necessary owing to Hollywood's international domination of the medium. The critical legacy left behind by this process irrevocably binds discussion of art cinema with theories of authorship, which provides a key theme in my survey of Lottery-funded art cinema in the late 1990s. Of particular interest here are those filmmakers whose authorial presence crossed the boundaries between different types of Lottery-funded art cinema practice; thus Lynne Ramsey's acclaimed short films provided a bridge towards her feature debut, the art film *Ratcatcher* (1999), whilst Andrew Kötting fused a distinctive avant-garde sensibility with the picaresque documentary in *Gallivant* (1997).

A second important strand to the critical discussion of art cinema has concentrated upon its formal characteristics. In contrast to the elitist, canon-building tendencies of art cinema, for formalist critics like David Bordwell, the term is intended to be primarily descriptive rather than evaluative. Bordwell's discussion of art cinema posits it as a mode of filmic narration with a distinct set of conventions, such as the loosening of narrative causality and elusive character motivation.[6] These conventions suggest the possibility of art cinema as genre: just one possible textual strategy within a range of equally valid alternatives. Whether this truly creates a level critical playing field is a matter for debate: the films which Bordwell uses to create his template are already valorised by their place within histories of European art cinema. Even so, this formulation is undeniably influential, partly because it echoes most audiences' understanding of the differences between mainstream and non-mainstream filmmaking. This work also provides invaluable starting points for my methodology in this chapter, which is driven by textual analysis. Common aesthetic and narrational strategies are drawn out and compared in order to evaluate the works' relationships to each other, as well as within wider currents of filmic activity. Bordwell's work is also limited to feature length examples of narrative art cinema; his model sometimes holds true within short film-making, but clearly has little relevance to artists' film and video work. The avant-garde sector has its own aesthetic tradition more closely allied to the visual arts than to mainstream cinema. Key

---

[6] David Bordwell, *Narration in the Fiction Film* (London: Methuen, 1985), 205–233.

elements here include the denial of narrative and attempts to redefine the relationship between artwork and audience.[7]

Both the canon-building and the formalist conceptions of art cinema can be criticised for removing films from their contexts, considering them either as transcendent works of human imagination on the one hand, or as ahistorical rehearsals of generic structures on the other. A third, more empirical viewpoint argues that a film's claim to the status of art may simply be a form of marketing or product differentiation, designed to attract niche audiences who feel excluded by the mainstream. Using this perspective, Steve Neale has argued that "Art Cinema, fundamentally, is a mechanism of discrimination… a division that functions economically, ideologically and aesthetically."[8] As an economic "division", art cinema is a specialised sector within a broader film industry—one with its own models of production, distribution and exhibition. The art-house cinema itself is a vital element in this equation, housing a community of cinemagoers seeking a different kind of experience than is typically available through the dominant exhibition mechanism, currently the multiplex. These venues also create space for "film culture": educational events, discussions between filmmakers and audiences, and festivals. In the context of this survey, the incorporation of details from the production histories, exhibition strategies and reception of the projects discussed provides more than just background colour; such information can be used to spark valuable questions concerning the nature of art cinema itself.

The fourth and final set of connections between art and cinema are particularly relevant towards the avant-garde end of the spectrum. Here the lack of an economic infrastructure has often forced the artist into the shelter of institutional support; universities and art schools have been especially important in this regard. In the British context, Michael Mazière has described the "educational nexus" of the Slade School of Art in the early 1960s, which begat a generation of artists and filmmakers, including Malcolm LeGrice.[9] Thus the "art" of "art cinema" also serves to stress the connections between film and the visual arts—in both theoretical and institutional terms. The boundaries between painting, photography and filmmaking have been blurred since cinema began, but in recent decades the process of exchange has been particularly visible as video installations

---

[7] For a discussion of the aesthetic strategies of the British avant-garde see A.L. Rees, *A History of Experimental Film and Video* (London: BFI, 1999).

[8] Steve Neale, "Art Cinema as Institution," *Screen*, 22:1 (1981): 37.

[9] Michael Mazière, "Institutional Support for Artists' Film and Video in England 1966-2003," *British Artists Film and Video Study Collection*, accessed April 2004, http://www.research.linst.ac.uk/ filmcentre//maziere/paper.html.

and multi-media experiments have become common fixtures in art galleries.[10] In the case of Lottery funding for film production, the institutional angle is particularly suggestive given the doubled remit of the Arts Councils, as the tension between its two major objectives is felt particularly keenly by Lottery-funded art cinema projects. Whilst public funding for popular cinema is largely driven by commercial imperatives unfamiliar to the traditional Arts Council, the producers of art cinema are closely aligned with the sentiment of John Maynard Keynes' inaugural BBC broadcast in 1946: "The purpose of the Arts Council of Great Britain is to create an environment to breed a spirit, to cultivate an opinion, to offer a stimulus".[11] That they do so in a medium which Keynes' disliked is somewhat ironic, as is their utilisation of a new funding source driven by populist rhetoric: the National Lottery.

The Artists' Film and Video Scheme

With its lengthy involvement in avant-garde film and video practice which originally emerged from a Visual Arts context, the "Artists" Film and Video' scheme saw the Arts Council of England on familiar territory. This work fits easily within the traditional high-art remit of the Councils, with the artists given a relatively free rein over content and means of exhibition. But even these low-budget, experimental projects were required to consider issues of "accessibility" in order to secure Lottery funding; installations were expected to be *in situ* in one or more locations for at least six weeks, and it was recommended that single-screen works should be toured to at least five venues in England.[12] Such projects were assessed separately from the other film production applications, and were all handled through the Arts Council of England. Therefore, they are recognised as forming an identifiable set of awards with their own particular characteristics, although further information on this material can be difficult to obtain, as can be the works themselves. Though heavily theorised, artists' film and video is an under-researched and sparsely documented field of practice, a problem which the AHRC Centre for

[10] One well-known example is Douglas Gordon's *24 Hour Psycho* (1993) which slowed down the projection of Hitchcock's 1960 horror film to create a series of still images.
[11] John Maynard Keynes, *The Collected Writings of John Maynard Keynes*, Vol. 28, ed. D. Moggridge (London: Macmillan Press, 1982), 372.
[12] Arts Council of England, *National Lottery Funding for Film: Application Pack* (London: ACE, 1997), 16.

British Cinema Studies began to address in the 2000s.[13] Most of the artists' film and video works listed in Table 5-1 can no longer be seen in their original context, which makes assessment of their contemporary impact more difficult. For this reason, it has sometimes been necessary to build up an account of a given piece through a combination of still images, the artists' own intentions, often laid out attractively in expensive exhibition catalogues, and what other artists and critics said about the work at the time. Conversely, other artists' film and video projects are now widely accessible through DVD releases (e.g. *Temenos*), television screenings (e.g. *The Alcohol Years*) or over the internet.

The 35 works receiving Lottery funding through the Artists Film and Video (AFV) scheme cost the Arts Council less than £800,000.[14] Although they are extremely diverse in terms of content, as Table 5-1 illustrates, they may nevertheless be grouped into recognisable types. The most common type of project (13 in total) was shot on video and projected as a single or multi-screen "installation" in an art gallery context. These works are the most easily transportable and can be projected at the same time across several venues. Other artists exhibited their work as part of a carefully arranged "space", with eight such projects incorporating set design and props to transform the neutral gallery setting. A further extension of this engagement with space saw three projects commissioned as "site-specific" works for a particular locale. These pieces frequently explored issues of architecture, history and memory. As a complete contrast, three other projects existed only in electronic space, using the internet or CD/DVD-ROM technology to create "interactive" experiences for their audiences. A further eight projects were placed somewhere between the avant-garde and other filmmaking modes, and embraced animation, short films, documentaries and features. These works were screened not only in art galleries but also at film festivals, in art-house cinemas, on television, or on DVD. Several of these projects can be closely related to the traditional visual arts (painting, photography and sculpture), whilst others work in entirely new media. The site-specific works usually represented one-off events, unrepeatable in any other location and hence unique experiences, whilst several of the interactive pieces were available any time in any location with an internet connection.

---

[13] The response was the small but invaluable British Artists' Film and Video Study Collection at Central St. Martins College of Art and Design in London. See *BAFVSC*, accessed December 2006, http://www. studycollection.co.uk/.

[14] See James Caterer, "The People's Pictures Appendices," *Google Sites*, https://sites.google.com/a/brookes.ac.uk/jamescaterer/.

Table 5-1: Lottery-funded "Artists' Film and Video" projects, 1995–2000.[15]

Applicant Name	Artist(s)	Title	Type[16]
Chaplaincy of Durham	Bill Viola	*The Messenger*	Site Specific
Maya Vision	Sandra Lahire	*Johnny Panic*	Short
Basilisk Communications	Nina Danino	*Temenos*	Feature
University of Central England	Michael Pinsky	*Transparent Room*	Space
Foundation for Art and Creative Technology (FACT)	Judith Goddard	*Night*	Installation
FACT—Video Positive '98	Willie Doherty	*Somewhere Else*	Installation
FACT—Video Positive '98	Keith Piper	*Robot Bodies*	Interactive
FACT—Video Positive '98	Butler Bros.	*Akkomodation*	Short
FACT—Video Positive '98	Kristin Lucas	*Screening Room*	Space
London Electronic Arts (LEA) Pandemonium	Clio Barnard	*Hardcut*	Installation
LEA - Pandemonium	Dryden Goodwin	*Within*	Installation
LEA - Pandemonium	Stephanie Smith & Edward Stewart	*Vent*	Installation
LEA - Pandemonium	Tracey Emin	*Sundown*	Installation
LEA - Pandemonium	Alison Craighead & Jon Thompson	*Speaking in Tongues*	Space
Bluecoat Arts Centre	Janet Hodgson	*History Lesson*	Site Specific
Film And Video Umbrella	Simon Biggs	*Halo*	Interactive
Finetake Productions	Robert Bradbrook	*Home Road Movies*	Animation
Steve Ross Foundation	Lulu Quinn	*Tidal*	Site Specific

---

[15] Source: David Curtis, British Artists' Film and Video Study Collection.
[16] "Type" collated from 'British Artists Moving Image Database', *BAFVSC*, accessed 2004-2006, http://www. studycollection.co.uk/bamid/; exhibition catalogues held at BAFVCS; artists websites e.g. *Dryden Goodwin*, accessed January 2007, http://www.drydengoodwin.com/.

Applicant Name	Artist(s)	Title	Type[16]
FACT—Video Positive '99	Dryden Goodwin	*Wait*	Installation
FACT—Video Positive '99	Monika Oechsler	*Johari's Window*	Installation
Lighthouse—Event Coast	Anna Hendrich & Leon Palmer	*Maximum Cube*	Space
Lighthouse—Event Coast	Paul Sermon	*There is no Simulation Like Home*	Space
Lighthouse—Event Coast	Simon Poulter	*Microhenge*	Space
Lighthouse—Event Coast	Susan Kozel	*Traces*	Space
Lighthouse—Event Coast	Tessa Elliot	*Incident*	Space
Bewitched	Sarah Turner	*Cut*	Short
Cannon And Morley Productions	Carol Morley	*The Alcohol Years*	Documentary
Film And Video Umbrella	Mark Lewis	*Peeping Tom*	Installation
Serpentine Gallery	Jane & Louise Wilson	*Parliament*	Installation
Site Gallery	Breda Beban	*Backstory*	Installation
Site Gallery	Forced Entertainment	*Hotel Binary*	Interactive
Film And Video Umbrella	Matthew Cornford & David Cross	*Childhood's End*	Installation
Mid Pennine Arts	TEA	*The Cut*	Installation
Spectre Films Ltd.	Phil Mulloy	*Intolerance*	Animation
Tigerlily Films	Clio Barnard	*Bright as Fire*	Short

Several of the single- or multi-screen installation works share a fascination with the human body—a similar figurative impulse to that found in portraiture or photography but with the added dimensions of time and movement. The specific qualities of the *video* image (as opposed to the *cinematic* image) and its meanings within both the public and private spheres were also a vital influence. For example, London-based video artist Dryden Goodwin was involved in two Lottery-funded exhibitions: Pandemonium (1998) and Video Positive (1999). In the case of the latter, his piece *Wait* (1999) was vividly described by *Guardian* journalist Chris Arnot:

> Two slobbish faces are in close-up on adjacent video monitors in the Tate Gallery, Liverpool. One belongs to a bloated football fan, the other to a dealer on the floor of a futures exchange. Both men have hard, unblinking eyes. But it is the mouths that command attention. One is clamped shut with tension while the other - the dealer's - is rotating so violently that he seems in danger of dislocating his jaw. Everything is in slow motion, so we can see across the glistening expanse of his tongue to the back of his throat.[17]

Hence the confrontational feel of the direct-to-camera close-up is made strange by the use of slow-motion, thus allowing the spectator to observe the minute details of non-verbal communication. Stephanie Smith and Edward Stewart's *Vent* (1997) is also orally-fixated: "an image is seen showing the view from deep inside the oral cavity outwards. Here, a sensory organ changes its purpose: the mouth can see."[18] The most widely known artist to receive AFV funding, Tracey Emin, used the video installation form to create another revealing self-portrait, *Sundown* (1998), illustrating her fascination with horse-riding.[19] By contrast, Willie Doherty's work is about landscape rather than portraiture, and his *Somewhere Else* (1998) envelops the spectator in footage of the urban and rural environments of Northern Ireland.[20]

Perhaps the most spectacular and certainly the most controversial of the Artists' Film and Video projects placed the naked human body directly into a religious setting. Bill Viola's site-specific piece *The Messenger* (1996) received £69,000—the largest Lottery award for a single AFV project. Commissioned by the Chaplaincy of Durham as part of the celebrations for the UK Year of the Visual Arts, it consists of a looped 25 minute piece of video in which a nude male figure slowly rises to the surface of a deep pool of water, takes a deep, gasping breath, and then begins to sink back to the bottom again. This video was projected onto an

---

[17] Chris Arnot, "Shooting Stars," *Guardian Unlimited*, March 23, 2000, accessed March 2005, http://www.guardian. co.uk/arts/story/0,,181477,00.html.

[18] Portikus Gallery, Frankfurt am Main, Germany, "Exhibition 97: Smith/Stuart Video Works," *Portikus*, accessed March 2005, http://www.portikus.de/Archive A0097.html.

[19] Nelly Voorhuis, "Pandemonium 1998," *Mute Magazine*, October 7, 2004, accessed January 2007, http://www.metamute.org/en/Pandaemonium-1998.

[20] Camilla Jackson and Ian Hunt, *Willie Doherty: Somewhere Else* (Liverpool: Tate Gallery, 1998).

enormous screen placed on the Great West Wall of Durham Cathedral. According to theology professor David Jasper, "*The Messenger* resonates within the spaces of Durham Cathedral both easily and as a challenge to its specific theological tradition."[21] The high-tech nature of Viola's video art reminds Jasper of the "magnificent medieval achievement"[22] of the Cathedral itself, but he also suggests that whilst the traditions upon which *The Messenger* draws may be deeply religious, they are not uniquely Christian. Public debate surrounding the work was less interested in theological interpretation than in the perceived obscenity of a naked figure in the sacred space, which generated enough of an outcry to warrant the placing of canvas screens around the image to shield unsuspecting eyes from the shocking nudity. In this case, it seems likely that the high-profile nature of Lottery-funded artwork directly contributed to an unfortunate neutering of the artist's intentions.

Another of the site-specific projects, Janet Hodgson's *History Lesson* (1999), plays with issues of childhood and memory in a manner which pays respect to its venerable location, an approach emphasised by the title's pedagogical slant. Hodgson's body of work as a whole typically focuses on place and architecture, as she "uncovers, unearths, retrieves and recovers."[23] This piece in particular grew out of the history of the Grade One Listed Building, which is now the Bluecoat Gallery in Liverpool, originally built as an eighteenth century school. The building lays claim to the title of the oldest arts centre in Britain, as it passed into the hands of the Bluecoat Arts Society in 1927.[24] Intrigued by the rich educational and artistic heritage of the gallery space, Hodgson used actors in authentic costuming to shoot period vignettes, which were then projected onto eight hidden screens placed throughout the building. In its use of tropes from historical drama, Hodgson's work begins to blur the boundaries between non-narrative artists' film and more conventional storytelling structures. Another piece which self-consciously relates to broader currents of film history—and, specifically, to Michael Powell's violent thriller of the same name—is Mark Lewis' *Peeping Tom* (1999). Mark Lewis is also the name of Powell's voyeuristic killer, and here the artist Lewis extends this coincidence to hysterical effect by attempting to recreate the film-within-

---

[21] David Jasper, "Screening Angels," in *The Art of Bill Viola*, ed. Chris Townsend (London: Thames and Hudson, 2004), 184.
[22] Jasper, "Screening Angels," 191.
[23] Fiona Bradley, "History Lesson," in Cindy Hubert, *Janet Hodgson: History Lesson* (Liverpool: Bluecoat Gallery, 1999), 3.
[24] See John Willett's study of the arts in Liverpool, *Art In A City* (London: Methuen, 1967).

the-film being made by his character namesake. Shot on 35mm, this was an expensive AFV project which also used professional actors to produce a 5 minute 30 second film, which was then transferred to DVD and exhibited on a loop in a gallery context.[25]

Other works fit more easily into the experimental film mode, and were shown outside galleries, at festivals, and in one-off screenings. Before her death in 2001, Sandra Lahire was a renowned and prolific avant-garde filmmaker working with themes of corporality and female consciousness.[26] One obituary placed Lahire's work within a tradition of feminist creativity, which includes the painter Frida Kahlo and the poet Sylvia Plath.[27] *Johnny Panic* (1995), funded by the AFV scheme, takes its title from a short story written by Plath and integrates other elements of her life and work into an abstract 45-minute film shot with a combination of 16 mm film and digital video.[28] Plath is embodied by an actress who delivers poetic speeches in a deadpan style, direct to camera against a backdrop of projected images: "Page by page, dream by dream, my intake books fatten." Other recurring motifs flash by, notably a split-screen close-up, illustrating gender duality with a combination of male and female features. Like Sandra Lahire, Sarah Turner is an academic and filmmaker whose work is informed by radical queer theory. Her piece for the AFV scheme, *Cut* (1999), is a co-production with Film Four, and is very similar in form and scope to several of the films having received Lottery money through the traditional shorts route.[29] *Cut* has a loose narrative structure and tells the story of a young gay woman living in an unspecified urban environment. The film begins with images of the coastline and sea, and a dreamlike voiceover from actress Julie Cox: "I get dressed, slowly." A bar scene, which begins happily, eventually illustrates the woman's dysfunctional relationship with her female partner. The final section of the film returns to impressionistic montage, including graphic shots of self-harm and flashbacks to childhood innocence.

---

[25] Stephen Bode, *Mark Lewis: Films 1995–2000* (London: Film and Video Umbrella, 2001).

[26] For a filmography and clips of *Johnny Panic* see "Sandra Lahire," *Luxonline,* accessed March 2005, http://www.luxonline.org.uk /work/id/915663/index.html.

[27] Jacqueline Rose, "Obituary: Sandra Lahire," *Guardian Unlimited*, August 13, 2001, accessed March 2005, http://www.guardian.co.uk/obituaries/story/0,,535780 ,00.html.

[28] Sylvia Plath, *"Johnny Panic and the Bible of Dreams" and other prose writings* (London, Faber, 1977).

[29] e.g. the Lottery-funded short films made by Virginia Heath and Pratibha Parmar, see "Short Films" section, 199–208.

At 75 minutes, Nina Danino's *Temenos* (1997) is an artists' film which approaches the running time of a feature. *Temenos* is also very unusual in the context of avant-garde filmmaking in that, after being screened at the London Film Festival and the Lux Cinema, it went on to receive a limited art-house theatrical release as a standalone film, thanks to BFI distribution. With a budget of £112,000, 50% of which was provided by the Lottery, it was also the most expensive one-off AFV project. The ability to raise this money is testament both to Danino's reputation as a leader in her artistic field and to her previous relationship with the Arts Council, who jointly funded *Now I Am Yours* (1993), her project for the *Experimenta* strand on Channel Four.[30] Her major work to date, *Temenos* is a film justifying its theatrical ambitions by immersing the viewer within a series of dramatic landscapes accompanied by a complex and disturbing vocal soundtrack. The dreamlike surrender of the cinematic audience is connected to Danino's theme of religious visionary experience. "Temenos" means sacred place, and Danino's landscapes are sites where visitations of the Virgin Mary have been recorded. Snowy scenes or baked mountainsides are shot in grainy black-and-white, which swirls with the texture of both video and the weather; eerie deserted panoramas which make the eventual appearance of human figures feel revelatory. At the film's conclusion, Danino directly cites a sequence from Pasolini's *Gospel According to St. Matthew* (1965), reinforcing the work's hybrid nature, somewhere between cinema and the visual arts.[31]

By contrast, Carol Morley's documentary *The Alcohol Years* (2000) feels quite at home on the small screen.[32] Its predominant form, the "talking heads" style interview, is strongly televisual, and its warts-and-all, confessional ethos is as close to reality TV as it is to conceptual art. The project sees former wild child Morley going back to her 1980s Manchester roots, where she extracts stories, confessions and insults from a cast of characters, including club promoter Alan Wise and musician Pete Shelley. The resulting portrait is an unflinching exploration of her bisexual promiscuity, inviting comparisons with Tracey Emin's notorious gallery

---

[30] Danino also has standing in the academic community with a lectureship in Fine Art at Goldsmiths College, and a period spent as editor for the journal for experimental film and video, *Undercut*. See Nina Danino and Michael Maziere (eds.), *The Undercut Reader* (London: Wallflower, 2003).

[31] "Nina Danino," *Luxonline*, accessed March 2005, http://www.luxonline.org.uk/artists/id/607902/. Clips of *Temenos* are available to view here.

[32] Indeed the film resulted in Morley being nominated for a BAFTA *television* award in 2002.

work.[33] However, unlike Emin's filmmaking, which tends to turn the camera upon herself, Morley is largely absent from the screen in *The Alcohol Years*—a decision which, according to *Guardian* critic Fiona Morrow,

> provides a large part of the film's power… For this is a film about attitude and myth: in presenting their perceptions of Morley as they remembered her, the men and women on screen become part of a study of both the power of memory and the endurance of received morality.[34]

The documentary consists of interviews on digital video mixed with Super 8 footage, which reconstructs past events in a style varying from playful to nightmarish. One interviewee points out the richness of Manchester as a setting owing to its colourful mythology, and Morley's film says at least as much about the city and its vibrant youth culture as it does about herself. In this respect, it makes for an interesting and ostensibly more realistic companion piece to Michael Winterbottom's free-wheeling treatment of the "Madchester" moment, *24 Hour Party People* (2000).

If *Temonos* and *The Alcohol Years* work within the well-established media of cinema and television, then at the other end of the AFV spectrum were those moving image projects that bypass the technology of film and video altogether. Keith Piper's work explores the relationships between humanity and technology, and his contribution to FACT's Video Positive 1998 exhibition was called *Robot Bodies*, a digital, CD-ROM exploration of the ideological connections between race and robotics. Australian-born artist Simon Biggs makes much of his art for consumption over the internet, although his interactive AFV-funded piece *Halo* (1998) worked with real gallery space rather than cyber-space. Like Bill Viola's *The Messenger*, *Halo* places the human figure in a quasi-religious context; the Fabrica Gallery in Brighton, a converted Victorian church. However Biggs' figures feature in an immersive environment covering walls and ceiling, and the artist/programmer uses computers to provide an interactive experience for the viewer/participant.[35] Robert Bradbrook uses home computers to create digitally animated works, such as *Home Road Movies* (1998), a co-production with Channel 4. This is an accessible narrative

---

[33] e.g. Emin's tent embroidered with the names of "Everyone I Ever Slept With, 1963–1995".

[34] Fiona Morrow, "Going back to the Bottle," *Guardian Unlimited*, June 5, 2000, accessed June 2005, http://www.guardian.co.uk/print/0,3858,4025579103691,00.html.

[35] Simon Biggs, "Halo," accessed January 2005, http://hosted.simonbiggs.easynet.co.uk/installations/halo /halo.htm.

short film about nostalgia for childhood holidays spent driving across Europe. It blends lavishly-coloured and textured backgrounds with photographs and digital video to create a strange, hyper-real atmosphere.[36] These new media projects embrace the possibilities presented by rapid technological change in an era when the term "Artists' Film and Video" was already beginning to have a quaintly old-fashioned ring to it. In his summary of the experimental film and video scene in the late 1990s, A.L. Rees describes a lively debate between those practitioners who felt that the internet meant the death of the "old" media and those who simply saw it as adding to the range of artistic possibilities available.[37] The Lottery-funded work of this period represents a snapshot of this rapidly evolving mediascape.

It is well worth reiterating that the total amount of Lottery money awarded to these 35 Artists' Film and Video projects was less than £800,000. This was the kind of sum which was routinely awarded to single feature film projects, such as *Get Real*. The scheme was therefore extremely cost-effective and scored highly in terms of value for money. These projects represent the Arts Council of England making the most of its traditional strengths, such as building relationships with artists, and experimenting with new technologies and their aesthetic implications, but such objectives are arguably a very long way away from the populism of "the people's Lottery". The originator of the scheme, David Curtis, relates how he convinced then Head of the Lottery Film department, Carolyn Lambert, to support his idea for an Artists' Film and Video scheme funded by the Lottery.[38] Lambert's initial reservations were overcome by the automatic "distribution", which the projects would receive as a result of the Visual Arts department's touring initiatives. Although this was simpler than organising commercial distribution for feature films, it could effectively help the Film department to meet their targets surrounding accessibility and public benefit. This is somewhat ironic given the specialist nature of these projects and their audiences, but it is also important to remember that many of these works will have a far longer "shelf life" than most commercial feature films. Although there is no way of accurately quantifying how many people have seen or experienced these

[36] Production details: "Home Road Movies," accessed January 2005, http://freespace.virgin.net/robert.bradfilms/hrm.html.

[37] Rees cites TV producer John Wyver's view that the traditional media faced a "meltdown" as the internet grew exponentially. Rees, *A History of Experimental Film and Video* (London: BFI, 1999), 104–5.

[38] David Curtis, interview with the author, October 2004.

works, the numbers are likely to be low, but it is equally likely that they will continue to grow for many years to come.

Short Films

The short film is by definition a mongrel form, given that it is characterised primarily by its brevity rather than any other formal criterion.[39] As noted above, it has a continued presence within the contemporary artists' film and video sector, which echoes its importance in the history of avant-garde practice. The short is economical—both financially and aesthetically—and has often enabled filmmakers to make the maximum impact with the minimum means. But its use is by no means exclusive to the cinematic underground, animated or documentary shorts, being a vital element of mixed exhibition schedules, common in cinemas until the single feature screening model was adopted across the industry. Since this change, the purpose of the short film for the industry as a whole has been largely restricted to training and development. The graduation films of trainee directors or producers can function as important "calling cards", evidence of a filmmaker's ability, which facilitates the move into other, more commercially viable forms. Partly as a result, shorts have an established presence on television, where they help to fulfil the public service ethos of several major broadcasters.[40] Since the mid-1990s, the short film form has been through a revival thanks to its suitability for transmission over the internet, with websites such as *Atom Films* catering to established filmmakers, and more recently, a deluge of user-generated content on *You Tube*. Meanwhile, digital projection in cinemas offers a possible return to mixed programming schedules and a means of overcoming the prohibitive costs of producing 35mm prints for low-budget filmmakers.[41] Given these developments, the investment of National Lottery money in short filmmaking can be justified both by the medium's history and by its future.

Unlike the Artists' Film and Video awards, short films were assessed by the same criteria as longer feature films, and were supported by each of the four Arts Councils. The Scottish Arts Council placed a special emphasis

[39] Eileen Elsey and Andrew Kelly restrict their study of the form to films lasting 30 minutes or less. See Elsey and Kelly, *In Short: A Guide to Short Film-Making in the Digital Age* (London: BFI, 2002).

[40] e.g. BBC Scotland's *Tartan Shorts* series or Channel Four's *Shooting Gallery*.

[41] Funding the transition to digital projection is one of the UK Film Council's key priorities. See UK Film Council, "Digital Screen Network," *UKFC*, accessed March 2006, http://www.ukfilmcouncil.org.uk/funding/distributionandexhibition/dsn/.

on shorts by enabling organisations to apply for funding for several films at one time, as well as offering help to select the films they wished to make.[42] As detailed in Chapter Three, between 1995 and 2000, the Arts Councils spent £4.8m on 174 shorts which had a total budget of £11.8m. Many of these were screened as part of festivals, on television, or over the internet, and a lucky few were seen in mainstream cinemas, "packaged" with other Lottery-funded product. Graham Fink's *Z* (2000), for example, was shown before Kenneth Branagh's *Love's Labour's Lost* (2000) in some cinemas.[43] Very few are commercially available, although Luke Morris' critically acclaimed DVD compilation series *Cinema 16* contains Lynne Ramsey's *Gasman* (1997) with a useful director's commentary.[44] In order to provide an overview of Lottery-funded short films, a random selection of 20 of those held at the National Film and Television Archive was sampled, as detailed in Table 5-2. The most common running time of these films is around 12 minutes; the shortest, *Father and Daughter*, only 8 minutes, and the longest, Bill Douglas' posthumously filmed script *The Ring of Truth*, 30 minutes' long. The average budget for live action shorts was around £68,000, whilst animated shorts were considerably more expensive, costing around £150,000 each.[45] There is no strong generic trend across the films, with drama, comedy, animation and other genres all represented in proportions comparable to their frequency in mainstream features.

Animated films represented a significant area of overlap between the Artists' Film and Video scheme and Lottery funding for short films. Liverpudlian animator Phil Mulloy received awards from both sources: *Season's Greetings* (1999) was funded as a short, whilst a year later, the first part of his *Intolerance* trilogy found favour from the AFV panel. Mulloy's partner, the feminist artist and filmmaker Vera Neubauer, was awarded £75,000 from the Arts Council of Wales in 1996 to make *La Luna* (*Over the Moon*), which was completed and screened at film festivals in 1999. Both Mulloy and Neubauer make confrontational films informed by sexual politics, and *La Luna* is no exception; the film attacks the role of storytelling in the ideological process of reinforcing gender roles

---

[42] Scottish Arts Council, *National Lottery Film Production Guidelines* (Edinburgh: SAC, 1998), 6–7.
[43] Source: SIFT database, BFI Information Services.
[44] *Cinema 16: British Short Films*, compiled by Luke Morris, Momac Films Ltd., 2003. For more information see *Cinema 16*, http://www.cinema16.co.uk, accessed January 2007.
[45] For financial details of each award see James Caterer, "The People's Pictures Appendices," *Google Sites*, https://sites.google.com/a/brookes.ac.uk/jamescaterer/.

Table 5-2: Sample of twenty Lottery-funded short films.

AC	Year	Production Company	*Title*	Director	Genre
SAC	1996	Lomand TV	*The Ring of Truth*	Richard Downes	drama
SAC	1997	Sigma Films	*California Sunshine*	David MacKenzie	thriller
SAC	1997	Holy Cow /BBC/SFPF	*Gasman*	Lynne Ramsey	drama
SAC	1997	Fresh Film & TV	*Karmic Mothers*	John Tiffany	black comedy
ACE	1997	Illuminated Films	*T.R.A.N.S.I.T.*	Piet Kroon	animated
ACE	1997	Tapson Steel/BBC	*The Future Lasts A Long Time*	David Jackson	road movie
ACE	1997	Hot Property Films	*Wavelengths*	Pratibha Parmar	gay interest
ACW	1998	Tiger Lilly/BFI/C4	*Anthrakitis*	Sara Sugarman	black comedy
SAC	1998	Cormorant/C4	*Darkness in the Afternoon*	Christine Winford	drama
ACE	1998	Faction Films	*Deep Freeze*	Virginia Heath	drama
SAC	1998	Screenbase	*Lay of the Land*	Fraser Macdonald	gay interest
ACW	1999	Fiction Factory/BBC	*Edith's Finger*	Jon Jones	black comedy
ACW	1999	Spectre Films	*La Luna/Over The Moon*	Vera Neubauer	animated
ACE	1999	Sparkler Films	*Panic*	Omid Nooshin	thriller
ACE	1999	Wiggin O'Neal Films	*Safer*	Rachel Tillotson	drama
ACW	2000	Little Dragon Films	*A Day Out*	Helen Grace	drama
ACE	2000	Cloudrunner	*Father And Daughter*	Michael Dudok de Wit	animated
ACE	2000	Alchymie	*Ho Ho Ho*	J. J. Keith	drama
ACE	2000	Little Dancer Films	*The Uninvited*	Daniel Simpson	horror
ACE	2000	Panopticon Pictures	*To Have And To Hold*	John Hardwick	black comedy

for growing female subjects. Blending heavily stylised live action with animation featuring a dysfunctional family of handmade puppet rats, the film gives Neubauer the unusual but accurate credit of "knitted and directed by…" *La Luna* therefore works within the feminist tradition of revalorising modes of creativity often demoted to the private domestic sphere. In this case, both handicraft and bedtime stories become the media for a nightmarish revisionist fairy tale about vivisection, sexual violence and domestic abuse. This is certainly not animation for children, but other Lottery-funded animated shorts fit more easily into a tradition of family-oriented storytelling. Dudok De Wit's *Father and Daughter*, for instance, an Anglo-Dutch co-production made by a Dutch animator then based in London, is a gentle, melancholic tale of a young girl growing into old age as she waits for the return of her absent father, told without dialogue and featuring tiny hand-drawn figures in silhouette against dramatic sepia or indigo washes.[46] It won an Academy Award for best animated short film in 2001.

In terms of live-action filmmaking, the short can provide a valuable space for articulating the concerns of groups excluded from mainstream narrative practice. Amongst the shorts which received Lottery funding, Neubauer's feminist concerns were echoed by academic and filmmaker Virginia Heath's *Deep Freeze* (1998) which tells a strange story of a young woman's obsession with her fridge. The domestic appliance was left to her in her suicidal father's will, becoming a literal embodiment of patriarchal control which ruins the woman's sexual relationship and drives her close to madness. Another tale of female desire and technology, *Wavelengths* (1997), explores the potential for cyberspace encounters within the lesbian community. Mona (Indra Oré) gets over the end of a previous relationship and begins a possible new one after an experiment with cybersex in a gay chat room. The film is light-hearted and frothy, possibly in an attempt to counter the somewhat dour reputation of lesbian avant-garde filmmaking. Fraser Macdonald's *Lay of the Land* (1998), takes the opposite approach by bringing danger and darkness into a site of frivolity and celebration. Examining the notion of homophobia as repressed homosexual desire, this naturalistic drama is played out in real time in a Glasgow gay bar. Drag queen John (Steven Rimkus) is both fascinated and repelled by an aggressive bar-fly who claims to have taken part in gay-bashing and yet appears to be flirting with him. A co-production

---

[46] *Father and Daughter* was also supported by European funding from public and television sources. See *Acme Filmworks*, accessed January 2007, http://www.acmefilmworks.com/.

between the BFI, C4 and the Scottish Arts Council, the film's credits have a long list of "Thanks to…" which suggests a network of benefactors from the gay community, including *The Pink Paper* and the Terrence Higgins Trust.

Not all short filmmaking is concerned with formal experimentation or pushing the ideological envelope. Many "calling card" shorts are genre films in miniature, as the use of generic conventions can provide a valuable narrative shorthand for filmmakers operating within the short's temporal confines. English writer/director Daniel Simpson's *The Uninvited* (2000) invokes both the gothic fantasy of Hammer Horror and the uncanny slasher films of Dario Argento. It opens in a dark, creepy apartment at night as a storm rages outside, and a decrepit landlord shows around a new female tenant—a French student. The film has little dialogue, instead using sound effects and dense *mise-en-scène* to build an atmosphere of menace around the resourceful but clearly vulnerable student. The monster revealed at the climax is created through a stop-motion computer animation technique, which makes it move like the fantasy creatures in films such as *Jason and the Argonauts* (1963). *The Uninvited* is therefore an exercise in nostalgia for a more innocent and less self-referential era of horror. Omid Nooshin's *Panic* (1999) is a thriller which pays homage to Hitchcock with a bold credits sequence, ending with a visual match between a close-up of a startled woman's eyes and the headlights of an oncoming car. The limited running time of the short cannot deliver the pleasures of a labyrinthine, twist-laden plot structure, and so instead Nooshin focuses upon one simple but terrifying incident: the accidental kidnapping of a boy during a car-jacking from a garage forecourt. Costing just £40,000—half of which was provided by the Lottery—the film has surprisingly high production values with some convincing stunt work, careful editing, and a polished orchestral score.

Other shorts work with genre in a less straight-forward, more playful fashion. *The Future Lasts a Long Time* (1997) takes its title from the autobiography of French political philosopher Louis Althusser, but is determinedly apolitical and nihilistic in tone. A knowing voice-over openly references *Bonnie and Clyde* (1967), and the film, as a whole, is soaked in the American independent sensibility. Young lovers May and Jimmy (played by then real-life couple Samantha Morton and Hans Matheson) leave the city behind in an attempt to score drugs, and become involved in a fatal shooting. But the English road movie can never have too far to go, and neither do the young couple, their criminal odyssey fizzling out into boredom. Developed by the BFI and Channel 4, the film was co-directed by Coky Giedroyc, who went on to make the Lottery-funded feature *Stella Does Tricks* (1997). Another filmmaker who used the short format to refine his style before moving into features was David Mackenzie. His *California Sunshine* (1997) similarly deflates the gangster pretensions of its young Scottish couple, whose small-time drug-dealing almost gets them into serious trouble. The film plays their dilemma for comedy, with a case of mistaken identity leading to a pair of visiting Christians discovering the wonders of ecstasy. The witty conclusion has one character state that the 1990s are "just the sixties upside down", an ironic reference to the atmosphere of "Cool Britannia" current at the time of filming. Mackenzie made two more shorts before his feature-length reworking of the Scottish gothic, *The Last Great Wilderness* (2002), and the critically-acclaimed art film *Young Adam* (2003).

California Sunshine is one of a group of films that suggest a particular affinity with black comedy in the shorts made with the help of Lottery funding. Two films made in Wales, *Edith's Finger* (1998) and *Anthrakitis* (1998) feature headstrong elderly women dealing with death in very different ways. In Jon Jones' film, Edith is a stroke victim only able to communicate through tapping her finger and visibly frustrated with her existence in an old people's home. She appears delighted with her new electric wheelchair, gifted by fundraisers, but only because it allows her to escape the well-wishers and drive herself into the lake. The film benefits from impressive naturalistic central performances, particularly from Shelagh Fraser as Edith, and has strong cinematography which is unafraid of examining her world-weary visage. Sara Sugarman would later make the mainstream Welsh comedy *Very Annie Mary* (2000), but her *Anthrakitis* is an altogether darker and more disturbing portrait of old age. Sugarman cast veteran comedy actress Liz Smith in the lead role of Dolly, a deranged crone living in squalor in rural Wales. Dolly has been hoarding coal since her husband was killed down the pit, and is so paranoid about her straight-talking niece stealing it that she fantasises about beating her to death. The film's relatively high budget of £80,000 (half-funded by the Lottery with further funding from the BFI and Channel 4) is justified by its ornate and absolutely filthy set, crammed with rats, rotting food and dangerous wiring.

Compared to Sugarman's baroque excesses, John Hardwick's *To Have and to Hold* (2000) is a cold and brutal piece of stripped-down storytelling. A woman comes round after a car accident in a forest to find that not only is her partner dead, but also that she is unable to release his grey rigor mortis grip on her own hand. After two days going through shock, grief and fear alone amongst the trees, she is forced to take drastic and stomach-churning action in order to survive. Hardwick's background was in conceptual art, underground filmmaking and music videos before he began to find budgets for more ambitious pieces of work.[47] *To Have and to Hold* resulted from a commission from the BFI and Film Four Lab for an eleven-minute film costing £40,000. His subsequent award of a further £30,000 from the Arts Council enabled a longer pre-production period on what was a complex shoot:

> We shot for six days, because you only had useable light from ten in the morning to about three or four in the afternoon, so it was really tricky. We needed a lot of quad bikes to get people in and out of the wood, we destroyed a car, so yes it was pricey.[48]

The film also features a well-known German performer, Suzanne Lothar, who brought with her a flavour of European art cinema. However, Hardwick had difficulties dealing with the actor's ego: "I don't think she was happy, and I wasn't, but I think she delivered."[49] Despite the successful results (the film was a hit of the Edinburgh festival in 2000); Hardwick is openly uneasy with the demands of bigger-budget filmmaking, and dismissive of the idea that making a feature is the natural progression from shorts: "I wouldn't want to spend two years making *Con Air* or even *Secrets and Lies*."[50] He has since made more shorts, documentaries and pop videos.

Whilst *To Have and to Hold* is most certainly adult material, a surprisingly common thematic element in the Lottery-funded short films are the concerns of children. Of the short films sampled, Helen Grace's *A Day Out* (2000), J. J. Keith's *Ho Ho Ho* (2000), Richard Downes' *Ring of Truth* (1996), and Rachel Tillotson's *Safer* (1999) all feature lead roles for boys around the age of eight or nine. This trend might perhaps be attributed to the logic that posits the short as a space for those commonly excluded by mainstream narrative. One of the best-known of the Lottery funded shorts also centres on a childish protagonist, although this time a little girl is brought to the fore. *Gasman* (1997), Lynne Ramsey's third in a series of prize-winning shorts, depicts an eventful evening in the life of Lynne (played by Ramsey's niece), a young girl who discovers that her father has another family of which she was previously unaware. The film's

---

[47] Hardwick's background and the production history of *To Have and To Hold* are described in Elsey and Kelly, *In Short,* 93–102.
[48] John Hardwick interviewed in Elsey and Kelly, *In Short*, 98.
[49] Elsey and Kelly, *In Short*, 100.
[50] Elsey and Kelly, *In Short*, 102.

pivotal sequence is a family party where Lynne makes her discovery, which, as Ramsey describes, was shot using cinema verité techniques:

> This was a real party… this isn't scripted, this is really happening, all these kids having this mad time. I think what we were trying to capture was that feeling of really being there, all the fun and excitement, the hyperactivity, getting tired… Just a normal kids party, a bit crazy! So it directed itself really.[51]

This extreme naturalistic approach combines with the lyrical, slightly off-kilter cinematography of Alwin Kuchler to create a heightened, "poetic" realist style which has become Ramsey's directorial trademark. In *Gasman*, this visual texture is closely allied to a child's point of view, and this is the element which most clearly prefigures Ramsey's subsequent piece of fully-fledged, Lottery-funded art cinema, *Ratcatcher* (1999), which I go on to discuss in the following section.

The Lottery-funded short films sampled above give an indication of a lively field of filmmaking practice, which deserves to receive more attention. Although these films were more expensive to produce than the artists' film and video works highlighted in the previous section, their public benefit is easier to define in terms of vital "research and development" for the UK film industry. Without the training ground of short films, many young directors would be unable to refine their style and demonstrate their readiness to move into large-scale filmmaking. From this sample alone, Lynne Ramsey, David MacKenzie, Sara Sugarman and Coky Giedroyc all went on to make Lottery-funded feature films.[52] However, the comments made by John Hardwick—who had no interest in "spending two years making *Con Air*, or even *Secrets and Lies*"—illustrate that, for many filmmakers, the short film is considered an end in itself; a pure and immediate form allowing much greater creative freedom than feature films.[53] Markedly, it is difficult to imagine artists and animators such as Phil Mulloy or Vera Neubauer working in any other form. It is also notable that, despite the large amounts of Lottery money awarded to prestigious talents, such as Kenneth Branagh, Mike Leigh and Michael Winterbottom, so far the only director to win an Oscar for a

---

[51] Lynne Ramsey, director's commentary, "Gasman," *Cinema 16 - British Short Films DVD* (Momac Films Ltd, 2002).
[52] These were *Ratcatcher* (1999), *The Last Great Wilderness* (2000), *Very Annie Mary* (2000) and *Stella Does Tricks* (1997).
[53] Elsey and Kelly, *In Short*, 102.

Lottery-funded film is Dutch animator Michael Dudok de Wit for the minimalist *Father and Daughter.*

Feature-length Art Cinema

The category of Lottery-funded feature-length art cinema is less rigid and more diffuse than those of artists' film and video or shorts films. Differing and sometimes conflicting criteria exist with which to identify such projects, although they tend to have lower-than-average budgets, be exhibited at festivals and art-house cinemas, and focus upon the director in their marketing, rather than their stars or genre. A further set of criteria exist with regard to the formal qualities of art cinema, such as the narrational and aesthetic strategies identified by David Bordwell. Individually, these yardsticks are not adequate: for example, the problems of obtaining wide distribution for many UK feature films means that some literary adaptations or independently produced dramas are shown only in art-houses when they might have been equally at home in the multiplexes. However, used in combination with one another, they can provide a reasonably coherent group of Lottery-funded films which are recognisable as "art cinema". This is not a large group of films, depending on how rigidly the criteria are applied somewhere between 10 and 15 films qualify out of the 95 Lottery-funded features which were released between 1995 and 2000.[54] Their budgets are indeed lower than average, tending to be around £2m or less, and they each received between one-third and half of their budgets from the Arts Councils. There were no clear examples of art cinema features produced by the smaller home nations of Northern Ireland and Wales, suggesting that it may take a larger and more diverse production slate to make room for these projects.

In Scotland however, there was a distinctive flowering of art cinema in the 1990s.[55] Lynne Ramsey's *Ratcatcher* (1999) is amongst the most highly praised of the Lottery-funded films, and its critical success is due, in no small part, to Ramsey's familiarity with the history and codes of European art cinema.[56] Ramsey came to filmmaking through photography,

---

[54] For more details of the 95 Lottery-funded features see James Caterer, "The People's Pictures Appendices," *Google Sites*, https://sites.google.com/a/brookes .ac.uk/jamescaterer/.

[55] See Duncan Petrie, "Devolving British Cinema: The New Scottish Cinema and the European Art Film," *Cinéaste,* 26:4 (Autumn 2001): 55–57.

[56] *Ratcatcher* reviews: Andrew O'Hagan, "This is my film of the year," *Daily Telegraph*, November 12, 1999, 25; Peter Bradshaw, "Poetry from the rubbish tip," *Guardian Unlimited*, November 12, 1999, accessed June 2003, http://

and although she trained at the National Film and Television School, her enrolment was in cinematography rather than directing. Whilst her films follow in the social realist tradition of Ken Loach, in many ways, they also have an unusual visual quality, shifting them away from naturalism. Ramsey's career has closely followed the paradigm of the art cinema auteur, with her authorial signature clearly placed on each work she produces, but she also understands the marketing value of playing this role. Whilst discussing the potential audience for *Ratcatcher*, she claimed to be "chasing the European art-house market" in order to keep her first film "as pure as possible."[57] This desire for purity was aided in its early stages by BBC Scotland, and particularly by Head of Drama Andrea Calderwood, who then went on to run one of the three Lottery "franchises", Pathé Pictures.[58] Calderwood's brought three well-developed projects with her to kick-start Pathé's production slate—*An Ideal Husband*, *The Darkest Light*, and *Ratcatcher*, which gained access to Lottery funding of £615,000 towards its budget of £2m. Her French bosses expressed most enthusiasm about *The Darkest Light*, Simon Beaufoy's first script since *The Full Monty*, but it was the combination of the popular success enjoyed by their glossy Oscar Wilde adaptation and the critical acclaim heaped on Ramsey's debut which initially made Pathé the most impressive of the three franchise companies.[59]

Ratcatcher is structured as a series of atmospheric episodes where moment is more important than plot, and character takes precedence over narrative tension. The story begins with a genuinely dramatic incident, the accidental drowning of a small boy in a dingy Glasgow canal, but this is less important as a plot device than as a tonal key and a source of guilt for the film's young protagonist James (William Eadie). Although the film's bleak working-class environment and use of non-professional actors are familiar realist techniques, Ramsey and her director of photography Alwin Kuchler make use of low-key natural lighting, unusual framing, and subtle temporal effects, such as a languorous slowmotion to create a sense of heightened realism. Similarly, the period setting of the 1970s public sector strikes, which saw rubbish bags pile up across Glasgow generates little of the explicit political commentary of social realist drama. Rather, it

---

film.guardian.co.uk/News_Story/Critic_Review/Guardian_Film_of_the_week/0,4267,102485,00.html; Alexander Walker, "Spellbound in Glasgow's ghetto', *Evening Standard*, November 11, 1999, 30.

[57] Ramsey cited in Nick James, "Medium Cool," *Sight and Sound,* 8:8, August 1998, 15.

[58] For more information see the case study of Pathé Pictures in Chapter 3.

[59] Andrea Calderwood, interview with the author, January 2006.

provides an other-worldly, almost medieval backdrop to James' childhood innocence and cruelty. *Ratcatcher* also has vivid glimpses of fantasy related to James' unspoken urge to escape. Whilst playing in a new, unfinished house, James leaps enthusiastically out of a window frame into a golden yellow cornfield under a bright blue sky; in effect, temporarily jumping into an idealised notion of sunny, carefree childhood. The same cornfield features in the happier half of the film's double-ending, which is a good example of the narrative device of ambiguity, as described by David Bordwell.[60] The final shot is a direct homage to Francois Truffaut's *Les Quatre Cents Coups* (1959), as James looks directly into the camera and breaks into a childish grin. *Ratcatcher* thus represents a bridge between the traditions of British documentary realism and those of European art cinema.

Ramsey's background in photography gives her film a quality of stillness and silence, two elements almost entirely lacking from Andrew Kötting's frenetic, anarchic *Gallivant* (1997). Kötting also came to filmmaking from a visual arts perspective, but one which grew out of the avant-garde video and performance art sectors which flourished in the 1980s. His persona as an artist, as described by *The Independent*, is "the ordinary geezer… who just happens to have an MA from the Slade and an interest in conceptual art."[61] He has a relationship with the Arts Council which stretches back as far as 1986, when his degree film short *Klippity-Klop* (1984) was bought for the Council's collection, and in 1990, another short *Hoi Polloi* was jointly funded by the Visual Arts department and the BBC.[62] In 1994, he made an eight-minute "pilot" version of *Gallivant*, which was used as a pitch to the Arts Council in the very early days of Lottery -funding for film production. In the period before David Curtis set up his specialised Artists' Film and Video scheme, for which *Gallivant* would surely have been ideal, there was little enthusiasm for the film. Ben Gibson at the BFI Production Board suggested that Kötting's abstract idea about filming a journey all the way around the coast of Britain would benefit from having central characters.[63] Kötting decided that the journey should become a generational road trip, with the artist being accompanied

[60] David Bordwell, "The Art Cinema as a Mode of Film Practice," *Film Criticism,* 4:1 (Fall 1979): 56–64.

[61] Liese Spencer, "Travels With My Gran," *The Independent*, September 26, 1997, 14.

[62] See "Andrew Kötting," *Luxonline*, accessed 3 March 2005, http://www.luxonline.org.uk/artists/id/ 900985/,.

[63] Wally Hammond, "'Gallivant' is a Coast-to-coast Study of British Eccentricity," *Time Out*, September 3, 1997, 23.

by his grandmother, Gladys, and his seven year old daughter, Eden. This more emotive and personal proposal won the approval of Lottery funding to the tune of £170,000—around half its total budget.

Kötting, his relatives, and a small crew spent three months travelling over 6,000 miles, from Bexhill-on-Sea in East Sussex, along the south coast to Land's End, up through Wales, Northern England and Scotland, and then back down the east coast of Britain. Using a mixture of Super 8 and 16 mm film stocks as well as digital video, the finished film contains a rich variety of visual textures, colour and black-and-white, time-lapse footage, and strange disjunctures between image and sound.[64] As Gibson predicted, *Gallivant*'s emotional centre is the relationship between Gladys and Eden, both of whom, as Kötting's voice-over communicates, have a limited life expectancy: Eden has a rare genetic disorder called Joubert's Syndrome, which makes sign language her principal means of communication; and Gladys may be an elderly lady, but she is also a useful foil for her grandson's art school tomfoolery: when he dives into freezing cold Scottish seawater to make his daughter laugh, she berates him as a "silly bugger, daft as they make 'em." Alongside these familial episodes, Kötting interviews characters they meet along the way, giving a clear preference to eccentrics, such as the attendant at the public lavatory in the Scottish Glens, who has turned his convenience into an art gallery. The filmmaker's interventions become increasingly strange; in Suffolk, he stops a confused lollipop lady just to ask her whether he looks like a monk.[65] In the end, *Gallivant* completes its circular journey and structure with Gladys and Eden back on the beach at Bexhill in matching red overcoats, an image needing no avant-garde trickery to be both forceful and arresting. Nonetheless, Kötting's film is proof of the potential for cross-fertilisation between the Arts Council's long-standing artists' film expertise and their new Lottery-funded feature filmmaking.

The autobiographical elements of *Gallivant* are presented in a playful documentary mode. By contrast, Sally Potter's *The Tango Lesson* (1997) uses a self-reflexive fictional frame and the narrative possibilities of dance to tell an equally personal story. Potter not only wrote and directed the film but also stars in it, playing a film director called Sally who is trying to make a film about the tango whilst having a love affair with her dancing partner, Pablo Veron. By taking on the lead role in the film herself, Potter

---

[64] Iain Sinclair describes Kötting's technical achievements in "Big Granny and Little Eden," *Sight and Sound*, 7:9, September 1997, 20.

[65] For Margaret Dickinson, the film suffers from Kötting's presence as he tends to silence the potential multiplicity of voices. "Gallivant," *Vertigo*, 1:7 (Autumn 1997): 28–9.

sparked off a surprisingly vigorous critical debate surrounding "self-indulgence".[66] *The Independent*'s Matthew Sweet was typical of those angered by the move, calling *The Tango Lesson* "Potter's passionate love letter to herself", and accusing her of "appalling narcissism."[67] Potter countered this hostility with pragmatism, pointing out that the role called for an English woman about her age who could be believable as a filmmaker and have studied tango to a professional level. In other interviews, clearly exasperated, she went on the counter-attack: "What's wrong with perusing something you're passionate about? I think *everybody* should be more self-indulgent."[68] Geoff Andrew accurately describes the film as "far less authorially reserved than most home-grown product", arguing that, whilst British audiences and critics might expect this level of personal content from European filmmakers, we seem less forgiving with our own auteurs.[69] Financial logic would suggest that the success enjoyed by Potter's previous feature *Orlando* (1992) should have made her follow-up project an attractive proposition for investors. However, Potter struggled to find resources until the Arts Council of England committed around one-third of the £3.2m budget, and this struggle became a central theme of her new autobiographical work.

The Tango Lesson contains explicit commentary on the difficulties of film financing and the potential for conflict between personal vision and business acumen. As the film begins, Sally is attempting to write a script about the fashion industry called *Rage*, described as a "treatise on beauty and the glamorisation of death". This is glimpsed on-screen in flashes of excessively stylish colour to contrast with the rest of the film's austere black-and-white. Following a scene illustrating the director's discomfort with the film's Hollywood producers, she abandons her script, impulsively deciding to explore her passion for the tango instead. She later comments to her dancing teacher, lover and co-star Veron that the money for her dance film will not arrive until "people have as much faith in me as I do in you." This dialogue is in keeping with the spirit of the film's homage to the classic Hollywood musical. Lucy Fischer reads Potter's rejection of her own intellectual thriller in favour of the exuberance and spontaneity of

---

[66] Anne Bilson called the film "a top contender for most self-indulgent movie of the decade." Bilson, "The Tango Lesson," *Sunday Telegraph*, November 30, 1997, review section, 11.

[67] Matthew Sweet, "The Tango Lesson," *The Independent on Sunday*, November 30, 1997, section 2, 11.

[68] Liese Spencer, "Out of Step," *The Independent*, November 29, 1997, 17.

[69] Geoff Andrew, "Sense and sensuality," *Time Out*, November 12, 1997, 25–6.

the musical in relation to a shifting dynamic within feminist discourse.[70] Noting that ideas of "pleasure" in viewing paradigms had been rehabilitated since Laura Mulvey's influential critique of the 1970s, "Visual Pleasure and Narrative Cinema", Fischer locates *The Tango Lesson* within a framework informed by both politics and passion. This strategy won Potter notable support from *The Evening Standard*'s Alexander Walker, who praised the film as a "wonderfully uplifting bit of entertainment".[71] Walker could overcome his aversion to Lottery-funded films provided they were suitably highbrow—although he gives the Arts Council no credit for *The Tango Lesson*.

Potter's film skips along the boundary between dance and cinema, whilst another Lottery-funded art film, *I Could Read the Sky* (1999) represents the culmination of an expansive multi-media project encompassing photography, prose, theatre, music and film. It began with photographer Steve Pyke's interest in the large Irish émigré population resident in his local London borough of Camden.[72] Many of these men left home after World War II and subsequently became vital workers in the rebuilding of England's post-war infrastructure, with their faces and stories becoming a recurring theme in Pyke's work. When Pyke met Irish writer Timothy O'Grady, they began to collaborate on a book where images and text would work together in ways outside of the usual caption/illustration relationship: the result, *I Could Read the Sky*, was published in 1997.[73] The book integrates Pyke's black-and-white images of faces, landscapes or enigmatic details with O'Grady's lyrical prose; the memories of an Irish man lying alone in his room, taking stock of his life as it approaches an end. A series of live events grew out of the book, combining O'Grady's reading of the text with slide shows of Pyke's photographs, and adding Celtic music from vocalist and composer Iarla O'Lionaird. Pyke's partner, the artist Nichola Bruce, helped to put the book together, and whilst doing so had begun to see the potential for a moving image version of the material. Quickly creating a storyboard style-script based on illustrations, she won the support of independent film

---

70 Lucy Fischer, "'Dancing through the Minefield': Passion, Pedagogy, Politics, and Production in *The Tango Lesson*," *Cinema Journal*, 43:3 (Spring 1994): 42–58.

71 Alexander Walker, "Sally puts on her dancing shoes," *Evening Standard*, November 27, 1997, 27.

72 This narrative of the project's conception and growth is built from the extensive biographies and interviews included with the DVD release of *I Could Read The Sky* (Artificial Eye, 2003).

73 Timothy O'Grady and Steve Pyke, *I Could Read The Sky* (London: Harvill, 1997).

producer Janine Marmot, who subsequently convinced the BFI, the Irish Film Board and then the Arts Council of England to contribute towards an extremely tight budget of around £470,000.

The finished film is an intricate construction interweaving layers of film and digital footage, anchored around a monologue performed by the grizzled Irish poet Dermot Healey, playing "The Man". His memories are rendered through fragments of overlapping images and sounds, often shot with the camera approximating the physical point of view of the central character. Digital editing techniques built up a distinctive visual approach, here described by the film's editor Catherine Creed:

> I was using a lot of superimposition and maybe an image would drift up to 60%, drift back down to 20% and up to 30%, which gave this lovely ghosting effect which became integral to the film's style.[74]

The film largely eschews the crisp monochrome of Pyke's photographs, being shot in colour with occasional tinting, but O'Grady's words survive intact, if in a somewhat truncated version. There is a very loose chronology based around the life story of The Man, whose memories begin in childhood in rural Ireland and end with a tragic love affair cut short by death. Music is provided by O'Lionaird, who had previously worked on the live events, adding to the impression that the film is fundamentally a useful conduit for a set of ideas which grew out of a network of collaborations between artists from different disciplines. Significantly, this network was able to draw upon public funding mechanisms at almost each step of the way. Pyke's award from the Arts Council in 1995 to work on a project called "Acts of Memory" built towards the book published with the assistance of the Arts Council of England. The film was then made almost entirely with public subsidy, enabling artistic freedom but on rather meagre financial resources. Nichola Bruce has since been awarded a fellowship from the National Endowment for Science, Technology and the Arts (NESTA) to support her continuing work on perception and memory.[75] In this sense, *I Could Read the Sky* represents a successful marriage between art and public finance.

Art cinema features such as *I Could Read the Sky*, *The Tango Lesson*, *Gallivant* and *Ratcatcher* are not generally made with the expectations of

---

[74] Catherine Creed interviewed by Jeanine Hurley, "Cutting the Sky," *Film Ireland*, 75 (April/May 2000): 40.

[75] NESTA was set up after the other main Lottery distributors, in 1998. Its interdisciplinary structure was designed to allow a more targeted, strategic approach to funding. See www.nesta.org.uk.

large profits. Simply on the basis of their UK box-office returns, they were all financial failures; the biggest domestic gross went to *Ratcatcher*, which, even with the assistance of Pathé's dedicated distribution wing, could only return £432,000 of its £2m budget. However, it is important to consider not just the amounts generated, but also how much was spent on prints and advertising in order to generate them. *Ratcatcher* was released in the UK in November 1999 on 15 prints, generating a per-print average of £28,000. By comparison, the bigger budget commercial success *An Ideal Husband* generated £15,800 for each of its 182 prints. Thanks to Sally Potter's relatively high-profile, *The Tango Lesson* performed equally solidly, although it did not come close to covering its costs in the UK alone. However, its audience across Europe was more impressive, overall generating around 10 times as many admissions as it received in the UK.[76] Both *Gallivant* and *I Could Read the Sky* fared less well at the box office.[77] These latter two films are much closer to the artists' film sector, with projects valued by different sets of cultural criteria. These are connected to the Arts Councils' traditional values of promoting artistic excellence outside of the constraints of financial risk and return.

However, the Arts Councils are also responsible for making art more accessible to the general public, and the allocation of Lottery funding for bigger-budget middlebrow feature films brought with it a new and unexpected means of meeting this objective in the shape of biopics concerning artists. These films engaged with British literary, musical, theatrical or artistic heritage through the lives of famous or infamous practitioners. For example, *Hilary and Jackie* (1997) is the story of the difficult relationship between the cellist Jacqueline du Pré and her sister Hilary. This was a notable critical success for the Lottery film scheme as it saw both its lead actresses, Emily Watson and Rachel Griffiths, nominated for Academy Awards in 1999. The film also attracted some controversy owing to its unflinching portrayal of Jackie's unattractive behaviour, the details of which were drawn from the book published by her sister after the cellist's death. *Pandaemonium* (2000) is an account of the romantic poets William Wordsworth and Samuel Taylor Coleridge, and their involvement with the French revolution. Other cultural figures represented in Lottery-funded biopics included Oscar Wilde and the popular playwrights Gilbert and Sullivan. The following case study considers how John Maybury's *Love is the Devil* brought Francis Bacon's work and

---

[76] *The Tango Lesson* admissions: UK: 53 696, France: 51 332, Germany: 124,486, Italy: 126,764. Total in 36 European markets: 539,360. Source: *Lumiere Database*.

[77] Although *Gallivant*'s lavish DVD release suggests that there is demand for such projects across other release formats.

private life back into the public sphere, and the challenge this posed to the Arts Council of England's responsibility for the nation's artistic heritage.

Defying the Sanctity of the Past: *Love is the Devil*

In 1963, as part of its programme of art documentaries, the visual arts department at the Arts Council of Great Britain commissioned a film called *Francis Bacon: Paintings 1944–62.*[78] This eleven-minute short has no commentary, and begins with a series of silent zooms into images pasted onto what looks like a studio wall. There are fragments of stills from Eisenstein's *Battleship Potemkin* (1925), a reproduction from Rembrandt, and a series of photographs of a dog walking by Eadweard Muybridge. Next comes a sudden cut from Eisenstein's famous close-up of the nurse with shattered spectacles to one of several interpretations of this image by Francis Bacon. Discordant orchestral music begins, and the remainder of the film uses camera movement and editing to explore a series of Bacon's disturbing figurative paintings created during the period of his rapid rise to acclaim and notoriety. Three decades later, in 1996, the Arts Council of England's Lottery Film department collaborated with the BFI and the BBC to produce *Love is the Devil: Study for a Portrait of Francis Bacon.* This feature-length drama stars Derek Jacobi as Bacon and centres on the artist's sadomasochistic relationship with East End petty crook George Dyer (Daniel Craig). Directed by John Maybury, a former acolyte of Derek Jarman, it is a visually stylised piece of British art cinema.[79] Bacon's paintings, which formed the whole content of the earlier documentary, are entirely absent from the later biopic.[80] Instead Maybury incorporates motifs and techniques reminiscent of the artist's work, making the film a self-conscious representation of both Bacon's life and his art.

---

[78] Credits: Script and Film Treatment by David Thompson; Photographed by David Muir; Edited by Kevin Brownlow; Music by Elisabeth Lutyens. Available to view online at "Francis Bacon: Paintings 1944-62," *The Roland Collection of Films and Videos on Art*, accessed 13 January 2005, http://www.Roland collection.com/rolandcollection /section/14/ 599A.htm.

[79] Maybury assisted on the set design of *Jubilee* (1977) and edited several other Jarman films including *The Last of England* (1988). See Michael O'Pray, *Derek Jarman: Dreams of England* (London: BFI, 1996), 153–154.

[80] The production was denied access to the works by Bacon's protective legal estate. See Geoffrey Macnab, "Bohemian Rhapsody," *Sight and Sound,* 7:7, July 1997, 18–20.

There is more to unite these two films than their subject and shared institutional point of origin, with both using cinema to create a mediated experience of Bacon's art. The earlier documentary aims to recreate the feeling of viewing Bacon's work in a gallery context, but is not simply a slide show. The camera picks out details of the paintings and compares them through juxtaposition. The music is applied both to create rhythmic patterns of editing and also as a harsh aural equivalent of the violent nature of the imagery.[81] Maybury's film physically recreates images from Bacon's *oeuvre*, sometimes distorting figures and faces with thick glass filters and unusual lenses, or breaking the space of the frame into the triptych composition favoured in the paintings. Like the shots of the studio wall in the documentary, *Love is the Devil* also explores Bacon's visual influences, even featuring a scene depicting the artist's perverse pleasure whilst watching the Odessa steps massacre from *Battleship Potemkin*. But this sequence also reinforces the major difference between the two films: namely Bacon's presence or rather the illusion of such created through performance and narrative. So what knowledge is gained through this biographical approach to Bacon and his artistic legacy? What does the film have to say about the politics of artistic activity in 1960s Britain? And what, by implication, can it tell us about Lottery-funded artistic activity in the 1990s?

In formal terms, there are strong similarities between *Love is the Devil* and David Bordwell's template of art cinema narration. Bordwell points out that the biographical narrative is "especially apt for the art-film" owing to its episodic structure and tendency to be equivocal about character causality.[82] Bacon makes a charismatic protagonist, but his goals are wilfully obscure and events have a sense of randomness and unpredictability. This is clearly demonstrated in the sequence where Bacon first encounters George Dyer, when the thief breaks into the artist's studio. Bacon is completely unperturbed and casually invites Dyer to bed, thus beginning a relationship which develops only in terms of Dyer's disintegration.[83] The parallel narrative of Bacon's rise to fame is obliquely explained through a

[81] This music was by British modernist composer Elisabeth Lutyens, who went on to create scores for several Hammer Horror films including *The Skull* (1965).

[82] Bordwell's quoted examples are Satyajit Ray's *Apu* trilogy and François Truffaut's Antoine Doinel series. David Bordwell, *Narration In The Fiction Film* (London: Methuen, 1985), 207.

[83] This version of their meeting is probably apocryphal, although it is patterned around a tall tale attributed to Bacon himself in Andrew Sinclair's biography. See Sinclair, *Francis Bacon: His Life and Violent Times* (London: Sinclair-Stevenson, 1993), 197.

voice-over, which is philosophical rather than expositional in tone; there is little evidence here of the artist's ambition and drive, which is clearly described in other biographical texts. The film also fits Bordwell's schema of "expressive realism", which is used to "dramatize private mental processes."[84] This is particularly relevant to the sporadic insertion of Dyer's nightmares into the texture of the film, which are carefully rendered with visuals reminiscent of Bacon's imagery. In general, Maybury's direction seems much less interested in naturalism or period authenticity than in creating a heightened, stylised atmosphere. *Love is the Devil* also has a subtle layer of inter-textuality thanks to its cameos from a string of young British artists and designers from the 1990s, including Tracy Emin and Rifat Ozbek. This kind of anachronism serves, in Bordwell's terms, to signal "that the profilmic event is also a construct."[85] The result is a self-conscious mode of narration, inviting an intellectual as well as emotional response to the film's story.

The events making up the episodic narrative structure of *Love is the Devil* are taken from the memoirs written by Daniel Farson, who was a member of Bacon's infamous Soho entourage from 1951 onwards.[86] *The Gilded Gutter Life of Francis Bacon* is therefore unashamedly anecdotal in tone and openly affectionate of its subject: "I doubt if he was the greatest man I have ever known, but he was the most extraordinary."[87] However the focus of the film is not the friendship between Farson and Bacon, but rather the latter's sexual relationship with the troubled and eventually suicidal George Dyer. As Dyer also served as Bacon's model for a significant period, this dynamic invokes classical ideas of the artist and his muse.[88] By exploring the murky recesses of their violent and doomed relationship, the film seeks to explain—or even to dramatise—Bacon's art. This process triggers several of the key debates surrounding biography as a literary or cultural form: for instance, there is the issue of factual authenticity; Farson was not involved directly in this relationship, and therefore much of the information is second-hand and possibly

[84] Bordwell, *Narration*, 208.

[85] Bordwell, *Narration*, 210.

[86] Farson is rewarded for his services as "special consultant" to the film by becoming a character within it, who at one point interviews Bacon for his arts review television show.

[87] Daniel Farson, *The Gilded Gutter Life of Francis Bacon* (London: Century, 1993), 12.

[88] Dyer features repeatedly in Bacon's paintings from 1962 until his death in 1972, which in itself became the subject of "Triptych May–June 1973". See John Russell, *Francis Bacon* (London: Thames and Hudson, 1971), 166–7.

untrustworthy. In opposition to this empirical historical doubt is the post-structuralist critique of the importance placed upon the author (or artist) within literary (or artistic) criticism. As Peter France and William St. Clair note, this legacy has made it difficult to approach biography in a critical context "without some misgiving."[89] There are also important ethical questions surrounding the split between the private and the public spheres, and the thorny issue of reputation when reconstructing the life of a figure who is considered by some to be the greatest British artist of the twentieth century.

The opening sequence of *Love is the Devil* illustrates many of these tensions through a combination of expressionistic montage and historical reconstruction. Three different events are overlapped and woven together. In the first, an unidentified middle-aged man arrives home carrying a suitcase. He sits down on an unmade bed in a shabby room, strokes and then inhales from a pillow, into which he buries his head in a gesture of sadness. The second event is mysterious, both in its origin and in its connection with the first event: it is presented through a series of slow-motion fragments; a champagne bottle knocked to the floor, some pills, the lower half of an almost naked male figure staggering away from the camera. The sequence builds towards a third event, this time out of the bedroom and in the public arena of celebrity, signalled by shots of photographers and popping flashbulbs. A bright white space filled with an applauding crowd is the setting for Francis Bacon's formal introduction to the film's audience. A museum curator speaks in French, welcoming the artist to his exhibition at the Grand Palais in Paris: "This installation establishes Mr Bacon as one of the great painters of our time." Standing proudly next to the curator is the same middle-aged man who sat on the bed a few shots earlier, linking these two events together. Finally, the mystery of the fragmented second event is then reiterated through a motion-blurred close up of a male head, apparently in agonising pain, as the electronic soundtrack reaches a crescendo.

The pattern of editing suggests that the second event may have the status of memory or imagination in the mind of the central figure, who the audience now knows to be Bacon. There is also a voice-over which begins as Bacon buries his head in the pillow:

> Like a bomb exploding in reverse. Thoughts, ideas, fragments of images, shards of memory like shrapnel - all come back to me, and are forced back out in a cruel pastiche of experience.

---

[89] Peter France and William St Clair, "Introduction" in France and St Clair (eds.), *Mapping Lives: The Uses of Biography* (Oxford: Oxford University Press, 2002), 3.

This pronouncement has the characteristic feel of a Francis Bacon *bon mot* with its mixture of intelligence and violence. It could equally well describe two processes: the act of creating art, and the act of converting a life into a biography. In this sense, both processes are connected right from the beginning of the film. The unexplained second event therefore appears to be something tragic which has come to inform and shape Bacon's art, an impression which is strengthened by the final shot of the man in agony, soon to be confirmed as George Dyer. This image is the first to refer directly to Bacon's art—specifically, his portraiture. If this image is the link between the first and second events in the opening sequence (Bacon's life and his art), the relationship between the second and the third events is then more complex and troubling. There is an uncomfortable juxtaposition between the fragments of Dyer's suicide and the gallery scenes, which raises the ethical dilemma inherent in the film as a whole. Do Bacon's fame and attractiveness as a personality justify moving this sordid event into the public arena?

It was this type of ethical reaction to the film's content which shaped the film's unusual encounter with the Arts Council of England (ACE) and almost cost it the chance to receive half its budget from the National Lottery fund. Maybury had received early support for his project from both the BBC and the BFI, and it was Ben Gibson in his capacity as Head of Production at the BFI, who applied to the Arts Council for extra funding.[90] The project had been approved by both the Lottery film department and the Advisory Film Panel, and seemed set to be successful. Then, in an extremely unusual move, the Council itself—who meet to approve all decisions leading to financial commitment—decided to overturn the recommendations and reject the application. In a report in *The Observer*, an unnamed council member was quoted as saying: "Frankly, some of us did think the film was sensationalist, prurient stuff."[91] But Gibson was convinced that it was the personal views of the chairman, Lord Gowrie, who swung the decision. Gowrie had been a friend of Bacon's and reportedly felt that it was too soon for a film about the artist's life as he had only died four years before. Gibson released this story to the press and put the Arts Council's appeal process in motion. Six months

[90] The following story was related by Gibson during an interview with the author in March 2004 and is confirmed by the newspaper reports (which he claims to have leaked).

[91] Richard Brooks, "Bacon love-film funding blocked," *The Observer*, May 12, 1996, 3.

later, the Council changed its mind again, and awarded the sum of £365,000 to the project.[92]

Despite this apparent climb down, the Arts Council's reservations marked the project as controversial and difficult right from its early stages, and it retained this status upon its release two years later. Unsurprisingly, it was well-received by the broadsheets: *The Guardian* called it "a stunning debut" and "art almost as corrosive as Bacon's own."[93] *Time Out* had already championed the film, reporting that its makers were facing censorial restrictions at the hands of the BFI and BBC; upon its release, Geoff Andrew pronounced it "tough, tender, [and] wholly compelling."[94] Equally predictably, it became another *bête noire* for the *Evening Standard*'s Alexander Walker in his concerted campaign against Lottery funding for British cinema. Walker's principal objection was that:

> The Arts Council, whose National Lottery coin co-financed Love is the Devil with the British Film Institute and BBC TV, has really no right to put its logo on a movie that so signally omits all traces of art.[95]

The absence of any representation of Bacon's actual paintings makes the film ridiculous, Walker claims, and his personal experience of meeting the artist was one of discussing Verlaine rather than sodomy. There is a streak of barely repressed homophobia running through Walker's views, suggested by his article's title, "Beefcake but no Bacon", his dislike of the film's "bitchiness", and most clearly in his opening dismissal of the film as a "porno-biography".[96] It's difficult to know on what grounds Walker considers the film to be pornographic, especially as he had already conceded that "Physical sexiness… is featured less than one might have expected".[97] The one moment of nudity in the film features Daniel Craig laid out in the bath, shot from above and sideways on so that his body stretches the full length of the frame. This unusual angle reinforces the

---

[92] The award, according to ACE's records, was worth £364,551, although Maybury refers to it as a "measly £250,000". Macnab, "Bohemian Rhapsody," 19.

[93] Rob Mackie, "Video of the Week: Love is the Devil," *Guardian Unlimited*, March 19, 1999, accessed February 2005, http://film.guardian.co.uk/News_Story/Critic_Review/Guardian/0,, 36024,00.html.

[94] Sarah Kent, "A Slice of Bacon," *Time Out*, December 31, 1997, 12–13.

[95] Alexander Walker, "Beefcake but no Bacon," *Evening Standard*, May 8, 1998, 19.

[96] Alexander Walker, "Blank portrait of an Artist," *Evening Standard*, September 17, 1998, 22.

[97] Walker, "Beefcake," 19.

impression that here the camera is using Craig's body as Bacon used Dyer's in his paintings: as an aesthetic rather than a sexual object.

Nudity is also a familiar marker of art cinema and, given Maybury's association with Derek Jarman, male nudity in this context specifically references a queer aesthetic. If there is a recognisable, defined "movement" with which to connect *Love is the Devil*, it is then probably that of "New Queer Cinema", a term coined by R. Ruby Rich in 1992 in response to "a watershed year for independent gay and lesbian film and video."[98] One of the films to have provoked this critical interest was Jarman's revisionist period drama *Edward II* (1991), with Michele Aaron's taxonomy of the movement's main characteristics including the observation that many of its films "defy the sanctity of the past."[99] This is an interesting light in which to consider Maybury's film. Bacon never made a secret of his homosexuality, and his entourage was peopled with a rich variety of queer characters. And yet, as Farson recalls:

> homosexual London was very different in atmosphere from what it is now. For us it was a fact of life rather than a statement. However, it was against the law.[100]

Moreover, Bacon clearly relished the clandestine, underground character of homosexual culture during the period; this makes the telling of his life story rather an ambivalent exercise in terms of "defying the sanctity of the past"; on the one hand, he represents raw, naked honesty about oneself and one's tastes; but on the other hand, he only does this in private, behind the closed doors of his studio or the Colony Club. *Love is the Devil* can be much more easily aligned with another characteristic of New Queer Cinema; that its films "are unapologetic about their characters' faults or, rather, they eschew positive imagery."[101] Bacon's treatment of Dyer in public provides his most repulsive behaviour; in one episode at a crowded restaurant table, he taunts his lover with revelations about mental breakdown and attempts at "susan-cide". Here, Maybury highlights Bacon's monstrous qualities by shooting Jacobi slurping down oysters in extreme close-up through a fish-eye lens. Scenes like this certainly

---

[98] R. Ruby Rich, "New Queer Cinema," *Sight and Sound*, 2:5, September 1992, 32.
[99] Michele Aaron, "New Queer Cinema: An Introduction" in *New Queer Cinema: A Critical Reader*, ed. Michele Aaron, (Edinburgh: Edinburgh University Press, 2004), 4.
[100] Farson, *Gilded Gutter Life*, 23.
[101] Aaron, "Introduction," 4.

contributed to the film's problematic relationship with the Arts Council, as Maybury describes:

> The complaints I've had from the establishment have all been about facts. They've asked me to remove facts because *they* were offended. I do feel that someone like Bacon would be horrified to know that such gatekeepers of the culture were trying to pretty up his work.[102]

This criticism contains a suggestive instance of slippage between Maybury's conception of his film and Bacon's art. The gatekeepers are not trying to 'pretty up' Bacon's work, but are arguably attempting to maintain his public reputation by placing restrictions on Maybury's film. Nonetheless, for an artist who achieved almost unprecedented financial success within his lifetime, it is not surprising that Bacon's powerful estate (and friends in high places, such as Gowrie) should be rather defensive over his legacy. In a further twist to the tale, the Arts Council actually have a direct interest in Bacon's reputation, as they acquired two of his paintings in the 1950s, both of which now feature amongst their most valuable assets.[103]

Conclusion

Whilst it would almost certainly be unfair to accuse Gowrie of directly acting to safeguard the value of his organisation's endowments, there is clearly a great deal at stake here—not just financially but also in political terms. At the beginning of this chapter, the Arts Council's twofold remit was characterised in terms of a tension between elitist "improvement" and democratic "accessibility". A similar strain exists in the relationship between the Arts Council's traditional expertise and its newfound largesse, enabled by the populist National Lottery. The strongly-contested decision of whether or not to allocate Lottery funding to *Love is the Devil* represents these tensions in operation at the highest level within the Arts Council of England. In favour of supporting the film were several clear opportunities. Firstly, as this was a major new project from an artist and filmmaker whose avant-garde work had already been supported by the

[102] Maybury quoted in Geoffrey Macnab, "Bohemian Rhapsody," *Sight and Sound,* 7:7, July 1997, 18.

[103] The Arts Council collection comprises some 6,800 works which were valued at £25 million in the late 1990s, the two Bacons ("Head IV" (1949) and "Study for a Portrait of Van Gogh (1957)) alone are worth several million. Richard Witts, *Artists Unknown: An Alternative History of the Arts Council* (London: Little, Brown and Co., 1998), 374.

Arts Councils (e.g. *The Remembrance of Things Fast* (1994)), it offered the chance to follow in the footsteps of the Arts Council's long-standing engagement with artist's film and video. Secondly, the Council could also justify supporting the film through the logic of "accessibility" by potentially increasing public knowledge of the life of one of the nation's greatest modern painters. On the other hand, the fact that not all aspects of Bacon's life are palatable was problematic for the cultural gatekeepers. The project also brought new focus to the historical rift between the BFI and the Arts Council's film specialists. By the time of its release, BFI Production had effectively been shut down to pave the way for the new funding superbody, the Film Council.[104] *Love is the Devil* was therefore a pivotal film in terms of public support for art cinema in the UK.

Despite all these difficulties, *Love is the Devil* did make it through the production process and into the public arena. It has received considerable critical attention, and its continued usefulness as an exercise in art historiography is demonstrated by its screening alongside a major exhibition of Bacon's work in 2006.[105] It now stands as a legacy of a very brief period when both the Arts Councils and the BFI had a direct influence on large-scale film production in the UK. This element of overlap or even competition between the two institutions begs the final question: did the Arts Council make a significant and unique contribution to art cinema during this period? After all, many of the features it supported with Lottery-funding had been previously developed elsewhere, by the BFI, the BBC or other smaller bodies. Pre-1995, there was already a reasonably healthy short film culture existing through the broadcasters and regional initiatives. The Lottery-funded artists' film and video projects, on the other hand, were very close to the Arts Council of England's heart, echoing the reason why it became involved with filmmaking in the first place; significantly, this was the only element of Lottery funding for film production to be retained by the organisation after the creation of the Film Council in 2000. The scale of the support for art cinema under the Lottery was far higher than had previously been available, and its centralisation within the Arts Councils meant that a degree of continuity was possible, with filmmakers such as Ramsey or Kötting moving between different

[104] Ben Gibson used the film's release to bring attention to the frozen funding of his department. See Gibson, "Lights, Camera, Axe Man," *The Guardian*, March 13, 1998, Section 2, 10–11.

[105] Sainsbury Centre for the Visual Arts, "Francis Bacon: Paintings from the 1950s," accessed January 2007, http://www.scva.org.uk/exhibitions/archive/?exhibition=28.

modes. In respect of art cinema, at least, the Arts Council briefly managed a level of integration to which the Film Council would later aspire.

CONCLUSION

THE PEOPLE'S VERDICT

In November 2005, some ten years after National Lottery money began to be channelled into the film industry, the Department of Culture, Media and Sport (DCMS) instigated a consultation exercise to test public opinion on the use of the Lottery's proceeds, which then amounted to over £1 billion a year. In this manner, they elected to ask the people of the UK what they thought of the pictures being made with their money. One question highlighted the support of national cinema as an area for debate:

> Lottery money for film has enhanced the range of distinctive films available in the UK, stimulated creativity and moving image culture and education throughout England, enabled young people to develop their creative and social skills by participating in a UK wide scheme to make short films and developed talent through training and skills development support, all in a way not possible without the Lottery. Do you agree?[1]

As an attempt to sell the advantages of using Lottery funding to support film production, this question offers a useful insight into what the Government considers the scheme's greatest achievements—and perhaps more importantly, which aspects of the scheme are most likely to meet with public approval. It is notable that the summary avoids explicit reference to the "large-scale direct subsidy" feared in Gerald Kaufman's report on the film industry published ten years previously.[2]

Instead, the document chooses to highlight the enhanced range of films *available* in the UK, which is not only new British cinema, but also the foreign language films, the distribution of which is supported by the UK Film Council. This shift in emphasis echoes Andrew Higson's suggestion

---

[1] Department of Culture, Media and Sport (DCMS), "Summary of results from consultation on National Lottery money for Arts, Film, Heritage and Sport from 2009," *National Lottery Shares 2009*, June 2006, 4, accessed June 2006, http://www.lottery2009.culture.gov.uk.

[2] Department of National Heritage (DNH), *The British Film Industry,* Cmnd. 2884 (London: HMSO, 1995), 4.

that "the parameters of national cinema should be drawn at the site of consumption as much as at the site of production of films."[3] Apart from its reference to the development of talent through training, the consultation document locates the benefits of Lottery support for filmmaking mainly in the cultural arena. Such arguments are hardly new: for example, the focus upon education and the development of skills in young people is reminiscent of the 1932 report from the Adult Education Institute, which led to the creation of the BFI.[4] But above all, the question neglects to mention that the majority of National Lottery money for film continues to be spent on production: in 2005–2006, the UK Film Council made Lottery awards totalling £42.3 million, of which £23.2 million was for feature film production and development.[5] This omission suggests that the DCMS were unsure as to how popular this financial support would prove to be amongst the public who provide its funds.

The results of the consultation were made public in June 2006, when the DCMS reported that 11,476 surveys had been completed—significantly more than expected. The question on Lottery funding for film elicited a positive response: 71% agreed with the statement, of which 33% agreed strongly, whilst just 10% disagreed. This is a convincing level of public approval for an activity which attracted severe criticism from the press as recently as 2003.[6] Several of the specific comments published along with the headline figures are also worth considering:

- Lottery funding should support an increasingly diverse range of films and take risks.
- Lottery funding for film has lacked quality control and allowed some poor films to be made.
- Film should be supported by the market rather than the Lottery.[7]

This sample of opinion illustrates that, despite the coy phrasing of the question, the respondents *did* care about film production and were also well-informed about the major debates and issues surrounding Lottery funding for film.

---

3 Andrew Higson, "The Concept of National Cinema," *Screen*, 30:4 (1989): 36.
4 Commission on Educational and Cultural Films, Chair. Sir Benjamin Gott, *The Film in National Life* (London: Allen and Unwin, 1932).
5 UKFC, *Group and Lottery Annual Report and Financial Statements For the Year ended March 31, 2006* (London: TSO, 2006), 18.
6 See discussion of *Sex Lives of the Potato Men* (2003) on pages 117–118.
7 DCMS, "Summary of results from consultation on National Lottery," 4.

The suggestion that Lottery funding should support cinematic diversity and "take risks" is a logical extension of the principle of "additionality" into the realms of public funding for film. The National Lottery itself was created to help pay for society's "desirables" rather than its "essentials", and therefore relies upon the principle of additionality to ensure that Government or private expenditure will not simply be replaced by the Lottery's proceeds. Applying this principle to the complexities of film funding is not entirely straight-forward. For a mostly deregulated industry, there was very little existing state film funding to replace, although it is possible to argue that the Lottery did hasten the demise of both BFI Production and British Screen. The area where it is most difficult to enforce the principle of additionality is in cases of large-scale feature film production, where finance often comes from a variety of private sources. As Lottery Film Officer Mark Dunford puts it: "You are damned if you succeed for putting money into something which didn't need public support, and damned if you fail for waste."[8] Lottery-funded popular cinema was also expected, perhaps naively, to return significant amounts of money back into the system, eventually enabling sustainability. Although some Lottery-funded comedies such as *Shooting Fish* (1997) and *Mike Bassett: England Manager* (2001) performed reasonably well, and *Billy Elliot* (2000) was a runaway hit, these projects also tended to have less demonstrable need of public support, hence complicating their status in terms of "added value" for the UK film industry. Arguably, each of these relatively successful films was, in its own way, a risk, but they also provide evidence for those who believe that "film should be supported by the market rather than the Lottery."[9]

There are important elements of national film culture which tend not be supported by market forces alone, with such elements often cited as contributing to cinematic "diversity". Artists' film and video projects, short filmmaking and feature-length art cinema are all relatively marginal activities as far as the commercial film industry is concerned, but their presence is valued for other reasons: as educational tools, as spaces for formal experimentation or ideological intervention, for providing a voice for the culturally disadvantaged, or simply as "art". Again, claims for cinema as a form of art are not new, but they fit particularly neatly within the Arts Councils' remit. Established in 1945 and changed very little since, this remit is structured around a tension between an elitist desire to increase the quality of artistic provision and a populist drive towards

---

[8] Mark Dunford, interview with the author, July 16, 2004.
[9] DCMS, "Summary of results from consultation on National Lottery," 4.

accessibility. Consequently, the Arts Council's first ventures into filmmaking were documentaries produced with the aim of allowing more people to experience the nation's artistic treasures, but this later developed from making films *about* artists to funding films *by* artists. This historical connection meant that the Visual Arts department at the Arts Council of England was able to channel Lottery funds into a separate Artists' Film and Video scheme, with modest resources of around £800,000, but which nevertheless enabled 35 new and distinctive art works. The 2005 consultation exercise on Lottery-funding particularly emphasises the usefulness of short filmmaking due to a recent scheme involving children and young people.[10] This scheme grew out of the earlier provision for short films when almost 200 were made, many by first-time filmmakers seeking a path into the industry. A smaller number of art-house feature films were produced, but these were valuable for developing the careers of directors, such as Lynne Ramsey, Peter Mullan and Sally Potter.

Another sense in which Lottery funding was intended to create a more diverse national cinema was in relation to the types of people employed in filmmaking. On the whole, women are under-represented within the UK film industry: figures published by the UK Film Council in 2003 indicate that 32.6% of film and video production workers were female, but also estimate that, on film sets, this proportion was as low as 15%.[11] It would be very difficult to obtain comparable details on the entire production teams who worked on Lottery-funded films, but simply looking at the senior roles of director and producer reveals some interesting trends. Of the 95 features which had a cinema release, 12 were directed by women, but perhaps more surprisingly, 25 had female producers; four of these women had produced two films each.[12] Of the 20 short films sampled in Chapter Five, 8 had female directors. Most striking of all is the proportion of women who received Artists' Film and Video awards: 20 out of 37 artists.[13] The same Film Council report noted that only 1.6% of film and video production staff in the UK are from ethnic minorities, compared to

[10] This scheme, "First Light Movies," uses Lottery funding to support short films made by young people between the ages of 5 and 18. See *First Light Movies*, accessed February 2007, http://www.firstlightmovies.com/about_us/.
[11] UK Film Council, *Film in the UK 2002: Statistical Yearbook* (London: UKFC, 2003), 75.
[12] These were Michele Camarda (*Photographing Fairies* (1996), *This Year's Love* (1999)), Sarah Curtis (*Mansfield Park* (1999), *The Governess* (1997)), Sheryl Crown (*House of America* (1997), *Solomon and Gaenor* (1999)) and Rebecca O'Brian (*My Name Is Joe* (1997), *The Navigators* (2000)).
[13] See Table 5–1 on page 170.

6.1% of the general workforce. At directorial level at least, the Lottery funded features were more ethnically diverse than the industry average, with funding going to British black, Asian and Chinese filmmakers, including Julian Henriques (*Babymother* (1997)), Leong Po-Chih (*The Wisdom of Crocodiles* (1997)) and Uduyan Prassad (*My Son The Fanatic* (1997) and *Gabriel and Me* (2000)). Several lesbian and gay filmmakers also received Lottery support, such as Patricia Rozema (*Mansfield Park* (1999)) and Richard Kwietniowski (*Love and Death on Long Island* (1997)).

Overall then, the Arts Councils' selection procedures and broader strategic priorities worked towards shaping a national cinema, which more accurately reflected the diversity of the UK's population, providing pictures for more different types of people.[14] But probably the most palpable effect of the early years of Lottery-funding for film production was caused by the Arts Council of Great Britain's fully devolved structure, which was completed in 1994. Between 1995 and 2000, over £25 million was awarded to Scottish, Welsh and Northern Irish film projects, leaving a legacy of more than 100 short films and 33 completed features.[15] It is therefore perhaps more accurate to discuss national cinemas in the plural when evaluating Lottery funding for film. There are signs that large-scale feature-production in the smaller home nations has tailed off since 2000, echoing the UK Film Council's trend towards greater centralisation of resources. The film industry continues to be focused around London where approximately 70% of the film and video production workforce is based.[16] Nonetheless, it is important to remember that this workforce is a particularly mobile one, and that the cluster of skilled technicians, actors and producers in London is made up of workers from across the UK or beyond. In this sense, it is fitting that the Scottish Arts Council's most popular production of the period was the romantic comedy *This Year's Love* (1999), which was written and directed by the Scot David Kane, and starred Dougray Scott and Douglas Henshall, but was set entirely in Camden Town.

The devolved structure of Lottery-funding for film encouraged the production of 33 features outside of England between 1995 and 2000, but only 20 of these were released in UK cinemas. From an economic viewpoint, sometimes the correct decision is *not* to distribute a film which

---

[14] As John Hill notes, the UK Film Council have attempted to continue in this fashion. John Hill, "UK Film Policy, Cultural Capital and Social Exclusion," *Cultural Trends*, 13:50 (June 2004): 29–39.

[15] Source: awards database; production and distribution data: BFI.

[16] UK Film Council, *Film in the UK 2002*, 77.

is unlikely to be successful, but this hard-nosed logic is clearly problematic when the costs already sunk into a project are partly derived from public resources.[17] Overall, of the 121 Lottery-funded feature films produced across the UK, 96 received a theatrical release of one sort or another. Whilst around 20% of films failing to secure distribution may not sound like an achievement, this rate was significantly better than the UK industry average over the same period, which was closer to 30%.[18] This suggests that the Arts Councils' application procedures saw some success in giving preference to those projects which already had interest from distributors. However, as noted previously, the smaller home nations experienced more problems in this regard, as did films with strong ethnic minority identities. Such difficulties are symptomatic of the wider structural weaknesses within the UK film industry, which motivated the Lottery Franchise Scheme. This attempt to restructure the industry had a striking historical precedent: the "Group Production Plan" instigated by the National Film Finance Corporation in the early 1950s. Just like the Lottery Franchises, the Group Plan aimed to bring together independent producers into subsidised consortia "with the economies and other advantages of continuity."[19] Both schemes were also regarded as failures for producing too few films and even fewer popular hits. The fact that a remarkably similar scheme was tried twice and failed for comparable reasons can be read as evidence of a fundamental ahistoricity within film policy debates, which this book is, in part, an attempt to remedy.[20]

Despite the repeated large-scale interventions designed to tackle the industry's structural problems, there are those who argue that some Lottery-funded films fail to secure distribution simply because they aren't very good. The respondent to the DCMS consultation who cited a "lack of quality control" was invoking this discourse, which has a complex history within film policy debates. During the heyday of the "quota quickies" in the 1930s, notions of quality were connected to a film's budget as a yardstick of production values. The cheapness of the quickies was combated

[17] Richard E. Caves, *Creative Industries: Contracts between Art and Commerce* (Cambridge: Harvard University Press, 2000), 15.

[18] Source: BFI Yearbooks. Distribution ratios are discussed in more detail in Chapter Three.

[19] Lord Reith, *1st Annual Report of the National Film Finance Corporation* (5 April 1950) cited in Richard Dyer MacCann, "Subsidy for the Screen: Grierson and Group 3, 1951–55," *Sight and Sound*, 46:3, March 1977, 169.

[20] Also see James Caterer, "Reinventing the British film industry: the Group Production Plan and the National Lottery Franchise Scheme," *International Journal of Cultural Policy* 17:1 (2011): 94–105.

by a minimum cost per foot restriction in order to qualify for quota, despite the recommendations of an independent committee which found that an evaluative process would be necessary to ensure proper quality control.[21] The relative merits of selective or automatic mechanisms continue to be an issue for debate. The European film-funding measures introduced from the 1980s onwards are largely selective, and criticised widely for the amount of red tape they generate. Meanwhile, tax incentives, such as Section 48, have very little quality control, yet the amount poured into the film industry by this method is many times greater than the £135 million of Lottery funding spent between 1995 and 2000.[22] The Arts Councils' system of distributing Lottery money to filmmakers was both selective and bureaucratic, demanding substantial work from applicants and relying upon a series of committees and recommendations. Quality control was most certainly in place, but whether this produced the right kind of films was less obvious. The committee model is considered by its supporters as the best way of ensuring independence from government interference and making use of expertise from practitioners. Its detractors argue that it results in safe, conservative choices (which offend as few people as possible) and unexciting cinema.

The idea that funding national cinema "by committee" can lead to unadventurous films is an example of the interconnections assumed to exist between policies, institutions and the cultural artefacts made at their behest. One of the central objectives of this thesis has been to investigate and clarify these complex interactions through the close examination of a range of films made with the assistance of National Lottery funding. This objective was motivated partly by a need identified by Julian Petley, to counteract the overwhelmingly negative press reaction, which greeted the scheme as a whole, and many of its films in particular.[23] However, throughout the course of this project, I have become convinced that the study of cultural policy needs to be connected to its end products in order to be fully meaningful. The incorporation of textual analysis into a history

[21] The Moyne Committee Report of 1936 recommended a "quality test" overseen by a Films Commission, but its conclusions were successfully resisted by the film trade. See Margaret Dickinson and Sarah Street, *Cinema and State: The Film Industry and the British Government 1927–84* (London: BFI, 1985), 53–74.

[22] By 2004, Section 48 had benefited the industry to the tune of £6 billion. See HMSO, "House of Commons Standing Committee A (pt 5)," Column 367, *UK Parliament*, accessed April 2006, http://www.publications.parliament.uk/pa/cm200304/cmstand/a/st040525/am/40525s05.htm.

[23] See Julian Petley, "From Brit-flicks to Shit-flicks: The Cost of Public Subsidy," *Journal of Popular British Cinema,* 5 (2002): 37–52.

of film policy carries dangers that need to be avoided; it is neither desirable nor useful to impose reductive models of influence between policies and texts so that one becomes a simple reflection of the other. To describe a UK film as "Lottery-funded" does not necessarily mean that we can instantly infer anything about its narrative or visual style. Conversely, the frequent occurrence of comedies upon the list of Lottery-funded feature films is caused by a variety of factors—not just their shared financial status. Importantly, the label "funded by the National Lottery through the Arts Council of England" must mean something, otherwise the institution (and its equivalents across the UK) would not have insisted upon the presence of these words at the front of each supported feature's credit sequence.

So what exactly does this label mean? This pre-title credit, demanded by the gatekeeper organisations as a requirement of receiving an award, was intended to remind the public that the National Lottery was invigorating a national cinema within which they were stakeholders—both in a financial and a cultural sense. On the one hand, it offers the utopian possibility of a "people's" national cinema paid for by the "people's" Lottery" on the other hand, however, signalling the involvement of the Arts Councils carries a different—and possibly incompatible—set of highbrow connotations. For the general cinema-going public, the endorsement of organisations associated with either conservative traditionalism or avant-garde radicalism seems likely to have been mildly puzzling at best. Art-house audiences are supposed to pay more attention to such stamps of cultural legitimacy, but this degree of legitimacy became compromised as criticism of the scheme grew. In 2001, *The Guardian* film critic claimed that, "At critics' screenings, when the words 'In association with the Arts Council of Great Britain' flash up on the screen there is a low moan in the auditorium."[24] This "low moan" is the sound of the critical hostility directed towards the Lottery-funded films, but whether this attitude actually affected audiences is difficult to assess. An example of an expensive flop, *Amy Foster* (1998), which received £2 million of Lottery money but only generated £49,000 at the UK box office, was initially criticised for many reasons, but not for its waste of public money. If the approval received by Lottery funding for film in the DCMS' recent consultation exercise is a reliable indication, then perhaps audiences are (or have become) more accepting than critics in this regard.

---

[24] Peter Bradshaw, "How our movies lost their cool," *Guardian Unlimited*, November 16, 2001, accessed June 2003, http://www.guardian.co.uk/friday_review/story/0,3605,5940 01,00.html.

In any case, the relationship between critics and audiences is only one element of a complex system of influence and exchange linking policies to texts. Individual personalities often play a vital role in shaping how this system works, as the interviews with policy-makers contained within this thesis demonstrate. The levels of direct influence exerted by policy-makers vary—not least according to the scale of each project. For the low-budget and highly subjective Artists' Film and Video projects, the judgements of David Curtis' panel could dictate which projects reached an audience at all. Curtis' long-standing involvement in the visual arts sector and the relationships he had built up with individual artists were also important: for example, Nina Danino's ambitious *Temenos* (1997) should be considered as the culmination of a long period of institutional nurturing. However, Curtis would probably balk at the suggestion that he had influence over the artists' creative decision-making, whereas a "hands-on" producer, such as Ben Gibson at BFI Production, would expect filmmakers to listen to his ideas. This is illustrated most clearly in the BFI/Arts Council co-production *Gallivant* (1997), which was changed radically by Gibson's suggestion that Andrew Kötting focus his free-wheeling travelogue by concentrating upon the relationship between his grandmother and his daughter. This may have shifted the film away from Kötting's avant-garde roots, but it also ensured that it would be accessible to a wider section of the British public. In terms of institutional influence, the most complex projects are the large-budget commercial features, but it is often possible to observe the Lottery's public benefit remit working alongside other considerations, as with Pathé Picture's output overseen by Andrea Calderwood, who balanced the star-laden and accessible *An Ideal Husband* (1999) with the art-house appeal of projects such as *Ratcatcher* (1999).

At the broadest scale, the detailed study of cultural policies, such as National Lottery funding for film production, is a means of evaluating and quantifying the relationships between politics, institutions and texts. As such, the idea that *Billy Elliot* may be considered as the "emblematic New Labour film" can trigger analysis on several levels. [25] In an empirical sense, *Billy Elliot*'s financial arrangements were characteristic of a Blairite emphasis upon private-public partnerships, and the success of the film led to its being used as short-hand for the idea that high culture can help

---

[25] Tom Ryall, "New Labour and the cinema: Culture, politics and economics," *Journal of Popular British Cinema*, 5 (2002): 18.

regenerate deprived communities: the so-called "*Billy Elliot* revolution".[26] On a textual level, the film's narrative is driven by conflict between traditional socialist values, represented by the 1984 miners' strike within which Billy's family are embroiled, and the young ballet dancer's dreams of success in the cultural arena. Billy's trajectory is strongly reminiscent of New Labour rhetoric, exemplified by the affirmative individualism of objectives, such as "developing the extra-ordinary status of ordinary people."[27] However, the important question here is whether there are any connections between the film's political context, its publicly funded status, and its ideological manoeuvres. I would argue that there are, and that these can be found in the way that Government priorities shape policy procedures and affect committee decision-making. As an employee of the Arts Council of England during the late 1990s, I witnessed how Government buzzwords would filter down through the system and affect the institution's behaviour; a key example of which during this period was "social exclusion".[28] *Billy Elliot*'s industrial rags to cultural riches plot made it an irresistible indicator of the organisation's investment in this concept.[29]

The case of *Billy Elliot*'s route to National Lottery funding confirms Adrienne Scullion and Beatriz Garcia's assertion that cultural policy research "inhabits the gaps and fissures of making, doing and interpreting".[30] Investigating these "gaps" and "fissures" can provide vital insights into the workings of national cinema in the UK during the late 1990s. The controversy over the National Lottery award to *Love is the Devil* exposes how one of the central tensions of public funding—elitist "improvement" versus democratic "accessibility"—can flare up—even at the highest level of cultural institutions. The production histories of films remaining unfinished or unreleased are generally ignored, and yet knowing what went wrong with a Lottery-funded project, such as *Jack Sheppard and*

---

[26] Gaby Hinsliff, "'Billy Elliot' payout for poor pupils," *The Guardian*, February 11, 2001, accessed June 2003, http://society.guardian.co.uk/childreninpoverty/story/0,8150,436 869,00.html.

[27] Tony Blair, "Introduction: My Vision for Britain," in *What Needs to Change: New Visions for Britain*, ed. Giles Radice (London: Harper Collins, 1996), 6.

[28] See Cabinet Office, *Social Exclusion Unit*, accessed August 2006, http://www.socialexclusion.gov.uk/.

[29] Mark Dunford, the Lottery officer responsible for recommending *Billy Elliot*'s award, confirms that such concepts were useful tools in securing Council support. Interview with the author, July 2004.

[30] Adrienne Scullion and Beatriz Garcia, "What is Cultural Policy Research?" *International Journal of Cultural Policy*, 11:2 (2005): 125.

Jonathan Wild, can offer important lessons for film policy-makers. Those films which do reach audiences become open to many different modes of interpretation, but when viewed from the perspective of policy debates, many of the Lottery-funded features are particularly revealing. Several contain more-or-less explicit commentary on issues surrounding UK national cinema: the setting of *House!* in a glorious art deco cinema come dilapidated bingo hall; *The Tango Lesson*'s representation of Hollywood's relentless stupidity and yet endless physical charm; the transatlantic protagonists of *Shooting Fish* who use any available con-trick to write themselves into a heritage fantasy. Such examples help to illustrate my argument that the period when the four Arts Councils created pictures for the people using National Lottery funding was a time for experimentation; a chaotic and yet wonderfully unfixed moment in the history of UK film policy, gaps and fissures and all.

BIBLIOGRAPHY

The data collected for the purposes of this project from the four Arts Councils of the UK is available online at James Caterer, "The People's Pictures Appendices," *Google Sites*, https://sites.google.com/a/brookes.ac.uk/jamescaterer/.

Books and essays

Aaron, Michele, ed. *New Queer Cinema: A Critical Reader.* Edinburgh: Edinburgh University Press, 2004.

Abel, Richard. *The Ciné Goes to Town: French Cinema 1896-1914.* Berkley: University of California Press, 1994.

Ainsworth, William Henry. *Jack Sheppard: A Romance.* London: Routledge, 1898. First serialised in *Bentley's Miscellany*, 1839.

Allen, Robert C. and Douglas Gomery. *Film History, Theory and Practice.* New York: Newbury Award Records, 1985.

Anderson, Benedict. *Imagined communities: Reflections on the Origin and Spread of Nationalism.* London: Verso, 1983.

Balcon, Michael. *Michael Balcon Presents... A Lifetime of Films.* London: Hutchinson, 1969.

Barr, Charles. *Ealing Studios*, 2nd ed. London: Studio Vista, 1993. First published 1977.

—. "Introduction: Amnesia and Schizophrenia." In *All Our Yesterdays: 90 Years of British Cinema*, edited by Charles Barr, 1-29. London: BFI, 1986.

Billig, Michael. *Banal Nationalism.* London: Sage, 1995.

Blair, Tony. "Introduction: My Vision for Britain." *What Needs to Change: New Visions for Britain,* edited by Giles Radice. London: Harper Collins, 1996.

Blanchard, Simon and Sylvia Harvey. "The Post-war Independent Cinema – Structure and Organisation." In *British Cinema History,* edited by James Curran and Vincent Porter. 226-227. London: Weidenfeld and Nicolson, 1983.

Bode, Stephen. *Mark Lewis: Films 1995-2000.* London: Film and Video Umbrella, 2001.

Bordwell, David. *Narration in the Fiction Film.* London: Methuen, 1985.

Bradley, Fiona. "History Lesson." In *Janet Hodgson: History Lesson,* edited by Cindy Hubert. 3. Liverpool: Bluecoat Gallery, 1999.

Brunsdon, Charlotte. "Not Having It All: Women and Film in the 1990s." In *British Cinema of the 90s*, edited by Robert Murphy. 167-177. London: BFI, 2000.

Butler, Ivan. *To Encourage the Art of the Film: The Story of the British Film Institute*. London: Robert Hale and Co., 1971.

Caterer, James. "The Mysterious Case of the House-Breaker, the Thief-Taker General and the National Lottery." In *Sights Unseen: Unfinished British Films*, edited by Dan North, 189-204. Newcastle: Cambridge Scholars Publishing, 2008.

Caves, Richard. E. *Creative Industries: Contracts between Art and Commerce.* Cambridge: Harvard University Press, 2000.

Crofts, Stephen. "Reconceptualizing National Cinema/s." In *Film and Nationalism,* edited by Alan Williams. 25-67. New Brunswick: Rutgers University Press, 2002.

Curtis, David. "English Avant-Garde Film: An Early Chronology." In *The British Avant-Garde Film 1926-1995*, edited by Michael O'Pray. 101-119. Luton: University of Luton Press, 1996.

Dale, Martin. *The Movie Game: The Film Industry in Britain, Europe and America*. London: Cassell, 1997.

Danino, Nina and Michael Mazière, eds. *The Undercut Reader: Critical Writings on Artists Film and Video*. London: Wallflower Press, 2003.

Dickinson, Margaret and Sarah Street. *Cinema and State: The Film Industry and the British Government 1927-84*. London: BFI, 1985.

Dickinson, Margaret, ed. *Rogue Reels: Oppositional Film in Britain, 1945-90*. London: BFI, 1999.

Douglas, Andrew. *British Charitable Gambling 1956-1994: Towards a National Lottery*. London: Athalone, 1995.

Dyer, Richard. *White*. London: Routledge, 1997.

Dyja, Eddie, ed. *BFI Film and Television Handbook 1996*. London: BFI, 1995. All subsequent annual editions until …*2003*. London: BFI, 2001.

Eberts, Jake and Terry Illot. *My Indecision is Final: The Rise and Fall of Goldcrest Films*. London: Faber and Faber, 1990.

Elsaesser, Thomas. *New German Cinema: A History*. London: BFI, 1989.

Elsey, Eileen and Andrew Kelly. *In Short: A Guide to Short Film-Making in the Digital Age*. London: BFI, 2002.

Ewen, C. L'Estrange. *Lotteries and Sweepstakes: an Historical, Legal and Ethical Survey of their Introduction, Suppression and Re-establishment in the British Isles.* London: Heath Cranton, 1932.

Farson, Daniel. *The Gilded Gutter Life of Francis Bacon*. London: Century, 1993.
Ferguson, Niall. *Empire: How Britain Made the Modern World*. London: Penguin, 2003.
Fielding, Henry. *The History of the life of the Late Mr. Jonathan Wild the Great*. Harmondsworth: Penguin, 1982. First published 1743.
Finney, Angus. "Support Mechanisms across Europe." In *The European Cinema Reader,* edited by Catherine Fowler. 212-222. London: Routledge, 2002.
France, Peter and William St Clair. *Mapping Lives: The Uses of Biography*. Oxford: Oxford University Press, 2002.
Franklin, Bob, ed. *British Television Policy: A Reader*. London: Routledge, 2001.
Frye, Northrop. *An Anatomy of Criticism*. Princeton: Princeton University Press, 1957.
Gifford, Denis. *The British Film Catalogue, Vol. 1: Fiction Film, 1895-1994,* 3rd ed. London: Fitzroy Dearborn, 2000.
Green, Ian. "Ealing: In the Comedy Frame." In *British Cinema History,* edited by James Curran and Vincent Porter. 294-302. London: Weidenfeld and Nicolson, 1983.
Hall, Stuart. "The Local and the Global: Globalization and Ethnicity." In *Culture, Globalization and the World-System,* edited by Anthony D. King. 19-39. Binghampton: Macmillan, 1991.
Hancock, David. "Profile of the Film Industry." In *The UK Cultural Sector: Profile and Policy Issues*, edited by Sara Selwood. 296-309. London: PSI, 2001.
Hanson, Stuart. "Spoilt for Choice? Multiplexes in the 90s." In *British Cinema of the 90s*, edited by Robert Murphy. 48-59. London: BFI, 2000.
Harper, Sue and Vincent Porter. *British Cinema of the 1950s: The Decline of Deference*. Oxford: Oxford University Press, 2003.
Harris, John. *The Last Party: Britpop, Blair and the Demise of English Rock*. London: Fourth Estate, 2003.
Harvey, Sylvia. "Channel Four Television: From Annan to Grade" In *British Television: A Reader*, edited by Ed Buscombe. 92-117. Oxford: Clarendon, 2000.
—. "The 'Other Cinema' in Britain: Unfinished Business in Oppositional and Independent Film, 1929-1984." In *All Our Yesterdays: 90 Years of British Cinema*, edited by Charles Barr. 225-251. London: BFI, 1986.
Higson, Andrew. *English Heritage, English Cinema: Costume Drama Since 1980*. Oxford: Oxford University Press, 2003.

—. *Waving the Flag: Constructing a National Cinema in Britain*. Oxford: Clarendon, 1995.

Hill, John. "British Film Policy." In *Film Policy: International, National and Regional Perspectives*, edited by Albert Moran. 101-113. London: Routledge, 1996.

—. "British Television and Film: The Making of a Relationship." In *Big Picture, Small Screen: The Relations Between Film and Television*, edited by John Hill and Martin McLoone. 151-176. Luton: University of Luton Press, 1996?

—. *British Cinema in the 1980s*. Oxford: Clarendon Press, 1999.

—. *Cinema and Northern Ireland: Film, Culture and Politics*. London: BFI, 2006.

Hjort, Mette and Scott MacKenzie, "Introduction." In *Cinema and Nation*, edited by Mette Hjort and Scott MacKenzie. 1-16. London: Routledge, 2000.

Hoggart, Richard. *The Tyranny of Relativism: Culture and Politics in Contemporary English Society*. New Brunswick: Transaction, 1998.

Holmes, Richard, ed. *Defoe on Sheppard and Wild*. London: Harper Perennial, 2004. First published 1724, 1725.

Hone, William. *The Every Day Book, Or, A Guide to the Year, Vol. II*. London: William Tegg, 1868. First published weekly, January 1825 - December 1826.

Hood, Stuart. "John Grierson and the Documentary Film Movement." In *British Cinema History*, edited by James Curran and Vincent Porter. 99-112. London: Weidenfeld and Nicolson, 1983.

Illot, Terry. "UK Film, Television and Video: Overview." *BFI Film and Television Handbook 1996*. Ed. Eddie Dyja. London: BFI, 1995. 20-23.

Jäckel, Anne. "European Co-Production Strategies." In *Film Policy: International, National and Regional Perspectives*, edited by Albert Moran. 85-97. London: Routledge, 1996.

Jackson, Camilla and Ian Hunt. *Willie Doherty: Somewhere Else*. Liverpool: Tate Gallery, 1998.

Jasper, David. "Screening Angels." In *The Art of Bill Viola,* edited by Chris Townsend. 184-192. London: Thames and Hudson, 2004.

Jennings, Ros. "*Beautiful Thing*: British queer cinema, positive unoriginality and the everyday." In *British Queer Cinema,* edited by Robin Griffiths. 183-194. London: Routledge, 2006.

Julien, Isaac and Colin MacCabe. *Diary of a Young Soul Rebel*. London: BFI, 1990.

Keynes, John Maynard. *The Collected Writings of John Maynard Keynes*, Vol. 28, edited by D. Moggridge. London: Macmillan Press, 1982.
Krutnik, Frank. "Love Lies: Romantic Fabrications in Contemporary Romantic Comedy." In *Terms of Endearment: Hollywood Romantic Comedy of the 1980s and 1990s*, edited by Peter Williams Evans and Celestino Deleyto. 15-36. Edinburgh: Edinburgh University Press, 1998.
Kuhn, Michael. *One Hundred Films and a Funeral*. London: Thorogood, 2002.
Lawrence, Amy. *The Films of Peter Greenaway*. Cambridge: Cambridge University Press, 1997.
Lindgren, Ernest. *The Art of The Film*. London: George Allen and Unwin, 1948.
Lovell, Alan. "The Documentary Film Movement: John Grierson." In *Studies in Documentary*, edited by Alan Lovell and Jim Hillier. 9-35. London: Secker and Warburgh, 1972.
Macnab, Geoffrey. "Unseen British Cinema." In *British Cinema of the 90s,* edited by Robert Murphy. 135-144. London: BFI, 2000.
Major, John. *John Major: The Autobiography*. London: Harper Collins, 1999.
McFarlane, Brian, ed. *The Encyclopaedia of British Film*. London: Methuen, 2003.
McGuigan, Jim. *Cultural Populism*. London: Routledge, 1992.
—. *Rethinking Cultural Policy*. Maidenhead: Open University Press, 2004.
McLoone, Martin. "Boxed In?: The Aesthetics of Film and Television." In *Big Picture, Small Screen: The Relations Between Film and Television*, edited by John Hill and Martin McLoone. 76-106. Luton: University of Luton Press, 1996?
Miller, Toby and Nitin Govil, John McMurria, Richard Maxwell. *Global Hollywood*. London: BFI, 2003.
Miller, Toby. "The Film Industry and the Government: 'Endless Mr Beans and Mr Bonds.'" In *British Cinema of the 90s*, edited by Robert Murphy. 37-47. London: BFI, 2000.
Monk, Claire. "Men in the 90s." In *British Cinema of the 90s*, edited by Robert Murphy. 156-166. London: BFI, 2000.
Mulholland, Neil. *The Cultural Devolution: Art in Britain in the Late Twentieth Century*. Aldershot: Ashgate, 2003.
Mundy, John. *Popular Music on Screen: From the Hollywood Musical to Music Video*. Manchester: Manchester University Press, 1999.

Napper, Lawrence. "A despicable tradition? Quota-quickies in the 1930s." In *The British Cinema Book, 2nd ed*, edited by Robert Murphy. 45-59. London: BFI, 2001.
O'Grady, Timothy and Steve Pyke. *I Could Read The Sky*. London: Harvill, 1997.
O'Pray, Michael. "The British Avant-Garde and Art Cinema from the 1970s to the 1990s." In *Dissolving Views: Key Writings on British Cinema*, edited by Andrew Higson. London: Cassell, 1996.
—. *Derek Jarman: Dreams of England*. London: BFI, 1996.
Oborne, Peter. *Alistair Campbell: New Labour and the Rise of the Media Class*. London: Aurum, 1999.
Orwell, George. *The Road to Wigan Pier*. London: Secker and Warburg, 1983. First published 1937.
Petley, Julian. "Cinema and State." In *All Our Yesterdays: 90 Years of British Cinema*, edited by Charles Barr. 31-46. London: BFI, 1986.
Petrie, Duncan and Robert Kruger, eds. *The Paul Rotha Reader*. Exeter: University of Exeter Press, 1999.
Petrie, Duncan. *Screening Scotland*. London: BFI, 2000.
Pick, John. *The Arts in a State: A Study of Government Arts Policies from Ancient Greece to the Present*. Bristol: Bristol Classical Press, 1988.
Plath, Sylvia. *Johnny Panic and the Bible of Dreams, and other Prose Writings*. London, Faber, 1977.
Prince, Stephen. *A New Pot of Gold: Hollywood Under the Electronic Rainbow, 1980-1989*. Berkeley: University of California Press, 2000.
Rees, A.L. *A History of Experimental Film and Video*. London: BFI, 1999.
Richards, Jeffrey. "Frank Capra and the Cinema of Populism." In *Movies and Methods, Volume One,* edited by Bill Nicholls. 65-77. Berkeley: University of California Press, 1976.
Russell, John. *Francis Bacon*. London: Thames and Hudson, 1971.
Russo, Vitto. *The Celluloid Closet: Homosexuality in the Movies*. New York: Harper and Row, 1987.
Sainsbury, Peter. "Independent British Filmmaking and the Production Board." In *Catalogue*: *British Film Institute Productions 1951-1976.* 11-16. London: BFI, 1977.
—. "Production Policy." In *The New Social Function of Cinema – Catalogue: British Film Institute Productions, 79/80*. 9-11. London: BFI, 1981.
Scannell, Paddy. "Public Service Broadcasting: The History of a Concept." In *Understanding Television*, edited by Andrew Goodwin and Garry Whannel. London: Routledge, 1990.

Schlesinger, Phillip. "The Sociological Scope of 'National Cinema.'" In *Cinema and Nation*, edited by Mette Hjort and Scott Mackenzie. 19-31. London: Routledge, 2000.

Sexton, Jamie. "The Film Society and the Creation of an Alternative Film Culture in Britain." In *Young and Innocent: The Cinema in Britain 1896-1930,* edited by Andrew Higson. 291-305. Exeter: University of Exeter Press, 2002.

Sinclair, Andrew. *Arts and Cultures: The History of the 50 Years of the Arts Council of Great Britain.* London: Sinclair-Stevenson, 1995.

—. *Francis Bacon: His Life and Violent Times.* London: Sinclair-Stevenson, 1993.

Smith, Anthony D. *National Identity*. Harmondsworth: Penguin, 1991.

Smith, Chris. *Creative Britain*. London: Faber and Faber, 1998.

Smith, Claire. "Travelling Light: New Art Cinema in the 90s." In *British Cinema of the 90s*, edited by Robert Murphy. 145-155. London: BFI, 2000.

Snoddy, Raymond and John Ashworth. *It Could Be You: The Untold Story of the National Lottery*. London: Faber and Faber, 2000.

Stephens, H. Pottinger and William Yardley. *Little Jack Sheppard.* London: W.S. Johnson, 1885.

Stoneman, Rod. "Incursions and inclusions: the avant-garde on Channel Four 1983-93." In *The British Avant-Garde Film, 1926-1995: An Anthology of Writings,* edited by Michael O'Pray. 285-296. Luton: University of Luton Press, 1996.

Street, Sarah. *British National Cinema.* London: Routledge, 1997.

Swann, Paul. *The British Documentary Film Movement, 1926-1946.* Cambridge: Cambridge University Press, 1989.

Taggart, Paul. *Populism*. Buckingham: Open University Press, 2000.

Vincendeau, Ginette. "Pathé, Charles." In *Encyclopaedia of European Cinema*, edited by Ginette Vincendeau. 328. London: BFI, 1995.

Waker, Alexander. *Icons in the Fire: The Rise and Fall of Practically Everybody in the British Film Industry 1984-2000.* London: Orion, 2004.

Walker, John A. *Art and Artists on Screen*. Manchester: University of Manchester Press, 1993.

Walsh, Michael. "Allegories of Thatcherism: The Films of Peter Greenaway." In *British Cinema and Thatcherism: Fires Were Started,* edited by Lester Friedman. 255-277. London: University College Press, 1993.

White, Eric. *The Arts Council of Great Britain.* London: Denis Poynter, 1975.

Wickham, Phil. *Producing the Goods? UK Film Production Since 1991: An Information Briefing*. London: BFI Information Services, 2003.

Wilde, Patrick. "Author's Introduction to *What's Wrong With Angry?*" In *Staging Gay Lives: An Anthology of Gay Theater*, edited by John N. Clum. 64-65. Boulder, Colorado: Westview, 1996.

Willett, John. *Art In A City*. London: Methuen, 1967.

Williams, Raymond. *Culture*. London: Fontana, 1981.

—. *Keywords: A Vocabulary of Culture and Society, 2nd Edition*. London: Fontana, 1983. First published 1976.

Witts, Richard. *Artist Unknown: An Alternative History of the Arts Council*. London: Little, Brown and Co., 1998.

Wollen, Peter. "The Last New Wave: Modernism in the British Films of the Thatcher Era." In *British Cinema and Thatcherism: Fires Were Started*, edited by Lester Friedman. 35-51. London: University College Press, 1993.

—. *Readings and Writings: Semiotic Counter Strategies*. London: Verso, 1982.

Journal Articles

Akomfrah, John. "Wishful Filming." *Black Film Bulletin* (Summer 1993): 14.

Bordwell, David. "The Art Cinema as a Mode of Film Practice." *Film Criticism* 4:1 (Fall 1979): 56-64.

Caterer, James. "Playing the Lottery Twice: The Dual-Nationality of *Stella Does Tricks*." *Journal of Media Practice* 5:3 (2004): 133-143.

Caterer, James. "Reinventing the British film industry: the Group Production Plan and the National Lottery Franchise Scheme," *International Journal of Cultural Policy* 17:1 (2011): 94-105.

Dickinson, Margaret and Sylvia Harvey, "Public policy and public funding for film: some recent policy developments in the UK." *Screen* 46:1 (Spring 2005): 87-95.

Dickinson, Margaret. "Gallivant." *Vertigo* 1:7 (Autumn 1997): 28-29.

Dupin, Christophe. "Early Days of Short Film Production at the British Film Institute: Origins and Evolution of the BFI Experimental Film Fund (1952-66)." *Journal of Media Practice* 4:2 (2003): 77-91.

Fischer, Lucy. "'Dancing through the Minefield': Passion, Pedagogy, Politics, and Production in *The Tango Lesson*." *Cinema Journal* 43:3 (Spring 1994): 42-58.

Gibson, Ben. "Independence and Politics." *Vertigo* 1:8 (Summer 1998): 57-61.

Higson, Andrew. "The Concept of National Cinema." *Screen* 30:4 (1989): 36-46.
Hill, John. "'Changing of the Guard': Channel 4, Film Four and film policy." *Journal of Popular British Cinema* 5 (2002): 53-63.
—. "Contemporary British Cinema: Industry, Policy, Identity." *Cinéaste* 26:4 (Autumn 2001): 30-33.
—. "UK Film Policy, Cultural Capital and Social Exclusion." *Cultural Trends* 13:50 (June 2004): 29-39.
Hurley, Jeanine. "Cutting the Sky." *Film Ireland* 75 (April/May 2000): 40.
Kramer, Peter. "Women First: *Titanic*, action-adventure films, and Hollywood's female audience." *Historical Journal of Film, Radio and Television* 18:4 (1998): 599-618.
Magor, Maggie and Philip Schlesinger. "'For this relief much thanks.' Taxation, film policy and the UK government." *Screen* 50:3 (2009): 299-317.
Marris, Paul. "Northern Realism: An Exhausted Tradition?" *Cinéaste* 26:4 (Autumn 2001): 47-50.
Mazière, Michael. "Institutional Support for Artists' Film and Video in England 1966-2003." *British Artists Film and Video Study Collection.* Accessed April 2004. http://www.research.linst.ac.uk/filmcentre// maziere/paper.html.
McIntyre, Steve. "The Lottery: Where Will All the Money Go?." *Vertigo* 1:7 (Autumn 1997): 3-7.
McLaughlin, Noel. "Short Sighted: Short Filmmaking in Britain." *Cinéaste* 26:4 (Autumn 2001): 62-64.
Mueller, John E. "Fred Astaire and the Integrated Musical." *Cinema Journal* 24:1 (Fall 1984) 28-40.
Murphy, Robert. "Another False Dawn? The Film Consortium and the Franchise Scheme." *Journal of Popular British Cinema* 5 (2002): 31-35.
—. "Popular British Cinema." *Journal of Popular British Cinema* 1 (1998): 6-12
Neale, Steve. "Art Cinema as Institution." *Screen* 22:1 (1981): 11-39.
—. "Questions of Genre." *Screen* 31:1 (Spring 1990): 45-66.
Nowell-Smith, Geoffrey. "Radio On." *Screen* 20:3/4 (Winter 1979/80): 29-40.
Petley, Julian. "From Brit-flicks to Shit-flicks: The Cost of Public Subsidy." *Journal of Popular British Cinema* 5 (2002): 37-52.
Petrie, Duncan. "Devolving British Cinema: The New Scottish Cinema and the European Art Film." *Cinéaste* 26:4 (Autumn 2001): 55-57.

Pratten, Stephen and Simon Deakin. "Compettiveness Policy and Economic Organisation: the Case of the British Film Industry." *Screen* 41:2 (Summer 2000): 217-237.

Rowson, Simon. "A Statistical Survey of the Cinema Industry in Great Britain in 1934." *Journal of The Royal Statistical Society* 99 (1936): 67-119.

Ryall, Tom. "New Labour and the Cinema: Culture, Politics and Economics." *Journal of Popular British Cinema* 5 (2002): 5-20.

Sainsbury, Peter. "The Financial Base of Independent Film Production in the UK." *Screen* 22:1 (1981): 41-53.

Scullion, Adrienne and Beatriz Garcia. "What is Cultural Policy Research?" *International Journal of Cultural Policy* 11:2 (2005): 113-127.

Stoneman, Rod. "Sins of Commissioning." *Screen* 33:2 (Summer 1992): 127-144.

Stubbs, Jon. "The Eady Levy: A Runaway Bribe? Hollywood Production and British Subsidy in the Early 1960s." *Journal of British Cinema and Television* 6:1 (2009): 1–20.

Upchurch, Anna. "John Maynard Keynes, The Bloomsbury Group and the Origins of the Arts Council Movement." *International Journal of Cultural Policy* 10:2 (2004): 203-217.

Urquhart, Peter. "You should know something — *anything* — about this movie. You paid for it." *Canadian Journal of Film Studies* 12:2 (Fall 2003): 64-80.

Walsh, Michael. "Fighting the American Invasion with Cricket, Roses, and Marmalade for Breakfast." *The Velvet Light Trap* 40 (Fall 1997): 3-17.

Wees, William. "On Defining Avant-Garde Film." *Opsis* (Spring 1984): 7-12.

Willemen, Paul. "An Avant Garde for the Eighties." *Framework* 24 (Spring 1984): 53-73.

Trade Press Articles

Anon. "Films of 1998." *Screen Finance* 13:8, May 11, 2000, 5.

Anon. "Jack Sheppard Newest Highwayman Picture." *Kinematograph Weekly*, February 8, 1923, 60.

Anon. "Lottery Funding: Who Decides?" *The PACT Magazine* 47, November 1995, 13.

Anon. "Low budget films clog overloaded Brit distribution chain." *Screen Finance* 12:9, May 13, 1999, 1, 6.

Anon. "National Lottery Funding for British films: the PACT Proposals." *The PACT Magazine* 50, March 96, 18.

Anon. "Open for business." *The PACT Magazine* 69, Dec 1997, 10-12.

Anon. "Checklist 1: UK Film." *Screen Finance*, 17:11, June 16, 2004, 7.

Anon. "F.B.I.'s "plans" under the microscope: Trade views and counter-suggestions." *Kinematograph Weekly*, 102:956, August 13, 1925, 49-52.

Anon. "Pathé Shake-up Divides Producers." *Screen Finance*, 12:9, May 13, 1999, 2-3.

Adler, Tim. "Lottery recouping accounts for 15% of UKFC Income." *Screen Finance*, December 2004, 4.

Adler, Tim. "Film Industry worth £4.3 bil. To UK GDP." *Screen Finance*, July 2007, 2.

Andrew, Geoff. "Four Better, Four Worse." *Broadcast*, November 1992, 28-29.

Bateman, Louise. "Council Tips." *The PACT Magazine*, 14, September 1998, 15.

Blaney, Martin. "Subsidy Heaven." *Screen International,* 980, October 21, 1994, 8.

Boehm, Erich. "Mixed review on Brit pix fund." *Variety.com*, December 15, 1998. Accessed December 2005. http://www.variety.com/story.asp?l=story&a=VR1117489401&c=13.

Dawtry, Adam. "Brit Pix Win Lottery Subsidy Money." *Variety*, April 10, 1995, 21.

—. "Denton tops Council film arm." *Variety*, October 14, 1996, 24.

—. "HAL, Miramax Confirm Split." *Variety.com*, February 2, 2000. Accessed January 2007. http://www.variety.com/article/VR1117776056.html?categoryid=18&cs=1.

—. "Searchlight to Shine for British DNA." *Variety.com*, September 4, 2003. Accessed December 2006. http://www.variety.com/article/VR1117891965.html?categoryid=1236&cs=1.

—. "Shuttered Film Council reaps rewards for BFI," *Variety*, March 14, 2011, 4.

—. "U.K. Arts Council Plays it Safe." *Variety*, May 6, 1996, 23, 26.

—. "Whole Lotto Shakin' in Brit Film Funding." *Variety*, May 6, 1996, 26.

Dobson, Patricia. "Case Study: *Billy Elliot*." *Screen International,* 1268, July 21, 2000, 15.

Elley, Derek. "*Get Real* review." *Variety.com*, September 21, 1998. Accessed October 2006. http://www.variety.com/review/VE1117913335.html?categoryID=31&cs=1.

—. "Reviews - *House!*" *Variety.com*, May 8, 2000. Accessed August 2006. http://www.variety.com/review/VE1117915760.html?categoryid=31&cs =1.

Federation of British Industries, "To revive production: F.B.I.'s summary of the rival plans." *Kinematograph Weekly*, 102:955, August 6, 1925, 30-1.

Fraser, Nicholas. "Staying Rude." *Broadcast*, November 1992, 43-44.

Fry, Andy. "Interview with Charles Denton." *The PACT Magazine*, 60, February 1997, 12.

Katz, Richard. "BET Movies Fest to Bow 7 Pix." *Variety.com*, June 24, 1999. Accessed February 2006. http://www.variety.com/article/ VR1117503413.

Keighron, Peter. "Radical Departure: Interview with Adam Barker." *Broadcast*, February 12, 1999, 22.

Kemp, Stuart. "Many Happy Returns?" *Screen International*, 1158, May 15, 1998, 12.

Kledy, Leonard. "Quality doesn't always mean B.O. quantity." *Variety.com,* September 24, 1997. Accessed January 2006. http://www. variety.com/article/ VR111662671?=13&cs=1.

Lapworth, Charles. "Production – and the exhibitor." *Kinematograph Weekly*, 102:955, August 6, 1925, 26.

Lodderhouse, Diana. "U.K. Gov't tells UKFC to stop lobbying." *Variety*, August 17, 2010. Accessed June 2010. http://www.variety.com /article/VR11180 23001?refCatId=3599.

Macnab, Geoffrey. "Rise of the Super-Slate." *Screen International*, October 27, 2006, 20.

Macnab, Geoffrey. "Film Council at the Crossroads." *Screen International*, April 24, 2009, 6-7.

Minns, Adam. "British Screen to be Folded into the Film Council." *Screendaily.com*, January 20, 2000. Accessed December 2005. http://www.screendaily.com /storyid=87.

—. "FilmFour, Calderwood first-look deal shapes up." *Screen International*, June 9, 2000, 14.

—. "Gov't writes British Film script." *Screen International*, 1189, December 18, 1998, 1.

—. "Pathé lures BBC talent." *Screen International*, January 30, 1998, 5.

—. "UK Independent Voices Struggle to be Heard." *Screen International*, 1271, September 1, 2000, 22.

—. "UK's Film Council sets aside $16m for bigger films." *Screendaily. com*, May 2, 2000. Accessed December 2005. http://www.screendaily. com/storyid= 1229.

—. "VNews: Jon Finn and Natasha Wharton on WT2." *Variety.com*, May 3, 2001. Accessed September 2006. http://www.variety.com/article/VR1117798516 .html.

Tutt, Louise. "Greater Expectations." *Screen International*, 1142, January 23, 1998, 24.

Newspaper and Magazine Articles

Anon. "Don't Tax the Poor to Amuse the Rich." *Daily Mail*, November 15, 1994, 8.

Anon. "Films a Lottery." *Sight and Sound,* 5:7, July 1995, 3.

Anon. "Is this the worst film ever made?" *The Times*, February 20, 2004, 1.

Anon. "State Lottery." *The Times*, October 19, 1826, 3.

Anon. "The Great Bonanza Race." *The Voice*, November 15, 1994, 6.

Alberge, Dalya. "Director attacks film institute." *The Times*, September 8, 1998, 9.

Ardendt, Paul. "Last Reel for Soho Cinema?" *Guardian Unlimited,* October 21, 2004. Accessed April 2005. http://www.guardian.co.uk/arts/news/story/0,,1331943,00.html.

Arnot, Chris. "Shooting Stars." *Guardian Unlimited*, March 23, 2000. Accessed March 2005. http://www.guardian.co.uk/arts/story/0,,181477,00.html.

Arroyo, José. "*Get Real.*" *Sight and Sound*, 9:5, May 1999, 48.

Bilson, Anne. "The Tango Lesson." *Sunday Telegraph*, November 30, 1997, review section, 11.

Binyon, Michael. "Denis the Menace and the Great Lotto Rip-Off." *Times Online,* December 29, 2003. Accessed January 2004. http://www.timesonline.co.uk/article /0,,585-942548,00.html.

Bradshaw, Peter. "How our movies lost their cool." *Guardian Unlimited,* November 16, 2001. Accessed June 2003. http://www.guardian.co.uk/friday_review/story/0,3605,594001,00.html.

—. "Poetry from the rubbish tip." *Guardian Unlimited*, November 12, 1999. Accessed 3 June 2003. http://film.guardian.co.uk/News_Story/Critic_Review/Guardian _Film _of_the_week/0,4267,102485,00.html.

Brooks, Richard. "Bacon love-film funding blocked." *The Observer*, May 12, 1996, 3.

Busfield, Steve. "£140,000 of Lottery Cash for more Vice on Four." *Daily Mail*, April 22, 1996, 27.

Catherine Millner, "Arts Council to cut a third of its staff." *The Telegraph*, June 30, 2002. Accessed March 2006. http://www.telegraph.co.uk/news/main.jhtml?xml= /news/2002/06/30/nart130.xml.

Christopher, James. "Masterclass in nauseous ineptitude." *The Times*, February 20, 2004, 3.

—. "More than a bit of a laugh." *The Times*, August 10, 2001, 8.

Church, Michael. "The Arm's Length Way to Wave Goodbye." *The Observer*, January 17, 1993, 45.

Cooper, Robert. "All right Jack." *The Guardian*, October 1, 1998, 23.

Dawson, Tina. "Sorry Minnie." *Daily Mail,* 19 March 2001, 7.

Dawtry, Adam. "How is the BFI suddenly able to take over from the UK Film Council?" *The Guardian*, November 29, 2010. Accessed June 2011. http://www.guardian.co.uk/film/filmblog/2010/nov/29/uk-film-council-bfi-ed-vaizey?INTCMP=ILCNETTXT3487.

Ebert, Roger. *Chicago Sun-Times*, January 23, 1998. Accessed January 2006. http://rogerebert.suntimes.com/apps/pbcs.dll/article?AID= /19980123/REVIEWS/801230304/1023.

Everitt, Anthony. "Catch-22 of the Lottery." *The Guardian*, May 30, 1994, Section 2, 11.

Fisher, Nick.

—. "One Trick Not To Be Missed." *The Sun*, January 30, 1998, 21.

—. "This Year's Loser." *The Sun*, February 20, 1999, 24.

Gibson, Ben. "Lights, Camera, Axe Man." *The Guardian*, March 13, 1998, Section 2, 10-11.

Glaister, Dan. "Fast fade into the black by feelgood comedy." *The Guardian*, May 29, 1997, 12.

Gowrie, Grey. "Let the Bids Roll In." *The Guardian*, August 6, 1996, 13.

Guthmann, Edward. "'Swept from the Sea' is Lush and Moody, but heavy handed plot is predictable." *San Francisco Chronicle*, January 23, 1998. Accessed January 2006. http://www.sfgate.com/cgibin/article.cgi?f=/c/a/1998/01/23/ DD4951.DTL.

Gutten, David. "Amy Foster." *Daily Telegraph*, May 8, 1998, 24.

Hammond, Wally. "'Gallivant' is a Coast-to-coast Study of British Eccentricity." *Time Out*, September 3, 1997, 23.

—. "Fishy Business." *Time Out*, October 15, 1997, 75.

Harding, James. "Film Makers Jostle to take Credit for *Billy Elliot.*" *Financial Times*, September 30, 2000, 3.

Hibbin, Sally. "Britain has a New Film Establishment." *New Statesman*, 127:4378, March 27, 1998, 40.

Hinsliff, Gaby. "'Billy Elliot' payout for poor pupils." *Guardian Unlimited*, February 11, 2001. Accessed June 2003. http://society.guardian.co.uk/childreninpoverty/story/0,8150,436869,00.html.

Holden, Stephen. "'Swept from the Sea': A Romance in the Rain." *New York Times,* January 23, 1998. Accessed January 2006. http://www.nytimes.com/library/film/ 012398swept-film-review.html.

Hunt, Jeremy. "I've cut the UK Film Council so that the money goes to the industry." *The Observer*, August 8, 2010, 5.

Iley, Chrissey. "Bell de Jour." *Guardian Unlimited*, November 27, 2005. Accessed July 2006. http://film.guardian.co.uk/interview/interviewpages/0,,1651459,0.html.

James, Nick. "Medium Cool." *Sight and Sound*, 8:8, August 1998, 12-15.

Jays, David. "Blues in the Night." *Sight and Sound*, 10:9, September 2000, 18-20.

Jury, Louise. "Millions spent on British films no one wants to see." *The Independent on Sunday*, April 9, 2000, 14.

Kent, Sarah. "A Slice of Bacon." *Time Out*, December 31, 1997, 12-13.

Kermode, Mark. "Sorry Ma'am, but you don't belong in a picture palace." *Guardian Unlimited,* September 24, 2006. Accessed October 2006. http://arts.guardian.co.uk/comment/story/0,, 1879500,00.html.

Lawrenson, Edward. "Cosmic Dancer." *Sight and Sound,* 10:10, October 2000, 12-13.

Leake, Christopher. "Britain's Luckiest Numbers." *Mail on Sunday*, November 20, 1994, 1.

Lennon, Peter. "The Composer, the Lottery and the Fat Cats who will Hit the Jackpot." *The Guardian*, September 24, 1994, 27.

Lister, David. "'Correct' Films to get Lottery Cash." *The Independent*, April 6, 1995, 8.

MacCann, Richard Dyer. "Subsidy for the Screen: Grierson and Group 3, 1951-55." *Sight and Sound*, 46:3, March 1977, 168-173.

MacDonald, Marianne. "Lottery goes into the Blockbuster Business." *The Independent*, September 18, 1995, 1.

Mackie, Rob. "Video of the Week: Love is the Devil." *Guardian Unlimited,* 19 March 1999. Accessed February 2005. http://film.guardian.co.uk/News_Story/Critic_Review/Guardian/0,36024,00.html.

Macnab, Geoffrey. "Bohemian Rhapsody." *Sight and Sound,* 7:7, July 1997, 18.

Macnab, Geoffrey. "Five years of flack." *Guardian Unlimited*, October 25, 2002. Accessed December 2005. http://film.guardian.co.uk/features/featurepages/0,,818782,00. html.

McRae, Hamish. "Several Funerals and an Opportunity." *The Independent*, June 9, 1995, 19.
Newton, Jeremy. "Films that Serve the Public Good." *The Independent*, April 7, 1995, 18.
O'Carroll, Lisa. "Hot Under the Collar." *Evening Standard*, January 28, 1998, 3.
O'Hagan, Andrew. "This is my film of the year." *Daily Telegraph,* November 12, 1999, 25.
O'Sullivan, Charlotte. "Amy Foster." *Time Out*, May 6, 1998, 78.
Palmer, Martyn. "We Can Laugh About It Now." *The Times*, September 15, 2001, 36.
Patterson, Hannah. "Dealer's Choice." *Sight and Sound,* 18:4, April 2008: 30-33.
Pulver, Andrew. "The Hit Man." *Guardian Unlimited*, October 3, 2000. Accessed June 2003. http://www.guardian.co.uk/friday_review/story/0,3605,594001,0.html.
Quirke, Antonia. "*House* review." *Independent on Sunday*, May 7, 2000, Culture Section, 4.
Reynolds, Nigel. "French Connection mars Lottery award." *Daily Telegraph*, May 16, 1997, 4.
—. "Lottery's film cash nets a flying fish." *Daily Telegraph*, May 29, 1997, 10
Rice, Xan and Dalya Alberge. "Investors laugh at their unfunny film." *The Times*, February 20, 2004, 3.
Rich, R. Ruby. "New Queer Cinema." *Sight and Sound*, 2:5, September 1992, 32.
Romney, Jonathan. "Don't give up the day job, Steve." *Independent on Sunday*, August 12, 2001, 9.
—. "London's Pride." *The Guardian*, February 19, 1999, Section 2, 3.
Rose, Jacqueline. "Obituary: Sandra Lahire." *Guardian Unlimited*, August 13, 2001. Accessed March 2005. http://www.guardian.co.uk/obituaries/story/0,,535780,00.html.
Seamark, Michael and Tom Kelly. "Fury as Lottery money funds vile sex film." *Daily Mail*, February 21, 2004, 1, 5.
Sinclair, Iain. "Big Granny and Little Eden." *Sight and Sound*, 7:9, September 1997, 20.
Spencer, Liese. "Out of Step." *The Independent*, November 29, 1997, 17.
—. "Travels With My Gran." *The Independent*, September 26, 1997, 14.
Stringer, Robin. "Now Showing: Film industry in dash for Lottery cash." *Evening Standard*, February 27, 1997, 4.

Summers, Sue. "Why the film crew call her Sir." *Daily Telegraph*, November 14, 1998, Arts, 7.

Sweet, Matthew. "The Tango Lesson." *Independent on Sunday*, November 30, 1997, Section 2, 11.

Sylvester, Rachel. "The blind boy who never stopped fighting." *Daily Telegraph*, December 16, 2004, 6.

Tharps, Lori L. "Foul Plié." *Entertainment Weekly*, 566, October 27, 2000, 24.

Thorncroft, Antony. "Movies Cash in on the Lottery." *Financial Times*, April 15, 1995, 10.

Tookey, Christopher. "Vile beyond belief, and we paid for it." *Daily Mail*, February 21, 2004, 5.

Voorhuis, Nelly. "Pandemonium 1998." *Mute Magazine*, October 7, 2004. Accessed January 2007. http://www.metamute.org/en/Pandaemonium-1998.

Walker, Alexander. "Beefcake but no Bacon." *Evening Standard*, May 8, 1998, 19.

—. "Blank portrait of an Artist." *Evening Standard*, September 17, 1998, 22.

—. "Dreams that Money Can't Buy." *Evening Standard*, January 29, 1998, 29.

—. "Lottery Millions will be Wasted on Films." *Evening Standard*, November 24, 1995, 9.

—. "Sally puts on her dancing shoes." *Evening Standard*, November 27, 1997, 27.

—. "Spellbound in Glasgow's ghetto." *Evening Standard,* November 11, 1999, 30.

—. "You've got your £92m Lottery cash, now show us your films." *Evening Standard*, May 16, 1997, 4.

Williams, Rhys. "Lottery Handout for Film Projects." *The Independent*, August 26, 1995, 6.

Williams, Richard. "Amy Foster." *The Guardian*, May 8, 1998, 7.

Policy Documents and Official Publications

Arts Council of England (ACE). *National Lottery Funding for Film: Application Pack*. London: ACE, 1997.

—. *1st Annual Report and Accounts 1994/5*. London: ACE, 1995. All subsequent editions until 2000/2001.

—. "The Spectrum Report", *Lottery Film Franchising: A Feasibility Study*. London: ACE, 1996.

Arts Council of Great Britain (ACGB). *First Annual Report and Accounts, year ending March 1946*. London: ACGB, 1946. All subsequent editions until 1993/1994.

Arts Council of Northern Ireland (ACNI). *The National Lottery Arts Fund: Film Development and Film Production*. Belfast: ACNI, 1998.

Cabinet Office. *Social Exclusion Unit*. Accessed August 2006. http://www.socialexclusion.gov.uk/.

Commission on Educational and Cultural Films. Chair. Sir Benjamin Gott. *The Film in National Life*. London: Allen and Unwin, 1932.

Conservative Party. *The Best Future for Britain: The Conservative Manifesto 1992*. London: Conservative Central Office, 1992.

Department of Culture, Media and Sport (DCMS). "Summary of results from consultation on National Lottery money for Arts, Film, Heritage and Sport from 2009", *National Lottery Shares 2009*, June 2006.

—. "The Operation of the National Lottery", *The United Kingdom Parliament*, March 7, 2001. Accessed January 2004. http://www.parliament.thestationeryoffice.co.uk/pa/cm200001/cmselect/cmcumeds/56/5602.

—. *A Bigger Picture: The Report of the Film Policy Review Group*. London: DCMS, 1998.

Department of National Heritage (DNH). *The British Film Industry*. Cmnd. 2884. London: HMSO, 1995.

—. *Second Report from the National Heritage Committee: The British Film Industry, Vol. 1*. London: HMSO, 1995. xiv, xv.

European Parliament. "Factsheet 4.18.0 – Media and Sport Policy." *European Parliament*, September 30, 2004. Accessed February 2006. http://www.europarl .eu.int/facts/4_18_0_en.htm.

GB Advisory Committee on Film Finance. Chair: Sir Peter Middleton. *Report to the Secretary of State for National Heritage*. London: DNH, 1996.

Great Britain Home Office. *A National Lottery Raising Money for Good Causes*. Cmnd. 1861. London: HMSO, March 1992.

Great Britain. *Broadcasting Act 1980*. London: HMSO, 1980.

HM Treasury. *Reform of Film Tax Incentives: Promoting the Sustainable Production of Culturally British Films*. London: HMSO, 2005.

HMSO. "House of Commons Standing Committee A (pt 5)", Column 367, *UK Parliament*. Accessed April 2006. http://www.publications.parliament.uk/pa/cm200304/cmstand/a/st040525/am/40525s05.htm.

National Audit Office (NAO). "Improving Access To, and Education About, The Moving Image Through the British Film Institute", *NAO*,

April 11, 2003. Accessed 11 June 2003. http://www.nao.org.uk/pn/02-03/0203593.htm.

Office for National Statistics. "Census 2001: Population", *National Statistics Online.* Accessed March 2004. http://www.statistics.gov.uk/cci/nugget.asp?id=185.

Parker, Alan. "Towards a Sustainable Film Industry", *UK Film Council.* Accessed January 2006. http://www.ukfilmcouncil.org.uk/aboutus/towards/.

Policy Studies Institute (PSI), "Cultural Trends In Scotland: 1995", *PSI.* Accessed 8 February 2004. http://www.psi.org.uk/publications/archivedpdfs/Ctscot2/SCOT6.pdf.

Robinson, Gerry. "Achieving a New Era for the Arts." *The Arts Council of England Annual Review 1999.* London: ACE, 1999. 2.

Scottish Arts Council (SAC). *National Lottery Film Production Guidelines.* Edinburgh: SAC, 1998.

UK Film Council (UKFC). "Distribution and Exhibition", *UK Film Council.* Accessed 1 April 2004. http://www.ukfilmcouncil.org.uk/funding/distributionand exhibition/.

—. *Film in the UK 2002: Statistical Yearbook.* London: UKFC, 2003. All subsequent editions until 2005.

—. "Tax Relief for the production of low budget British films." *UK Film Council.* Accessed September 2005. http://www.ukfilmcouncil.org.uk /usr/downloads/BFC_UKFCI/finance/Tax_Relief_Sale_Leaseback.pdf.

—. *Report and Group Accounts for the Year ended 31 March 2001.* London: UKFC, 2001. All subsequent editions until 2005/2006.

Interviews

Allison, Deborah. Programmer for City Screen. July 13, 2011.

Barker, Adam. Producer of *Stella Does Tricks.* February 11, 2004.

Calderwood, Andrea. Former Head of Production at Pathé Pictures. January 11, 2006.

Curtis, David. Former Visual Arts Officer at the Arts Council of England. October 22, 2004.

Dunford, Mark. Former Lottery Film Officer at the Arts Council of England. July 16, 2004.

Gibson, Ben. Former Head of BFI Production. March 19, 2004.

Preston, John. Co-writer of *Jack Sheppard and Jonathan Wild.* August 2, 2005.

Ross, Benjamin. Writer-director of *Jack Sheppard and Jonathan Wild.* October 7, 2005.

Solomon, Frances-Ann. Producer of *Peggy Su!* January 28, 2006.
Taylor, Richard. Former Head of The Northern Ireland Film and Television Commission. February 9, 2006.
Taylor, Samantha. Producer of *Jack Sheppard and Jonathan Wild.* February 2, 2006.

Unpublished material

Columbia-TriStar. "*Amy Foster*: Production Notes." Held at the BFI National Library, London.
Ross, Benjamin and John Preston. *Screenplay: Jack Sheppard and Jonathan Wild.* July 2001. Supplied by Luc Roeg at Artists Independent.
Taylor, Sam. *National Lottery Application Form: Jack Sheppard and Jonathan Wild.* May 1997. Held at the UK Film Council, London.

INDEX